MW01279958

...

Ancient Knowledge

By George E Curtis

Revealing things which have been kept secret from the foundation of the world.

Copyright

ISBN-13: 978-1506127781

ISBN-10: 1506127789

Health warning and disclaimer

The discovery described in this book is real, and if the reader understands the calculations and the unavoidable implications it is possible that 'the shock of the new' might induce some degree of cerebral disquiet.

The author of this work will not accept responsibility for any psychological or emotional distress caused or claimed to be caused by the mathematics detailed in chapter ten, or by any other content of this book.

G.Curtis

Acknowledgements

I must acknowledge the help of the late Dr. P. Hunt, a very good friend and talented academic mathematician who very kindly checked my calculations.

I was also greatly helped by the talent of another good friend, Jack Lewis, who produced some of the illustrations in this book, and because of his pestering, caused this book to be written.

Jack is also responsible for the foreword.

I would like to acknowledge the work of Professor R.J.C.Atkinson who published 'Stonehenge', (Penguin 1979, & 1990) from which the descriptions and measurement details in this current book are obtained.

The construction method and other views expressed in the following pages of 'Ancient Knowledge' concerning Stonehenge are my own, and should not be taken to reflect on Professor Atkinson or anyone else.

I must also acknowledge the work of all those astronomers and mathematicians who measured the orbits of the planets, together with that publication known as 'Norton's Star Atlas'.

All Biblical quotes are from the King James Authorized Version of the Holy Bible.

All alternative meanings of words in the Bible are from Strong's concordance.

Content

Page

List of figures 11

Foreword by Jack Lewis 13

Author's Introduction 19

Part One – In the Beginning

Chapter 1 Antediluvians - Antediluvian Civilization....25

Chapter 2 Babel – Is Babel real? 63

Chapter 3 Stonehenge - The same as Babel?..............91

Chapter 4 Order in the Orbits 137

Chapter 5 Of Gods and Men – general discussion. ...161

Chapter 6 Cargo Cult – general discussion 193

Chapter 7 The Unction of Sanctity – general 221

Part Two - Technical chapters

Chapter 8 Of Pegs and String - Technical details 243

Chapter 9 Sticks, Stones and Space-Technical 281

Chapter 10 **A New Heaven** -Technical details 301

Part Three - Science implications

Chapter 11 The Hard Facts of the Matter – review....339

Chapter 12 Such a Little Change – Carbon dates 379

Part Four - Religion

Chapter 13 The Grand Plan – Smoke and Mirrors 433

Chapter 14 The Culmination – the Kingdom 467

Chapter 15 A Horror of Great Darkness 517

THE END

Appendix 1 - '***In unto'*** as a sexual euphemism 543

Appendix 2 - Conventional Mathematics 549

Index 559

List of Figures, Graphs, and Tables

Fig 1 Drawing 56 points on circle 251

Fig 2 Draw vernier Circle 253

Fig 3 Drawing 30 radials 257

Fig 4 'Y' feature and 30 radials in progress 259

Fig 5 Outer monument peg & string pattern 265

Fig 6 Inner monument 271

Fig 7 Combined inner and outer 275

Fig 8 Correlation with planets – Sketch 296

Fig 8a First crude graphs 111

Fig 8b First application of exponents 123

Graph Fig 9 Function of main Equation 333

Graph Fig 10 - Relating all the orbits 335

Graph Fig 10b - Design your own Solar System 349

Graph Fig 11 Simplification of Fig 9 146

Fig 12 Illustrating 'dumb clue' 131

Table 1 Orbital data 299

Table 2 Look-up ready worked data 307

Table 3 Table of Percentage Differences 327

Plate 1 Modern View of Stonehenge 100

Plates 2 & 3 Aspects of Stonehenge 110

Foreword

by Jack Lewis

I'm sure that it cannot be very often that he who is asked to write a foreword to a book was also a contributor to that book and also that he had never met the author in his life. I am such a person. My contribution to George's book is that I did many of the illustrations; however, the fact that I have never actually met George must be bizarre in the least.

I have been corresponding with George for about three years and all by email. He saw my email address on the top of a letter that I had posted on an Internet discussion forum. It was remiss of me to leave my address on that letter because there are so many malevolent people who could have done me mischief as a result. In the event I suffered no cyber-attacks except from George.

George picked up my email address and wrote to me.

This is where this whole thing gets very interesting. George contacted me because of something I left in view by mistake, however George was not beyond making the same mistake himself!

In his first email to me there was a website link underneath his name at the end of the email. Being of a curious nature, I clicked on it to see what it would reveal.

What I saw was the most astonishing set of calculations that I had ever seen!

Not fully understanding what they were demonstrating I emailed George and asked him what they were all about. George's reaction was like that of someone who had been caught-out doing something terrible in secret. I really had to press George very hard to tell me what it was all about. This book, I like to think, is the result of that pressure although it took three years for it to happen.

George is retired by profession and by nature - a quiet kind of man who is devoted to his wife. He is intelligent and no slouch when it comes to mathematics. He was skilled in electronics and that is where his interest in science was probably birthed.

He is also an amateur geologist and likes to live dangerously, climbing up and down cliffs and old tin mines looking for interesting minerals.

I mentioned earlier that George asked me to undertake all his illustration work, but I have to say that George is also a very good oil painter. My expertise in illustration was that I was a technical illustrator for over 30 years and I also ran my own graphic design company. I too am now retired.

This book has a great deal of George's life tied up in it. When he first published his thesis he was subjected to many personal attacks and ridicule. His personal life also suffered badly. These attacks weren't against the science or the reasoning but because he dared to challenge beliefs which are part and parcel of the accepted scientific wisdom of the day.

This wisdom may be just the same today but one hopes that it may have moved on. Scientists are human and as such have the same foibles and prejudices as ordinary people. When a scientist undertakes new research he never starts with a blank sheet of paper. He starts with a blank sheet of paper and a given, probably unshakable, world-view. It is this worldview that will guide the way his research results are interpreted.

*

This book seriously challenges the perceived scientific and spiritual wisdom of today. It will take you from nothing more than a chat George had with two elderly ladies on his doorstep, to a realisation that something awesome has taken place in the past and the cause of which was still present today.

You will be challenged at every level of your understanding of that which is around you and in your mind. It is your mind that will be the most challenged. Make no mistake! On the one hand George will convince you that the greatest coincidence that you could possible conceive really did happen like that and then will sweep the carpet completely away from under you and suggest that this goes beyond materialism!

As much as I know that most people are content to accept what their senses tell them, there is something that exists and is true but is beyond the comprehension of our senses. George demonstrates, mathematically, that something that has always been considered as being 'natural' is in fact 'un-natural', or to put it in perhaps a more favourable way, 'artificial'. Artificial is not a word that is in the cosmologist's dictionary unless applied to man-made satellites. It cannot be used in any shape or form to describe any aspect of the cosmos.

What do we do? We can either accept the result and do the unthinkable and re-think everything we ever learned or we can do what ostriches do.

Jack Lewis

Author's Introduction

This is a true story.

This book is an adventure for the mind, but it is also a treasure hunt, where the treasure we are hunting is not gold or silver, nor precious stones. The precious thing we seek is 'ancient knowledge' which is far more valuable than mere material things. The trail that leads us to the treasure is obscured by prejudice and overgrown by the long ages of history. The clues we must follow are hidden beneath layers of legend, and camouflaged by a thick crust of tradition.

Many books have been written that claim to search for ancient knowledge but this one is a little different. This story actually succeeds in finding the treasure of knowledge, and holds it up for the entire world to see, should it care to look.

This is not intended to be a religious book, though it starts with a brief excursion into the Bible. Religion, as practiced today, is not a part of this work.

We start in the Bible, in Genesis, and unfortunately we need to discuss the flood, as many others have done before, but after that we go on an extended journey to other places where science prevails, and in the end, after discovering the secrets of antediluvian knowledge, we spend some time considering the implications, both for us as individuals and for the world in general.

The secrets revealed represent astronomy that is not previously known to modern science, and is shown to be valid by mathematics.

Mathematics makes for rather tedious reading for most people, so it is not included in the main text, but is relegated to the second part of this volume for the consideration of those readers who have an interest in it. For all others, the knowledge is described in narrative form.

This book tells the story, from its beginning, through the various stages of research and detective work, to the final discovery, and its implications.

There are two pillars of civilized life, one called 'science' and the other called 'religion'. These two are mutually antagonistic, and attempts to reconcile them are doomed to failure.

This book is not intended to be seen as critical of either, indeed, both these antagonists are searching for the nature of our human origins, and this writer can only applaud such an effort, even when he disagrees with the methodology employed.

Science requires that we use reason and logic, and throughout this book every attempt is made to adhere to the rules of science, and to follow the paths of reason and logic, but we do not feel obliged to accept the many and varied assumptions upon which much of modern science is founded.

As for religion, the subject matter of this volume is concerned only with a time period that preceded both Judaism and Christianity. For this reason, all modern doctrines and dogmas of these religions are held to be irrelevant.

This is not a religious work, though it may well appear to be, at times.

It is self-evidently true that in those parts of Genesis that give us the first clue, religion as we know it today did not exist. There was a form of religion, but it did not have a name, at least, not any name that is recorded in the Bible.

So we can say without fear of contradiction that this work does indeed fall between the two stools of science and religion. It will not satisfy science, because in the end it demonstrates that some scientific theories are wrong. It will not satisfy religion, because, for the most part, we ignore religion, and provide our own understanding of the words found written in the Bible.

I hope the reader enjoys the journey, even if he or she fails to appreciate the implications of the final conclusions. If my reader does not enjoy the read, then it is this writer who is at fault, for it is my job and my joy, to entertain as well as inform.

Chapter one will set the scene, and the rest is in the lap of the gods.

Ancient Knowledge.

Part One

In The Beginning

In which is narrated the events that led to the discovery of this treasure of Ancient Knowledge, how the discovery was made, and some of the implications.

Chapter One

Antediluvians

In the beginning, I was making myself a nice cup of tea when the doorbell rang. I cursed under my breath, wondering who would disturb my peace in the middle of the afternoon. I dropped the spoon in the sink and made my way to the front hall. Two shadowy blurred figures could be seen through the frosted glass.

On opening the door I saw before me a matching pair of elderly ladies clutching bags and Bibles. They were obviously from a well-known religious sect, and I felt a sudden urge to run back into my house and hide in a cupboard.

Manfully conquering my feelings of panic, I stood and stared blankly at them, noting their white hair and the gleam of salvation in their twinkling blue eyes.

"We wondered if you would like to discuss the troubles of this world?" one of them asked.

The conversation that ensued involved lots of talk about salvation, and there was mention of Jesus, of course, but I do not remember all the details.

*

That is how this story began. It is a true story that recounts how I discovered an ancient secret that is incredible and unbelievable.

The secret is not a 'spiritual' one, nor are my words to be taken as window dressing for some religious conversion. This book, this story, is not one of religion, nor is it 'creationist science' although religion and the Bible come into it.

The secret is one that could be called 'scientific', and concerns a physical and very real thing. It is proven with mathematics, and is rock solid.

Secret knowledge is always unbelievable, so I have included the mathematical proofs in part two of this book. I have done this to provide for those who doubt the content of part one, to enable them, if they are willing, to follow the same path that I ventured along.

I wish I could tell you that I discovered this secret in some far off part of the world, like Tibet, or Mongolia, or even up the Amazon. I wish I could tell you a story of an exciting adventure in Peru, but alas, all the discoveries took place in my own front room, here in civilized England.

That does not mean that I never left the house; of course not. It means that the secret was found by the reading of books.

The secret is revealed by a study of archaeology books, and astronomy books, but first in order of chronology, the Biblical book of Genesis.

However, do not be fooled into thinking that it is a safe journey just because you are sitting in an arm chair, do not think that, not for one minute.

If you understand the mathematics in part two, which is relatively simple, at '0' level or slightly above, then you may encounter frightful things you have never seen before.

This treasure hunt takes us into some strange and unfamiliar regions, and the treasure itself is found in a dark and dangerous place from which there is no return. It is far more perilous than Peru.

We start with a gentle stroll along the garden path, the Garden of Eden that is, after which we explore a little of the antediluvian period, but do not be deceived into thinking that this is just a despicable way to lure you into a Bible study class.

I am not a preacher, I am not an evangelist, and I am certainly not a 'Bible thumper', so try to remember that this book is not primarily about the Bible. We are engaged in a treasure hunt, and remain so until we find what we seek in that perilous place where no man has been before, and from which there is no escape, and no way back.

There is danger lurking in the mathematics, but if you do not understand the math, then there is no worry, no need for concern, you will be safe.

*

Every treasure hunt starts with a suggestion that such a treasure exists, or might exist, and there has to be a clue. The first clue might be an easy one or a hard one, but it inevitably leads to another clue, and then another, until if all the clues have been followed correctly, the treasure is found.

That is the nature of a treasure hunt, all of them start slowly. It isn't until the first few clues are solved that the way ahead becomes a little clearer, and the trail continues until we find the 'X' that marks the spot where we start to dig.

So it is with this little treasure hunt. It is no exception, it started slowly.

It is difficult for me to relate the story because as I write the treasure is already found, so I know how the story ends. The treasure has been found, the difficulty is not in the finding of it, but in trying to present it in a manner that will be understood.

It is a dull and slow start, and I make no apology for that, because it is needful that you should be told about the clues that led me to begin to think that there could be a treasure to search for.

If you find the initial discussion of the Genesis flood and other Biblical clues to be in any way tedious or boring, please feel free to skip to a later chapter. If you stay with me, try to understand that reading the Bible is not a sin. It just seems that way.

*

After the ladies had left, I more-or-less forgot the conversation, it was not important to me at all. There were only two or three things that I actually do remember.

During the polite argument that I engaged in, it became abundantly clear that I was in a very weak position; my ignorance of the subject gave the two ladies a distinct advantage.

One of the ladies, out of a desire to be helpful, had suggested I read the Bible for myself, since I obviously knew nothing about it. When I had objected that it was all myth and mumbo-jumbo, it was further suggested, quietly but with sparkling eyes, that it was actually the literal Truth, the unfailing inspired Word of God, and perhaps I should consider giving it the benefit of my doubt.

The thing I remember most was that the tea I was making had gone cold.

*

A little later, as I relaxed with another freshly made nice hot cup of tea, and a digestive biscuit, their words hung in my mind, like the remembered parts of a fading dream. I began to think about the Bible for the first time since I was a small child.

And so I set foot on a path of research that has led me inexorably to the writing of this book.

*

I was aware that the Bible had kept men enthralled for at least two thousand years, and had somehow survived where many other books had faded into obscurity.

Parts of the Bible have been with mankind, as a constant companion, since the dawn of recorded history, and the book has grown over the centuries to end up as it is today.

It has had a massive influence on humanity, and still determines much of what happens.

The Creation story gave us our seven day week, which is now observed all around the globe; and much of our Western heritage, our culture and traditions, and our laws, are founded on the content of the Bible.

The 'Holy Book' has inspired great works of art and has been responsible for the construction of magnificent cathedrals and other examples of fabulous architecture.

It has given us our morality, and has presided over the building of empires, inspired exploration, sent missionaries into every corner of the world, and encouraged conquering armies.

It has to be admitted that those sacred pages have also provoked many arguments and given rise to a great many wars, witch-hunts and the inquisition, and has been responsible for a huge amount of human suffering.

The 'Inspired Word of God' has the power to stir heated emotions in many, and leave others as cold as my forgotten cup of tea.

The sad thing for me is that all the troubles and strife, all the bloodshed and carnage, seems to have been about nothing more than the 'right way' to worship the One True God.

Nevertheless, for good or for mayhem, the Bible has shaped all our lives.

Many people do not realize that without even reading it, their lives are saturated by the content of the Bible.

Despite all this, many still regard it as a book of myth, as being untrue, and of no value.

I was such a person myself.

*

I considered that the ladies were right, perhaps I should read it, and perhaps I should keep an open mind and give it the benefit of the doubt.

I knew there was a copy of the King James Authorized Version in my house somewhere, one of my children had received it as a gift, many years previously, as far as I knew it had not been thrown away.

After a brief search I found it hiding in the same cupboard that I had desired to cower in.

I dug it out and cleaned off the cobwebs, and having made myself yet another pot of tea I put my feet up, opened the book at Genesis chapter one verse one, and started to read.

It was not what I had expected.

I hardly had time to take a sip of my tea before I noticed quite a few apparent inconsistencies between the things people believe and the words written.

I became enthralled, in the sense that my curiosity was tweaked; I became interested in what I was reading, though not in the religious sense.

That was my undoing. I soon became hooked, and found myself unable to put it down.

So many questions arose, that the very next day I went to the local religious book shop and bought a Strong's concordance, and a few other things.

*

At this point I would like to ask the reader if he or she would mind if I adopted a writing style that addresses them directly.

I wish to speak to you, my reader, as though you were my only reader, which might well be the case.

I want to do this for a number of reasons, firstly because it illustrates something that I will mention in a few paragraphs from now, and secondly because later in the book the subject matter gets more than a little complicated, and I feel it would be easier to explain these things if I adopt a more personal approach.

If you will allow me this honor, it will make things a great deal easier for both of us.

Of course you cannot refuse, you are unable to reply, and I have considered that.

This serves as something of an example to illustrate a problem with the Bible. It is not possible to engage God in direct conversation; we cannot ask Him to explain things. It is this ability to avoid questions that lends the Bible much of its authority.

The Bible talks to all of us, much as I am talking to you, in a one-sided, one way, communication.

The writer of the Bible has the advantage that we cannot contradict him. He decided what was written, much as I decide what is written in this book.

It is obvious that God did not actually write the Bible, though it is often claimed that He inspired the words. The pen that wrote those words was held by a human hand, and to distinguish that writer from this writer, I propose to call that writer 'the scribe', which does not exclude the likelihood that there was more than one.

This is just one of the observations I made when I started to read the book of Genesis. There were many more, and I would like to discuss some of the other difficulties I found, before moving on to more significant matters.

I could simply direct you to the passage of greatest interest, but that would leave you bereft of some important details. We will get there just the same, all in good time.

For now, I would like to continue with describing my first experiences with the Bible, which really do have a bearing on what happens later, if they did not, I would not mention them.

*

I am sure you are already aware of the meaning of the word 'antediluvian', but in case you are not, it simply means 'appertaining to before the flood'.

We start with a brief survey of the antediluvian period, which is contained in the very first chapters of Genesis, up to and including Genesis chapter 6, where the flood starts and the antediluvian age ends.

Towards the end of this book, after we have found and understood the secrets of the antediluvian age, we will be better placed to appreciate the earlier parts of the Bible, and those things which appear tedious and boring right now may become rather more interesting later.

*

My initial venture into Genesis may appear at first sight to be a 'hatchet job', to use the vernacular, but you would be mistaken to think that, I can assure you it is far more destructive.

I wish to introduce you to my way of working, my way of thinking, in the hope that it will induce you to do likewise.

Although we could jump straight to where the treasure is hidden, our time will be better spent if we take a few pages to consider the earlier chapters, because it will help to set the scene, it will ease us into the main theme without you really noticing.

To this end it would be helpful if you had a Bible available, so that you could read along with me, and check that what I say is true.

If you prefer not to, it doesn't matter much, but reading the Bible for yourself will make this present book come alive.

*

And here, straight away, we encounter another minor problem.

If you obtain a copy of the Bible, there is a good chance it will be different from mine, because there are so very many different versions of the Bible available.

It has been translated into just about every language on Earth, and within those languages there are different versions. Even in the English language, there are so many different versions they are hard to count.

We do not know what language the book of Genesis was originally written in. The version that has come down to us was likely written in ancient Hebrew, which differs considerably from Modern Hebrew.

But no matter what language it was written in, the words used all have different nuances of meaning. Words in all languages have nuances of meaning, which is why it is often difficult to win an argument with a politician.

This may seem like a trivial matter, but it is actually rather important, and relates to one of the things the ladies insisted on, that the Bible was the inspired Word of God.

There are religious people who vehemently claim that every word in the Bible is literally true.

Clearly, this cannot be a valid claim. Before they could even attempt to validate such a claim they would first have to establish which one of the countless differing versions is the one that they accept as being literally true.

*

There is another problem for people who believe in the literal truth of the inspired and unfailing Word of God. I had barely started to read the blessed pages when I came across an obvious anomaly.

In the very first chapter of the book of Genesis the plurality of God is very prominent. It cannot fail to draw the attention of a critical and secular reader.

If you read just a few verses on the first page, down to verse 26, you will see:

...***And God said, Let us make man in our image,***

The word used in the Hebrew for God is 'Elohim' which is a plural word, and literally means 'Mighty Ones'.

So, if these religious people insist that every word is literally true, then they must accept that their God is really a group of Mighty Ones.

If we are to take it literally it means:

.. And the Mighty Ones said, let us make man in our image,

From which we should deduce that these putative 'Mighty Ones' look like us. That is the outcome of a literal understanding.

In fact, in Genesis 1 v 1, the very first words of the Bible, the word translated as 'God' is actually the plural word 'Elohim' or Mighty Ones.

....In the beginning Mighty Ones created the heaven and the earth.

*

It gets worse, but already, while we are still on the very first page, it is possible to see that if we look closely at the Bible, a different story to the generally accepted religious one is emerging. As we read on, the anomalies continue to intrude on the story.

Still on the theme of a plurality of Gods, there is another instance in chapter three, verse 22.

...And the LORD God said, Behold, the man is become as **one of us**.

Clearly this is not to be taken literally, or is it?

The plurality of God is found elsewhere in the Bible, and we will come across it again later. It is not really a problem for me, but it may be a problem for others. For me, at the time, it was an indication that all was not as it seemed.

Religious people do not take the Word of God literally, not even those who claim to, because if they did, they would believe in a multitude of gods, not just the one. It is necessary to 'interpret' the words in the Bible if we wish to sustain the generally accepted view.

Since I had no interest in sustaining the general view, I continued to follow the ladies' advice, and take it literally.

*

As I studied these things, I gradually became aware that the book of Genesis had been 'retro-edited' if there is such a word. Perhaps the term 'redacted' would be more accurate.

It seemed fairly obvious that the original text used a plural form to denote multiple gods, but once the notion of monotheism had become established, a multiple god was not acceptable, so in translation the literal meaning 'Mighty Ones' was changed to 'God'.

It is even possible to see echoes here of the old pagan pantheons of gods, as in the Greek and Roman gods, which were many, and all looked like men. (Or men looked like them)

If we are made in the image of God, then it is to be presumed that God looks like us.

Even today, we still refer to a well-built man as being 'like a Greek god' or a good-looking woman as a 'goddess'.

Naturally, modern theologians will come up with many 'interpretations' of this straight-forward statement. It is explained by claiming that God made us in His 'spiritual' image, or in some other meaningless way.

Look again at what is actually written,

"Let us make man ***in our image, after our likeness****"* He repeats Himself, *"After our likeness"*

We see the plurality of God again, and if we are to take the written words literally, it means that the scribe who wrote them believed that the 'Elohim' or Mighty Ones, made us to look like them. We are made in the image of the Mighty Ones.

That is what it actually says.

If I jump ahead of the story a little, to Gen 5 v 3 where Adam the man created in the image of God, after God's likeness, himself fathers a boy child. We see a similar turn of phrase applied to Adam and his son.

'And Adam lived an hundred and thirty years, and begat a son ***in his own likeness, after his image****; and called his name Seth:'*

I noticed the similarity of the wording, and thought it was strange that the scribe would use the exact same words to describe a child born of biology, and a human created by the Mighty Ones.

The fact that the same human 'Adam' was involved in both comments made it all the more interesting.

The same sentiment is found yet again in

Genesis 9 v 6

....for in the image of God made he man.

Again the word translated as 'God' is 'Elohim' or Mighty Ones.

*

So if every word is to be taken literally, the picture that emerges is one that is quite different from the doctrine preached by modern clerics.

It is worth noting that if the scribe was writing what he believed to be true, then he and his antediluvian contemporaries believed that a group of 'Mighty Ones' created humans, and that the Mighty Ones looked like us, because they made us to look like themselves.

This is when my brain first whispered the word 'clone' into my unguarded mind, when that concept first intruded into my conscious thoughts. It was a word that I considered only briefly at that time, before putting it back where it came from.

I considered it, indeed I did, because I was not putting a presumptuous and atheistic interpretation on the ancient scribe's words; I was taking them literally, as instructed by the very religious ladies who came to my door.

The word 'clone' is a modern word, and we know what it means, but the ancient scribe was surely saying the same thing, though struggling to express himself?

I sat there sipping my tea and staring at the words I was reading in disbelief. I had only just started to read the holy pages and already I found myself thinking words like 'aliens' and 'clones'.

Something was not right somewhere.

*

We can delve a little deeper, and read another verse that puzzled me greatly.

Genesis chapter 3 verse 21 ***...Unto Adam also and to his wife did the LORD God make coats of skins, and clothed them...***

This is a very simple little statement, until we look closer. Where did the skins come from? One presumes they came from an animal that was freshly killed and skinned by the LORD God, prior to using the hides to make clothing.

Are we really supposed to accept that this blood-splattered figure who killed and skinned animals to make clothing for a couple of naked humans is the same as the Infinite Spirit, the Almighty God who created the universe and everything in it? Or is it possible that the Chief of the Mighty Ones was better equipped for the sanguinary task?

What exactly is going on here?

*

Then there is the problem that when the scribes write, they often quote God verbatim.

They write words like ***'And God said – Let there be light.'***

Quite obviously a scribe could not have heard those words, if they had ever been spoken, because they were spoken before humans existed.

The scribes believed what they wrote, and they wrote what they believed. It is up to us to try our best to understand what they believed without swamping what they say with our own preconceptions.

*

The experts of the modern world, the theologians and the scholars of comparative religion, bend over backwards and jump through hoops in their attempts to resolve the plurality issue.

'It is the Trinity, the three-in-one' appears meaningless to me.

'It is the royal ***We*** like the Queen would use.' We are not amused.

'God is talking to **us**; we are the ***us***.' Does this make sense to us?

My main objection to these so-called 'explanations' is that in proposing these convoluted distortions they credit the antediluvian scribe with a sophisticated understanding of academic theology, as if that ancient scribe had the mind of a modern scholar of divinity.

I say that it is not at all likely that the scribe was engaging in complex philosophical reasoning, he was just writing down what he believed.

The simplest and best answer to the plurality problem is to say that the scribe believed there were a group of Mighty Ones.

If I say to you "There is a man who dresses like one of us." Would you assume I was talking to myself about myself?

No, if I talk to you, I am talking to another person. When we talk to other people we are talking in much the same way as God is reported to be talking.

The religious pundits also explain how the scribe can quote God when there were no humans around to hear Him, by claiming that the words were by direct inspiration. That means that God dictated and the scribe wrote down what he said, much like a modern secretary.

It is more reasonable to say that the scribe wrote down what his people believed, and invented quotes from God as a shorthand way of explaining things.

The other passage I mentioned, where the Almighty Infinite Spirit Creator of the universe skinned animals and sewed the skins into clothing, is usually ignored by one and all, so has no explanation.

*

If this were a fictional treasure hunt, the opening scene would be deep underground in the bowels of the Earth, in a tunnel beneath an old and long-lost Cambodian temple. The heroine, a young blonde girl named Claudia, would be running for her life along a dark, bat infested, stone passageway, with the sounds of her pursuers echoing close behind her.

Her heart would be pounding in fear as she jumped across a strange symbol carved into a flagstone, dimly seen in the light of her failing torch...

I could write fiction as well as anyone, but this is a true story of a real treasure hunt, not a fictional adventure, so you will just have to put up with me sitting in an armchair reading books and sipping tea, or find a more exciting storybook to read. The Bible can be very tedious at times, this is acknowledged, but without patience and endurance on the part of both of us, it will not be possible for you to understand the finer points of the search, and later, you will not comprehend the full significance of that which we eventually find.

There are many seemingly dull and boring matters in the first three chapters of Genesis that I have deliberately missed out, mainly because they are not relevant to the theme of this book, and although they may be of concern to some, to my current endeavor they represent a distraction. I found them to be interesting at the time I first read them, but now, at this moment, we are on a treasure hunt, so those irrelevancies can be omitted.

Some of these things I have left out because I intend to return to this subject in a later chapter, after we have revealed our discovery, to see what difference it might make to our understanding.

There is one such apparent irrelevancy that I would like to mention, in passing, if I may.

In Genesis chapter 1, in the creation story, it says:-

9 And God said, Let the waters under the heaven be gathered together unto one place, and let the dry land appear: and it was so.

If we might notice here that we have a description of the water being together in one place. The words used paint a picture of one single ocean, 'gathered together unto one place', and one single continent.

It implies the modern scientific notion of a single huge continent, which the scientists call Pangaea.

I mention this, because this is one incident where there is a vague hint of advanced scientific knowledge in the Genesis story.

Modern science accepts the single ocean and single continent, as part of their understanding of the early world. It seems odd to me that it was so similar to the apparent belief of the ancients.

It is just a little thing, but is something that stuck in my mind as an early hint, a residual piece of information from a possible ancient science.

I would now like to move quickly on to Genesis chapter four and beyond.

*

In Genesis chapter four we leave the protected area of the Garden of Eden and move into the wild, untamed antediluvian world, and we see the start of a civilization.

Again there is a slight problem. The scribe gives us a picture of a population that is growing rapidly from just two people.

After Cain killed his brother Abel, it suddenly appears that Cain has a wife, and he has children. The scribe does not account for the sudden appearance of females on the scene, but we may assume that he is not telling us everything.

Like me, that ancient scribe may have felt the need to abbreviate his account, for fear of boring his reader, or perhaps large sections, whole pages, of his account have been lost, the gaps being filled in by subsequent editors.

The scribe also informs us that people in those days lived for hundreds of years, which is a claim that most moderns would laugh at, but there is no scientific ground for disbelief. On the contrary, modern science is striving to find the secret of longevity, knowing through research into genetics that it is scientifically possible, if not very probable at our current rate of progress.

The problem is that our DNA contains a self-destruct function. Scientists are aware of this fact; it is why we die of old age if nothing else kills us first.

If it were possible to rid our DNA of that particular coded instruction, we could theoretically live forever, so the claim that individual antediluvians could live for nine hundred years or more is not as fantastic as it first seems. Of course we would need to reject accepted history before we could encompass such a thought, which would be a problem for some, but the biological possibility of extreme longevity is not total nonsense.

*

The scribe goes on to give us hints of a technology that is more advanced than the stone-age.

Chapter 4

Verse 21 ...And his brother's name was Jubal: he was the father of all such as handle the harp and organ...

22 ...And Zillah, she also bare Tubal- cain, an instructer of every artificer in brass and iron...

This is the antediluvian age, and we are told that there are musicians, and instructors in the working of iron.

If we are to take this as literally true, inspired by God, we should remember that modern historians place the earliest use of iron in 1200 BC, which is long after the antediluvian age had passed into myth and legend.

Notwithstanding the objections of modern historians, the text informs us that before the flood there were facilities for mining and smelting iron and other metals, and for constructing musical instruments.

The musical instruments suggest that there is leisure time, time to sit around and play the harp, and of course if it were possible to make musical instruments and smelt iron, then it would have been equally possible to make a host of other useful items.

The scribe only gives us brief morsels of information, but the picture I get is one of an emerging technological civilization. The Bible speaks of a time long ago, long before the stone-age, when there was a civilized race of men, blessed with extreme longevity, who had developed a relatively advanced culture. This was a culture that has been forgotten, destroyed by a catastrophe and consigned to myth and legend. I do not need to inform you that the very notion of the possible reality of such a culture is dismissed by modern academics.

It was not always thus. Before the advent of modern scientific thought it was accepted that an antediluvian civilization once existed on Earth. It is a concept that was believed and accepted as fact ever since the scribe first wrote his words on parchment thousands of years ago.

Scientists would say that the reality of such a civilization can no longer be supported, because the catastrophic flood that destroyed them is regarded as nonsense. If there was no deluge, then there could not have been a 'before the deluge', ergo, no antediluvians, no civilization, just myth. The scribe who claimed that there was such a race of people 'must' be making it up.

Modern scientists are calling the ancient scribe a liar, without any justification other than simple disbelief.

These days we are all born into a world of mass communication, which is so much a part of our lives that we find it difficult to imagine a world where a scribe has to write his words on whatever comes to hand, and that is the end of it. He cannot duplicate it without making a handwritten copy. He cannot broadcast it, publish it, or have it printed, or read over the radio. He cannot post it on the net.

Imagine the scene where a lonely old scribe is wandering around the desert clutching his piece of parchment; trying to show it to anyone he comes across. That is the only method the ancient scribe had for the publishing of his handwritten historical material.

His is the only copy, so why would he write it if it were not an important part of his history? It is not a script for a disaster movie, it is a tale of the destruction of an entire civilization, and at the time it was written it would not have been dismissed as a joke. We should also ask ourselves how an ancient scribe could invent such a story. In his day, there was surely no such thing as science fiction?

The ancient scribe must have believed what he was writing, and his contemporaries would no doubt have believed the same, and I am of the opinion that they must have had a reason for believing what they did.

It is an undeniable fact that the earlier generations of modern humanity all valued it; and many people accepted it as a true story, or it would not have ended up in the Bible, it would not have survived the millennia full of critics.

Our modern-day scientists say that there is no evidence of a flood, ignoring the old truism that the absence of evidence is not evidence of absence.

What really makes me wonder about the integrity of science is the observation that if they dig up an old Babylonian clay tablet inscribed with cuneiform writing, or an old Egyptian pot with hieroglyphs on it, they enthuse over it and write learned papers on it, but here we have a lucid account of an ancient civilization which is equally old, if not older, and science just shrugs and dismisses it as myth.

Something is not right somewhere.

*

In the final verse of chapter four of Genesis we see the start of a formal religion:

...then began men to call upon the name of the LORD...

This suggests that prior to this verse, antediluvian men did ***not*** call on the name of the Lord, thus placing difficulty on the claim that scripture is by inspiration of God.

If men did not call upon His name previously, they are not likely to be inspired by Him are they? So how did they manage to write the creation story by direct inspiration? Perhaps God dictated it later.

So religion started, but we do not know what form it took. It was certainly not Judaism or Christianity, neither of which came about until thousands of years had passed by. Whatever forms the religion took; it did not do the worshippers much good, because they were all subsequently labelled as wicked and drowned in the flood which was soon to destroy their world.

*

If we move quickly on to Genesis chapter five, we can skim through a genealogy which takes us from Adam through to Noah, and we can observe that all of these antediluvian patriarchs are reported to have lived to a ripe old age.

Enoch is of passing interest, because he was taken away by God. Exactly what that means is a bit of a mystery, but many religious pundits will suggest that he did not die, but was physically taken to be with God.

Genesis 5 v. 24 ...And Enoch walked with God: and he was not; for God took him.

Both instances of 'God' in this verse are 'Elohim' – a plural word meaning Mighty Ones.

...And Enoch walked with the Mighty Ones: and he was not; for the Mighty Ones took him.

*

Of course, I am sure you realize that the text we are discussing dates from a very early time. If we are to give the scripture the 'benefit of the doubt' as suggested by the ladies at my door, then we would have to recognize that the scribe who originated the information, who first wrote these words, was himself an antediluvian, that is to say, he lived before the flood that destroyed his world.

*

Need I remind you that at this stage I did not take the Bible very seriously? Nobody treats it seriously anymore, not in England anyway. The only people who treat it seriously are those who are predisposed to religion, but it is usually ignored by the rest of us.

I was reading it because I had become interested, but that is not the same as taking it seriously.

It wasn't until much later that I discovered just how significant some of these seemingly irrational stories are.

There I was, sat in my armchair, with a cup of tea beside me and a Bible open on my lap, just amusing myself with casual thoughts about the words I was reading. Little did I know where it would all lead, I did not foresee just how much it would cost me in terms of my personal life, but that is another story.

We really must get on with it now, or we will never get there.

*

One important question that I asked myself was concerned with how the words the scribe wrote managed to survive the flood. It could be argued that the scribe who wrote the words we are reading lived after the flood, but that does not answer the question. He may have lived after the deluge, but the information he was writing down must have originated from before.

In the context of the Biblical story the only way such information could survive the flood would be via Noah and his Ark.

If we keep to the setting specified by the story, giving it the benefit of my doubt, Noah must have carried the information with him on the Ark, I presume written on scrolls, or perhaps he wrote some of the words himself.

The Bible gives us a story of the flood, a story that only Noah or one of his family could have known about or reported on, so the original author of the flood story was probably one of the people actually on board the Ark.

*

We are still engaged in our treasure hunt, I would like to remind you, in case you have forgotten and are getting bored, and this story is relevant to the hunt.

It came to my mind when reading this story of Noah and the flood, that as well as the scrolls recounting the stories of the antediluvian period, and the genealogies, Noah might well have been in possession of a treasury of ancient knowledge. It is reasonable to suppose that Noah would want to preserve the knowledge of his people, along with the animals, surely?

He certainly had enough time to collect the records of the achievements of his people, he had advance warning. He had time to build a monstrous great wooden Ark, and gather a load of animals together; so it is reasonable to suppose he would have had a little time spare to pop round to the local reference library and scoop up an armful of scrolls?

Surely he would have given some priority to preserving his people's legacy of scientific and other knowledge? I would have done, had I been in his sandals, wouldn't you?

It is fairly evident that the story has been abridged and sanitised by the passage of time, coupled with religious interpretation and scientific disbelief. I have this image in my head of women and children begging for passage on his Ark, and him replying that he has no room left; the last berth was taken up by a pair of sewer rats, and even then they had to share with the cockroaches.

Genesis 7 v. 16...and the LORD shut him in.

Noah must have been made of very stern stuff, considering he was able to ignore the pleas for help from his friends and neighbors, or perhaps, after the Elohim had shut the door, he was hermetically sealed into the Ark, safe and secure, and could not hear the sounds from outside?

Perhaps he was unaware of the thumping on the door and the piercing screams of terrified children?

I see crowds of unfortunate people clinging to the woodwork, swarming onto the roof as the waters rose, banging and shouting, begging in vain to be let in.

One could argue that if he let one of them in, he would soon be capsized with the weight of desperate drowning bodies. The entire population drowned like rats, whilst the rats themselves were safe, warm and snuggled up together in a nest of straw under Noah's bed.

To save or not to save his compatriots must have been a difficult decision for Noah to make, but an easier decision would be whether or not to save their cultural achievements.

To me it is inconceivable that he would not save knowledge. If there were any truth to the story, any grain of truth at all, then Noah would have tried to save the scientific knowledge of his people, even if only to atone for his guilt, so that in some way he could preserve the memory of the people he had abandoned to their watery fate.

If he did what any other human would do, if he tried to salvage the accumulated knowledge of his people, then he would have had that information with him while he was on the Ark, and *after he left it*.

I decided it might be fun to follow him, to watch him closely, to see where he goes and what he does.

Of course at this point I was still just playing a cynical game; I had no idea at the time that it was anything other than myth. The notion that there could have been secret knowledge on the Ark was just empty-headed speculation. I didn't know then what I know now; I didn't know that there really was a treasure of ancient knowledge; I was just toying with the idea, because the only way antediluvian secrets could survive the flood is by being on board the Ark with Noah.

*

The reality of the flood is denied by all and sundry, of course, but if we are to give the Bible the benefit of the doubt, then we are expected to consider it, because it is a fundamental part of the Genesis story.

For the sake of argument, for the sake of our research, we may assume that the scribes who wrote the Bible were honest. They wrote about their God, or Mighty

Ones, in fear and trembling, they would not lie about the flood, surely?

*

The flood is eternally connected with the continuing and futile argument between Creationists and Evolutionists. Theories and hypothetical suggestions about how the flood could have been real abound. I hesitate to add my suggestion because I would not wish anyone to think I was taking sides. I accept neither evolution nor Creationism; I simple say that I think there is a mechanism which would allow for the flood to have happened, without transgressing natural law.

I wish to make it abundantly clear; I am not on either side of the squabble.

*

The story of the infamous flood, which science knows nothing about, is found in Genesis chapters six and seven.

If we are to continue accepting the elderly ladies' suggestion that the scripture is the literal truth, then we should really attempt to show how this imaginary flood could have wiped out the entire population of the world, without leaving any traces for science to examine.

I think we owe it to the ancient scribe who wrote the story, and to satisfy my own need to move the treasure hunt forward. The treasure is to be found on our side of the inundation, so somehow, along with Noah, we must also survive the flood.

I am not in the position of knowing for certain, but I am prepared to give the scripture the benefit of the doubt once more. It is possible that there actually was a flood as described in the Bible, the mechanism exists and is known to science, but that does not prove that it really happened.

*

In Genesis chapter one verse seven, we read that there were two sets of 'waters', one below a 'firmament' and the other above.

Given that the firmament meant sky, we can say that the scribe is telling us that there were waters 'above the sky', or, in modern terminology, in space.

Water in space would be in the form of ice. Though a purist would argue that the scripture says 'water', I would maintain that ice is water, just solid water.

If we take this at face value, the scribe is telling us something he could not have known unless he had access to technology. He is telling us that the Earth had a cloud of ice around it, or rings of ice, like the planet Saturn. Again, we see a vague hint of advanced knowledge in the antediluvian age.

Ice in space in the vicinity of Earth is, in itself, not unlikely, as I am sure scientists would agree. Ice is plentiful in the Solar System, and rings are found around one or two planets.

It is even postulated that all the evidence of rivers of water on Mars can be explained by a flood brought about by a collapse of a ring system.

Let us suppose that Earth had a ring system like Saturn, made of lumps of ice. Such a ring system would not be very stable, because of the gravitational influence of the moon.

If the rings were to collapse, either because of the influence of the moon or some other perturbation, then the collapse would be relatively sudden and complete. Huge amounts of ice, in large lumps, would fall towards the Earth at high speed.

Friction caused by high velocity entry into the atmosphere would generate heat, which would melt much of the ice. The resulting water mingled with residual ice would fall in a deluge all over the world, raining in icy torrents onto the Earth below. Larger blocks of ice might survive entry into the atmosphere and crash into the ground, exploding into clouds of water and ice shrapnel. The kinetic energy of the impact would certainly shatter the lumps and generate more heat, so further melting would take place.

Ice chunks that fell into the sea might survive, floating as frozen rafts on the surface.

The scripture claims that the deluge lasted forty days and nights, which implies a large ring structure, taking a long time to complete its collapse. It is easy to see that a large ring structure of ice could easily produce enough melt-water to flood the planet to any arbitrary depth; it would depend entirely on how much ice there was in the original ring.

It is irrational and unreasonable to be dogmatic and declare that such an event could not happen.

Should such a disaster have happened then all trace of the putative antediluvian civilization would have been wiped from the Earth. If it happened today all evidence of our global civilization, along with any buildings or machinery would be erased. So it would also have been with the antediluvians, all evidence of them would have been eradicated.

Science will have none of this of course, but it is a possibility.

The question arises, what happened to all that water?

The answer is it is still here.

*

Beneath the continents and the oceans the Earth's mantle is a malleable magma. Modern science will tell us about plate tectonics, and how the continents float on this mantle, and those same scientists will also tell us about something they call 'isostatic adjustment'.

Water is heavy, very heavy, and it pushes down on the ocean floor, which is a flexible layer on the surface of the semi-molten flexible mantle.

The whole weight of water pushing down on the ocean floor will cause the ocean floor to sink, and the continents to rise. This is isostatic adjustment.

If we add water to the planet, in large amounts, then it will push down more on the ocean floor than it will on the land, because the land is higher and gets higher still. It is a little like a seesaw in a child's playground. If you push down on one end, the other end goes up.

As a result, all the extra water forced the ocean floor to sink down a bit more, and squeezed the flexible mantle such that the continents rose up further.

So the oceans got deeper and the continents rose a little higher, draining the extra water from the land into the deepening oceans.

This will continue until the weight of the extra water is balanced by the weight of the emerging continents, when they are said to be in 'isostatic equilibrium'.

The end result would be the world that we see today.

*

Scientists tell us that there is no evidence of such a flood, instead they point to evidence of an ice age.

If the flood happened as described, by a titanic blizzard of ice driving into the atmosphere, then much of that ice would end up floating on the surface of the floodwater. It would be much like the aftermath of a summer hail storm, only a bit bigger.

As the ice entered the atmosphere, as well as melting to form water that would fall as torrential rain, a part of the water would evaporate to form water vapour. All that water vapour in the high atmosphere would cover the world in a blanket of cloud, blocking the heat from the sun, and falling as thick snow in higher latitudes.

After the deluge stopped, the scripture claims that it took about a year before the first signs of receding waters were observed.

The world would have been a much colder place, with so much ice around. Ice floating on water would tend to last longer and be more concentrated at the Earth's poles, and as the floodwaters receded into the deepening ocean basin the floating ice would settle on the emerging land, building up to a huge thickness in many places. Much of it would end up going aground on mountains and forming glaciers.

With water vapour blocking the sun, and huge amounts of ice at the poles and elsewhere, snow falling thick and fast within and beyond the polar-circles, the total overall effect could be called an ice age.

This would also explain where all the ice came from to produce the scientist's ice age, for they cannot explain it by other means.

As a matter of minor interest, I did a little research into scientific accounts of the ice ages, and although it is easy to find numerous theories of how the world could get cold, I could find no sensible account of how so much ice could form. Under normal circumstances snow and ice cannot accumulate to a greater degree than is permitted by the amount of water vapour in the atmosphere, and this is controlled by the amount of heat evaporating water from the sea. If you wish to construct a conventional ice age, you need a lot of heat to evaporate the water from the oceans before you can get enough precipitation to build up a miles-thick layer of ice. In short, you need an awful lot of excess heat and a huge amount of extreme cold at one and the same time to make a 'scientist's ice age'. A 'flood' ice age provides the ice for free.

The ice from above would generate an ice age, and would leave all the same evidences as an ice age.

So you see it is possible that there really was a true global flood that destroyed just about everything on Earth, and left evidence to make geologists think it was just an ice age.

If we look a little more closely, there is even suggestion in the scripture that this mechanism was known to the scribe.

Gen 7 v 11 In the six hundredth year of Noah's life, in the second month, the seventeenth day of the month, the same day were all the fountains of the great deep broken up, and the windows of heaven were opened.

We can note that this was no ordinary rain. The windows of heaven, the sky, were opened, so the water came in through the windows, as if pouring in from above the sky, from space.

The fountains of the great deep were broken up, suggesting plate tectonics, volcanism, and similar disturbances.

It is a wonder anyone survived, but by a miracle, and because he built a huge and strong wooden box, Noah got through the ordeal. We may spare a passing thought for those of his compatriots who would have tried to gain entry to the Ark, and were left to drown in despair. If meteorites of ice smashing into the Earth were added to the deluge of rain and the maelstrom of rising waters, the tumultuous noise would add to the frenzy of panic and confusion. The disaster would truly have been of Biblical proportions.

All the antediluvians perished, except Noah and his family. Noah survived, along with any ancient secrets he may have carried with him.

*

We are nearly at the end of chapter one; and I would like to explain why I have left out rather a lot of scripture that you might have taken an interest in, if you had read it.

I missed out the bit about 'Sons of God' or Bene ha Elohim, sons of the Mighty Ones, because I will be mentioning it later.

I have missed out any significant comment about the animals in the box, ('Ark' means box) and there are many other details I have skipped over, because they do not help in our treasure hunt.

I am not engaged in an exposition of scripture, I am highlighting some of the passages that will become relevant later in our quest, and leaving out most of the religious aspects.

*

The flood marks the end of an era; it marks the end of the long-lived generations of a lost civilization. The antediluvian population have all been mangled and drowned and ground into mud and buried beneath miles of sediment on the ocean floor, along with all evidence that they were ever here. All of them destroyed, all except Noah and his immediate family.

The story tells us that Noah and his wife, and three sons with their wives, eight people in all, survived into the modern world.

*

Now someone is going to mention dinosaurs and fossils, there is no escape from that.

There is however a neat little answer to the question of dinosaurs, but it will have to wait until the end of this book.

We will leave the matter of the creation until last as well. We will return to all these subjects when we are better equipped to discuss them.

The world has just been totally destroyed by a devastating flood, but one man and seven family members survived, and we hope and suggest that these people had with them a library of antediluvian secrets.

To start with this was just a vague misty thought that occupied my mind while I was opening a packet of digestives, and making myself a fresh pot of tea, but it was not long before it began to take on a more solid form.

We will meet Noah again in the next chapter.

...

Chapter Two

The Migdal of Babel

---

1 And God remembered Noah, and every living thing, and all the cattle that was with him in the Ark: and God made a wind to pass over the earth, and the waters asswaged;

2 The fountains also of the deep and the windows of heaven were stopped, and the rain from heaven was restrained;

If you are still with me, then I thank you for your patience.

By now you should have an appreciation of my attitude to religion and the scripture. I think there is truth in the Bible, but not the same truth as the various churches would have us believe.

In the previous chapter we made mention of a global flood, the description of which we found in the book of Genesis.

It is a fairly well-known fact that there are many other global flood myths, prominent amongst them being the Babylonian Epic of Gilgamesh, which relates the story of a man named Utnapishtim who survived a global flood.

Testimony to the reality of such a flood is to be found in the sheer number of the myths and legends from around the world that recount the same story in different forms.

Modern pundits reject them all, ignoring the old maxim that there is no smoke without fire.

I confess I have not read all these myths, but I have tried to read the story of Utnapishtim, and I found it to be confused and irrational.

Why the pundits would suggest that the Biblical version was in imitation of the story in the Gilgamesh epic is beyond me.

The Babylonian nation did not come into existence until long after the flood took place, so it cannot claim precedence on the basis of age.

I judge the story by a kind of 'rationality index'.

Noah's story in the Bible is far more rational and coherent than the other myths, at least those that I have read. It has the additional advantage of being in the Biblical book of Genesis, which was the very book I was reading.

*

We left Noah adrift on a world of water, where there was no land visible, but gradually the waters abated, the principle of isostatic adjustment came into play, and slowly but surely the land emerged from the waters.

His huge wooden lifeboat runs aground on a mountain, which we have come to know as Ararat, but in truth it could have been anywhere.

If we accept that modern-day Ararat is the same place, then the Ark grounded on a mountain in what is now known as eastern Turkey.

If Noah had looked out of the window, he would presumably have seen a world awash with muddy water and floating ice.

The story informs us that Noah waited for a while; several months in fact, until some signs of plant growth were detected.

Genesis 8 v.11 ***And the dove came in to him in the evening; and, lo, in her mouth was an olive leaf pluckt off: so Noah knew that the waters were abated from off the earth.***

This makes it clear that some life had survived the flood; the olive leaf had to have come from a living olive tree, which was not planted by Noah.

Some very religious people would insist that no living thing survived the flood apart from those on the Ark, but the olive branch found by the dove and presented to Noah casts doubt on that rigid claim.

If olive trees could survive, so could other trees and plants, so could marine creatures, crocodiles, fish, birds, insects, bacteria, and a few lucky land animals, even men, who found safety on some floating islands of vegetation. In any disaster there are always survivors.

We really must try to be pragmatic in our view of these matters.

The ocean tides are caused by the gravitational influence of the sun and the moon, so we can expect tides to ebb and flow even at the highest point of the flood. There would still be tides as the flood receded, and each high tide would leave a strandline of seeds and shooting twigs and roots strewn over the land. Since the flood was slowly dropping, each strandline would be on a lower contour than the previous, so as tide follows receding tide, the whole land would gradually be seeded with the detritus of the flood, which could include insects and small animals.

It therefore seems possible that within a few years the world could have been green again, especially in regard to those species of plant that had seeds that floated, many of which would be edible fruit trees.

There are many arguments that have been put forward against the reality of the flood, for example it might be objected that the flood would be fresh water, and the sea is salt. Well, we do not know how salty the original ocean was, or how fresh the flood water was, so we do not know what salinity the resulting mix would be, or how much it has changed in the time that has passed since it happened.

Whatever the case for and against the flood, the story makes it clear that the antediluvian age is over and finished with, and a new age is about to begin.

*

We will skip forward a little way, to an event that I consider carries with it the 'ring of truth'. We are in Genesis chapter 9 now. The story has moved on a little.

In the far north the Ice Age is underway, but Noah is in a Mediterranean area, and for him the weather has improved. The clouds have cleared and the sun is warming the southern slopes of Mount Ararat, where we find him picking grapes.

He has settled down to recover from his ordeal, and one of the first things he does after giving thanks for his salvation is to grow some grapes, just so he could make some wine, and get falling-down drunk.

20 And Noah began to be an husbandman, and he planted a vineyard:

21 And he drank of the wine, and was drunken; and he was uncovered within his tent.

We are invited to assume that he had the grape vine rootstock with him on the Ark, and that he had to wait a year or so before he could pick a crop of grapes, and ferment wine, but nevertheless, if a man is determined enough!

Noah was supposedly a righteous man, but this little episode betrays a truth, for he does what any man surviving such an ordeal would do. He gets himself well and truly smashed at his earliest opportunity, even if he had to grow the grapes himself.

The story of Noah and the flood is often ridiculed because it has been turned into a child's story, a story that always leaves out the part where Noah is lying drunk and naked in his tent, with all his naughty bits on show. (Gen 9, vs. 20-23)

The child's story appears to have infected the modern critics and pundits, for rather childishly they usually concentrate on the animals, arguing senselessly about how many the Ark could accommodate, and what Noah did with all that manure. They invariably ignore the plight of the antediluvian people, who are simply dismissed as 'wicked'.

This is because creationists are inflexible in their belief in the literal truth of the Bible, and they cannot make pragmatic adjustments, they cannot do what I can do.

I say, Noah took some animals into the Ark, as anyone would, but I do not care how many or of what kind.

The story is one of survival, not the survival of people or animals, but the survival of *knowledge*; and that is the important point to come out of this tale.

*

Noah and his family represent the lost civilization of the antediluvian world. If there is any truth in the story, he and his family were the only people left alive on Earth. His entire world, all that he knew, had been destroyed.

When Noah stepped down from the Ark he didn't stand on the world he knew, he stood on the modern world. He stood on our world, on the world that we know today.

***Genesis 9 v 28 And Noah lived after the flood three hundred and fifty years*.**

If anyone was in possession of any of the scientific records of that lost antediluvian world, then it would have been him.

Did Noah possess antediluvian scientific secrets? I did not know at the time I was reading the words, but the point is that he *could* have, and if he did, then he walked this world, our world, for three and a half centuries with that knowledge in his possession, on his person, or in his head.

It is easily possible, within the terms laid down by the myth, that he could have hidden that scientific knowledge somewhere.

If it is really myth, we will never find such knowledge, because if it is really myth then the knowledge doesn't exist. But what if he did hide scientific knowledge? What if we do actually find it? Should we then feel obliged to accept the reality of the story?

The answers are; he did, and we do, and we should.

The Tower of Babel

The text then gives a long genealogy, which is broken in the middle by the story of the Tower of Babel, which is the first of the three principal themes of this book, and is where we want to be.

We have finally arrived at the starting point, the first clue of our treasure hunt. It is a great pity that the process of teasing out the clue is rather tedious, but had it been more obvious, and less irksome, others would have found it long ago.

It is possible that you are not familiar with the story of the building of the Tower of Babel, or you may have heard some entertaining but invented fictional tales, so shortly we will take a look at it in detail.

First I wish to show that Noah was still very much to the fore as we continue our tale.

*

I need to briefly mention the genealogy of the people involved in the building of Babel, and some people just hate numbers and mentally switch off when numbers are mentioned, so, just in case you are one of those people, I will not indulge in calculation.

The genealogies in scripture are just long lists; they give the ages and names of people and the names of their children and how long they lived, something like a 'family tree'.

These ages and names are used by some enthusiastic religious people to determine how long ago the creation happened. It is possible to add up all these time periods and come to a conclusion that the creation happened in 4,000 BC or thereabouts. Personally I do not care to calculate dates for the creation, but it is possible to do the same sort of thing with Noah, and determine that he was *still alive at the time Babel was built.*

I came to this conclusion by considering what the scripture says about a man named Nimrod.

If you can bear with me for a few paragraphs, I would like to explain.

*

According to the story, after Babel was built, the people had their language (tongues) confused and were subsequently scattered across the world.

Before the confusion of tongues there were no kingdoms, the people were one, but it is stated that Nimrod founded his kingdom on Babel, so he must have established his kingdom after the people were scattered. (Gen 10 vs. 9 & 10.)

It follows from this that work on the 'tower' must have ended before the time Nimrod was old enough to make himself king. This enables us to roughly estimate the relative time scale involved in the building of the 'Tower'.

If we care to consider the genealogy, Nimrod was the son of Cush, who was the son of Ham, who was one of Noah's three sons who took passage on the Ark. (Gen. 10, verses 6 & 8)

*

If you think I am taking this mythological nonsense just a little bit too seriously, then I apologise for deceiving you. I was not taking it seriously at all, not at the time. I was following my instincts, and treating the mythological story *as if* it were real, just to see where it might lead. The problem I have encountered is that as I write, I know full well where it leads, so the game of 'make-believe it is myth' is getting difficult to sustain in a convincing manner.

It turned out to be quite different from the myth everyone assumes it to be.

*

So Noah was Nimrod's great-grandfather, and it therefore follows that the 'Tower' was finished within two generations of the Ark's grounding on Ararat.

Even if we allow for longevity, the construction of Babel was started, at most, within one century of the famous flood, while Noah was still alive.

This is important, because a cultural trait observed to be in force in slightly later Biblical times was that in those days, the elder, the oldest patriarch, was the undisputed leader of the family or tribe. It is to be presumed that as long as Noah was alive, he was in charge of his tribe, and they did what he said.

It follows from this that Noah was in command when the Tower of Babel was built. It means that the Tower of Babel was not a pagan temple, because Noah was a righteous man, he would not build a pagan temple.

*

So now, we move into an important part of the search.

If I fail to put across the understanding that I have of this matter, then I blame myself. I know how important Babel is; you do not, not yet.

My suspicion was that if Noah was real, and not entirely myth, then he could have coded information into the structure of the 'Tower of Babel'.

This is what we seek, and this is what we shall find.

*

The first thing to notice is that the story of Babel is out of chronological sequence. It is not really all that important, but it is as well to get things in order, to better understand what is going on.

The previous chapter ends with a genealogy which covers a period extending beyond the time of Babel, so there is a chronological overlap.

The last verse of chapter ten says, -

..by these were the nations divided in the earth after the flood.

The dividing did not happen until after the story of Babel.

It is important to understand this because the story of Babel starts with this statement....

Genesis 11:

1 ... And the whole earth was of one language, and of one speech.

The words 'whole earth' here offer the opportunity for confusion. Time had passed since the grounding of the Ark, time had passed since Noah got drunk, and the family had multiplied. Noah now had grandchildren, and possibly great-great-grandchildren, and they were grown up to have children of their own.

Let us not forget that the scripture would have us believe that most of the offspring were gifted with longevity. Their life expectation was not as long as Noah's, but a lot longer than ours.

The tribe of Noah had increased in population, but it was still a very small group, I would guesstimate a few thousands at the most.

These were Noah's tribe, and since they were the only people on Earth, they represented the 'whole earth' in the above verse. This can be demonstrated by an analysis of the genealogy, but I feel sure you do not wish me to go into that sort of detail.

After they had established themselves, consolidated their position, and grown in numbers and in confidence, they set out from their mountain refuge to explore the new world.

2 ... And it came to pass, as they journeyed from the east, that they found a plain in the land of Shinar; and they dwelt there.

If we take this at face value, the whole group travelled from the east, which means they were moving towards the west. This reinforces the notion that we are dealing with a small group, representing the 'whole earth' because a widely populated world could not all move in the same direction at once.

After a journey of some unknown distance, they found a plain. It sounds a little like they were actually looking for a plain, for having found one, they settled there.

This plain was in the land of 'Shinar', and many commentators place Shinar in Babylon, simply because they assume Babel was in Babylon. They are wrong.

Who named this land? Immediately after a global disaster of such proportions all the geological landmarks and features would have been altered beyond recognition, and no place would have a name. The name 'Shinar' could only have been a later edit, someone trying to place Babel in Babylon. 'Shinar' is taken to mean 'two rivers', which in turn are taken to be Tigris & Euphrates.

Of course the same argument would apply to the name of Ararat, we cannot be sure that it is the same place as the modern Ararat, but we need a starting place.

The people were moving westward from Ararat, and if Ararat was where we think it was they were moving into Europe, in the opposite direction to Babylon, which didn't exist at that time anyway. To suggest that Babel was in Babylon is to produce an extreme chronological anomaly; Babylon did not exist until centuries had passed.

To equate the word 'Babel' with 'Babylon' is just not sensible. The pundits are bemused and confused by the similarity in the spelling.

This is actually a very important point, and I tried to find a translation for 'Babel' myself. The closest I could get is a combination of 'Bab' and 'el', (Bab-el) which can be understood to mean 'Gate of God'. This understanding may or may-not be correct, but it makes more sense to me than the orthodox one, and follows the same pattern as other Hebrew place-names of more certain meaning, like 'Beth-el', for example, which means 'House of God'. (Gen 12 v. 8 and many other references.)

Much of what has been said about Bab-el by the world's theologians and other experts is completely wrong, and all those dramatic pictures of a huge Babylonian ziggurat falling in ruins are a complete fiction.

There is no scriptural basis for any of it.

I am aware that it remains for me to demonstrate this, I cannot expect to just say it and get away with it, but if you can just accept what I say for now, and criticise later, it would be much appreciated.

I would also ask you to bear in mind that we are on a treasure-hunt; we are not engaged in a Biblical exegesis. In many ways it really isn't important if we get one or two scriptures wrong.

It is worth reminding ourselves of this. I could be getting the clues wrong, in which case I won't find the treasure. As long as we find the treasure, then we may with hindsight assume that the clues were correctly solved. That is all that matters for the time being.

3 ... And they said one to another, Go to, let us make brick, and burn them throughly. And they had brick for stone, and slime had they for morter.

4 ... And they said, Go to, let us build us a city and a tower,* whose top** *may reach* **unto heaven*; and let us make us a name, lest we be scattered abroad upon the face of the whole earth.

Verse three is rather unimportant. The important thing to note here is that these people built two things, a city, so called, and a tower. The word city is often used for just about any place of habitation for more than a few people. Ancient cities were what we would call hamlets or villages. Strong's concordance gives the word as meaning:-

'From עוּר (H5782) a city (a place guarded by waking or a watch) in the widest sense (even of a mere encampment or post)'

The 'city' would have been a collection of mud-brick

huts, where the builders of the 'Tower' would have lived.

The 'Tower' itself would have been more substantial, and I suspect it would have been made of stone. I say this because they give a reason for building it, ***'let us make us a name*** ', so that they would be remembered if they got scattered, which, of course, they were.

This 'migdal', often translated as 'tower' could also be a 'strong place', sometimes translated as fortress, was built as a memorial by and for the people of Noah, survivors of the lost antediluvian world.

It was not a temple.

I would also challenge the notion that it was a tall tower.

These people were intelligent. Noah and his children were all there, and they were survivors of a race of people that supposedly lived for hundreds of years.

They were not so stupid as to build a tall tower in the hope that its top would reach the heavens. Further, were they to be so stupid, they would have been better off building it on the mountain of Ararat, where they had just come from, rather than on a plain. At least, on a mountain, you are halfway to heaven to start with.

Indeed the words used in the description do not offer compelling support for the notion that it was a 'tower' in the traditional sense.

'Whose top ... unto heaven' the words *'may reach'* are an insertion of the translator, who was presumably trying to make sense of the statement.

Strong's concordance gives a few samples of alternative meanings for the word translated here as 'top'.

Some of these are; - *"head, top, summit, upper part, chief, total, sum, height, front, beginning,"* and quite a few more.

*

The verse under consideration could be legitimately rendered as *'whose* **sum** *unto heaven'*, or *'whose* **total** *unto heaven'*.

The translation we read in our Bible actually says its 'top unto heaven' but the original could well mean something else. It could mean, in architectural terms, the 'top view connects with the heavens'.

An alternative translation or understanding of the nuances in the wording 'top unto heaven' could be 'Top elevation relates to the heavens.'

It struck me as being a strangely flexible statement, and I thought to myself that it could possibly mean that the ground plan had some connection with the heavens.

If the words could be understood to mean that the 'top view', or ground plan, connected with the heavens, then my earlier suspicion could be upheld. It could be that it contained knowledge, knowledge that Noah had brought with him on the Ark. It could mean that the builders of Babel had incorporated antediluvian knowledge into the ground plan of the 'migdal'.

Right or wrong, I told myself that this was the case, that Noah had built the structure, this migdal, as a memorial for his people, and as a repository for their antediluvian knowledge.

For these people to build a monument that incorporated their ancient knowledge would be a memorial indeed. This suggestion is not as farfetched as it may seem, for it is supported by what happened next.

*

The Hebrew used for LORD is here the famous Tetragrammaton; the never-pronounced but very holy name of God.

"YHWH" came down.

5 … And the LORD came down to see the city and the tower, which the children of men builded.

6 … And the LORD said, Behold, the people is one, and they have all one language; and this they begin to do: and now nothing will be restrained from them, which they have imagined to do.

Why was God, or the Elohim, so upset by what He/they saw?

The Lord came down, from up above, in a physical sense, where He could have seen the plan view, and He was not amused.

"***This they begin to do***!" He seemed a little astonished, to say the least.

"***Now nothing will be restrained from them, which they have imagined to do!"***

I repeat the words of the Chief of the Mighty Ones (as recorded by a nameless scribe) to draw attention to the fact that this 'migdal' was something very unusual, something that God did not approve of.

From this, some commentators think that the 'tower' was a pagan temple, but there have been lots of pagan temples in the world since Babel, and God has not come down to see all the others.

A point of more pertinence is that it was Noah who was in charge, and he was a righteous man. Besides, it is already stated in the text, it was intended to function as a memorial.

My view was that there was some secret here. The people had incorporated some antediluvian scientific knowledge into their plan, intending that it should be a memorial that would pass the secret on down the generations.

The knowledge would be in the ground plan, and it would connect with the heavens.

The Chief of the Mighty Ones did not like what he saw.

7 ... Go to, let us go down, and there confound their language, that they may not understand one another's speech.

8 ... So the LORD scattered them abroad from thence upon the face of all the earth: and they left off to build the city.

When I saw this my eyes lit up, and the hairs on my neck tingled.

'***They left off to build the city'***, and presumably they stopped work on the 'migdal' as well.

Please note that God did not destroy anything. All He did was cause the people to stop working. No mention is made here of any destruction.

Those lurid pictures of toppling towers are a complete fantasy.

I remember reading the passage over and over again.

If the 'migdal' was not destroyed, then that opens up the possibility that it might still exist.

I had to pause here, for quite a long while. I studied the passage closely, trying to pinpoint and extricate every last detail.

It was clear what it said.

The impression was that there was something very special about it, something very important both to the men who were striving to build it, and to the Elohim who wanted to stop them.

Important in another sense was the observation that there was nothing in the passage to suggest that the structure had been deliberately destroyed, not by the Mighty Ones or by anyone else.

*

After those dramatic events the people were scattered, leaving only Nimrod to claim the area as his kingdom. The scripture itself then resumes the genealogy which leads all the way to Abram, (Abraham) the patriarch of the Jews, and whatever was built at Babel is never mentioned again.

As the centuries rolled by and turned into millennia, the migdal of Babel faded into the mists of history and was gradually forgotten, until eventually it became a myth.

*

I called to mind the stated fact that it was to serve as a memorial. If it really was a memorial, then it was built to last, one presumes. A memorial that doesn't last long isn't much of a memorial.

It could have been lost altogether, totally destroyed in wars or natural disasters, or simply ruined to rubble by the passage of thousands of years. With luck, it might still exist, but misidentified in later times by a generation who had no idea what it originally was.

With this kind of reasoning I managed to convince myself that it might still exist, or at the very least, some traces of it might remain.

If I could find it, I thought, and if I could unlock its secrets, well, who knows what might transpire.

At this point in time I began to get a little concerned for my sanity, to be honest. I was becoming very deeply involved, and I had to go into a quiet room and have a little word with myself. For a while I dismissed my own findings. I told myself it was silly, but then, I realised I couldn't just ignore it. I had to try to find it.

The Search for Babel

First things first, a nice cup of tea and a biscuit, and then I got started on reviewing everything I could deduce about Babel from the few short verses in the Bible.

If you are agreeable, I would like to do that again, and consolidate our position, which is something I did rather often.

We need to know what we are looking for, and where it might be.

The first thing to establish is the likely nature of the structure we are seeking. If it still exists, then we can be sure that nobody has recognised it as yet, for if they had, it would have been broadcast on the news.

I deemed it unlikely that I would be able to find the 'city', which would have been made of mud brick, and most likely eroded to dust by now, (In this I was wrong, some archaeologists found it.) but the 'tower' was a different matter. I believed it was intended as a memorial, as stated in the scripture, and so it would have been built to last. It would have been made out of durable material like stone.

I had to review my assertion that it was not a tall tower. The Hebrew is 'migdal', which is often translated as 'tower' but does not have to be. I believed the translators chose 'tower' over the other possibilities because they could see no other way in which the structure could connect with the heavens.

According to concordances 'migdal' can have a variety of meanings. It is a word used for any tower, fortress, castle, elevated platform, and such like places, and it did not escape my attention that all these places are usually built out of stone.

After review, I concluded that it was most likely not a tower, but would have been a strongly built structure of stone, perhaps on a platform, that vaguely resembled a fortress.

I also took some guidance from other scriptures, and from history, and from what I knew of Noah and his people.

Noah may well have been a very intelligent person, and he might possibly have been full of knowledge of all manner of highly technical matters, but he found himself in very primitive circumstances, without proper tools.

I concluded that no matter how well educated or technically advanced the builders might have been, the structure would have been built using primitive tools, and primitive methods. If it still existed, if it has survived the many millennia that have passed since it was built, it would appear to be very primitive.

It would appear to us as being 'Neolithic'.

The thought that the structure would look as though it was Neolithic because of the crude nature of the tools Noah was forced to use triggered another thought.

Whatever else one could say about the migdal of Babel, as long as we suspend disbelief and assume that the Bible is right, we have to admit it was the first structure of stone to be built on the post-flood Earth.

In other words, from the perspective of my Biblical premise, it had to be seen as the oldest stone structure on Earth.

This led to the thought that after the confusion of tongues; and after the people had been scattered across the world, the building of stone memorials might have become a cultural trait, leading to the erection of a great many other Neolithic stone monuments. These later ones would have been inferior to the first, because the people could no longer communicate with others, and within a few generations their life span would have dropped to the standard seventy years, and they would have degenerated, and forgotten what their own history was.

*

I have no doubt that you will think me to be completely crazy, but I really had nothing better to do at the time, so I set to work to try to identify it, or at least find a likely candidate.

Is it possible, even likely, that amongst all the Neolithic stone monuments in Europe, to the west of Turkey;

there might be one that is older and grander than all the rest?

If it is built on a plain, then it would be a good candidate.

Another thought that crossed my mind is that it would need to be fairly complex if it really was hiding ancient knowledge. A simple stone circle was not likely to be able to contain much in the way of knowledge.

So, I was looking for a rather complex, very ancient, Neolithic-looking, very robust stone monument that was built on a plain, somewhere in Europe to the west or northwest of eastern Turkey.

This was deduced from scripture. It is all there in the Bible, it just needs to be read properly, with an open and honest mind.

*

It would be nice if I could say, at this juncture, that I spent ages searching the continent of Europe for the 'tower', I would like to be able to say this so that I could take you on a conducted tour of all the stone monuments of Europe, and thus add some extra chapters to this otherwise very short book.

Sometimes it is disheartening being an honest man.

I cannot lead you on a wild goose chase.

I made a few rudimentary attempts to calculate how far the people could have walked, but there was little point. At the leisurely pace of 5 miles per day, it is possible to walk 4000 miles in as little as 2.5 years, and they lived for a very long time, they had all the time in the world.

It was obvious that within a few years of leaving Ararat,

they could have been anywhere; they could have reached any point in Europe.

A clue came from an enigmatic statement in the Bible, in Genesis 10 verse 5, it states:

By these were the isles of the Gentiles divided in their lands; every one after his tongue, after their families, in their nations.

This was another anachronism, since there were no 'Gentiles' in the time context of the story. The scribe was clearly from a later time, and inserting his own later knowledge to describe his understanding of where the 'Tower' was. I had no choice but to take him at his word.

There are not very many 'Isles of the Gentiles' in Europe that possess Neolithic remains of any merit. The only 'Isles' I could think of were the British Isles.

*

It must be very obvious to you, unless you live in a very isolated part of the world, that a prime candidate that fulfils all the requirements is that monument known to us today as - Stonehenge.

Stonehenge has everything that the scripture requires. It can genuinely be described by the Hebrew word 'migdal', so often translated as 'tower' when the word can mean so many other things.

It finally settled in my mind that if the memorial of Babel were to exist anywhere on the planet, it had to be Stonehenge. Despite all of my researches, I could find no other viable candidate for the role.

*

If my suppositions were anything like true, then it

suddenly brought the myth into the real world. If it were true, everything would change.

I was no longer toying with ideas in a mythological world of make-believe and children's stories; I was suggesting that the myth was real.

I did not believe my own thoughts, how could it be real?

It is one thing to pretend that the Bible is true, it is quite another to accept that it is a fact.

There was only one answer to this conundrum; - tea and biscuits!

I mulled it over for a long while.

*

If the story in the Bible had any basis in fact, then it was reasonable to suppose that the survivors of a global disaster would want their story to be remembered. It is not unreasonable to think that they would build a massive monument, and find a way to store information in it, perhaps in its design, or in its ground plan.

That all depended on the reality of the supposed global disaster, which was itself widely believed to be just a myth.

It all sounded reasonable, as long as it remained in the world of myth and legend, but it was crazy to try to bring it to life.

*

There I was sitting in my armchair drinking tea and munching digestives, with the Bible on my lap, thinking that mythological stories were to be found in England, standing on Salisbury Plain, looking as rock-solid as only tons of rock-solid rock can look.

It was insane, but I had been having fun with my investigation into the Biblical narrative, and I didn't want to stop my researches just because the world wouldn't believe where it led me.

*

If Stonehenge and Babel were the same, then Stonehenge had to have a ground plan that connected with the heavens in some way.

In order to prove my case, I knew I had to investigate Stonehenge.

Before I could even start on such an investigation, I needed to be sure I was not missing something important.

I ran over the points of detail once more.

1 Stonehenge is very old, though not generally recognised as being the oldest structure on Earth, it could be.

2 Stonehenge is robust, durable, and has lasted well, like any memorial should.

3 Stonehenge, according to archaeologists, was never finished. See Prof Atkinson, page 83-84 of *Stonehenge. 'They abandoned their work...and this abandonment was complete'*. Like Babel, the builders 'left off the building of it'.

4 There is a 'city' of mud brick nearby. Archaeologist recently reported finding it. It was a small mud village where the builders of Stonehenge lived. National Geographic says, 'A prehistoric village has been discovered in southern England that was likely home to the builders of Stonehenge, archaeologists announced on January 30, 2007'

5 Stonehenge displays a sophistication that other monuments lack. There are mortised joints in the stone lintels, and the curvature on those lintels is very precise.

6 Both Stonehenge and Babel are (falsely) accused of being temples.

7 Both are built on a plain.

8 Stonehenge could genuinely be described as a 'migdal'.

9 Even according to archaeologists, Stonehenge connects with the heavens. The 56 holes of the Aubrey circle (Named after John Aubrey...12 March 1626 – 7 June 1697) can be used to predict eclipses, and of course the well-known but false solstice alignment is 'heavenly'.

10 Stonehenge is complex enough to contain hidden knowledge.

There were a couple of other points that might be worth considering.

The plain that Stonehenge is built on is chalk. If the monument preserves knowledge in its ground plan, then the fact that it is built on a chalk base would be significant. Holes dug in chalk remain for thousands of years, so even if all the stones of the monument were to be removed, the plan would remain in the form of holes in the chalk. Even if the holes were to be filled in and grassed over, archaeologists could still find them.

Chalk has the added advantage that it is easy to dig with primitive tools, and it appears from the archaeology that deer antlers were used as pickaxes.

It seems possible that the journey Noah and his people made was expressly to find the right kind of plain on which to build their memorial.

I decided that I would like to investigate Stonehenge, and learn as much as I could about it, to see if I could find any connection with the heavens.

*

I brushed the biscuit crumbs from the pages of Genesis, closed the book, and put it to one side, because we are now leaving the Bible, and matters of myth, and entering the real world of grass and stone.

We say farewell to the scripture, for a little while.

Now we must trespass on the territory of archaeology and mathematics, but I will keep the math for part two.

I bought some books on Stonehenge, of which there are a great many, and learned all I could.

For you, my sole remaining reader, I will do my best to describe what I found, not in mathematical symbols, but in words.

*

The Tower of Babel is tentatively identified as being that monument in the British Isles known as Stonehenge.

It is suspected that the ground plan of this monument may contain coded information regarding the heavens, put there by an intelligent antediluvian named Noah.

It all sounds rather silly, but we press on regardless and see where it leads us.

Chapter Three

The Migdal of Stonehenge

The clue that led me to suspect that there was any treasure at all was found more in my imagined picture of the story of Noah, rather than in anything stated in the scripture. It was all in my head, a matter of wishful-thinking rather than one of fact.

I followed the imaginary clue out of boredom more than anything else, and it led me to consider the finer details of the wording in the story of Babel. This second clue was just semantics, a matter of choosing my preferred meaning from a range of possible meaning. I took it as a very vague hint that there might be something significant in the wording, and so I pursued further vague clues that led me to consider Stonehenge.

The story of my treasure hunt had such a flimsy start, that it would have been very easy for me to have dropped the whole thing, had it not been for my suspicious nature. There had to be some explanation for the survival of the stories in the first place. These stories were 'myths', but I asked myself what a 'myth' actually was if it was not the haunting after-image of a long forgotten truth.

I had nothing to lose by investigating Stonehenge anyway, so that is what I proceeded to do.

So far I had just sat in my armchair reading the early

chapters of the Bible and looking up a word or two in my concordance. I had progressed from the mythology of the Creation, through to the supposed global flood and Noah. Noah survived the flood and led me to Babel, and now I propose to leave the mythology, bringing us right up to date, into the twenty-first century to concern ourselves with factual matters that exist right now in the real world.

It may seem that I had done no actual work thus far, and that observation would be fully justified, but now is the time when real work must be considered.

Stonehenge is the second of the principal themes of this book, and is deserving of our close attention, for this is where we find the first real clue to our treasure, and I wish to be sure that you understand it, so that we will be better able to proceed.

It is not a mythological clue, it is not an imaginary clue; it is a real and genuine mathematical clue.

This is likely to be a challenging chapter, for although I understand it completely, it is going to be very difficult to explain.

This chapter, and the next one, are going to be very demanding chapters to write, but after that, things get a lot easier, until we get to part two.

I hope that you will be patient, help me through these two chapters, and then we can do some real work and investigate our treasure. I promise to do my very best to make it all clear, but if I should fail, if I cannot make you understand, it will be my fault, not yours.

So before I get started, I would like to remind the two of us what this is all about.

This chapter should have been very technical and

mathematical, but for the sake of keeping my only reader with me, I have decided that it would be best for both of us if I try to keep it interesting.

I have relegated the boring mathematics to part two, in chapters 8 & 9.

*

Sometimes we need to remind ourselves that all this started with a casual reading of the scripture and a somewhat cynical romp through the various claims made by religious people.

In doing this, I seem to have painted myself into a corner, because now I am entertaining the suggestion that at least a part of the story in the Bible could be real after all.

Of course when I started I didn't really believe it, I mean, everyone else knows the stories in the book of Genesis are just fiction; just myth and legend, fit only for children's colouring-in books, and bed-time reading for toddlers.

Hitherto my Biblical researches had been something of a game; I had not really thought there was anything serious behind it. The whole chain of thought had been started in reaction to the ladies' eager sincerity; a response stimulated by my recognition of my own ignorance of a subject that the ladies claimed was the literal Truth with a capital 'T'.

I wanted to educate myself, so that if they returned I would be better prepared to argue my case, stand my ground, and not desire to run and hide in my cupboard.

Now things are different; now we are about to attempt to bring the scripture into the real world. It is no longer hypothetical, real results are expected, so we need to be very careful.

If we venture into the world of archaeology, where many clever scholars have been before us, we obviously cannot compete with them on equal terms. We will need to be very stealthy, and not let the archaeologists know we are there, or what we are up to, so we won't tell them.

There will be times when I say something, or make an assumption, that the scholars would disagree with if they were aware of what I had said. I cannot help it if they would disagree, but I will always try to justify any such comment to you. You are the only reader I have left, you are very important to me. If you go, I will be on my own.

*

How did I start to investigate something like Stonehenge when I knew nothing about it? I had seen the pictures, but none of them showed the ground plan, which was the main focus of my interest.

To start such an investigation I first needed to familiarise myself with the monument, and I did this, of course.

The problem is that it is necessary for you to also be familiar with the monument if you wish to follow my researches. This is not mandatory, but it would help you to understand, and I cannot do it for you.

I needed information about the monument that I could not get just by looking at pictures. I needed to know what the monument is like, what its measurements are, and so on. Above all, and first and foremost, I needed to know what the original ground plan was.

To get all this information I needed to study books on

the archaeology, and of course, it would be nice if you could do the same, just to check what I say. You could take my word for it, but that would not be very scientific.

I regret that I cannot include an archaeological treatise in this little book, because it would take up too much space, and distract from the thread of the story, which is difficult enough as it is. It is also true that were I to attempt to include such chapters, they would do little more than plagiarise Professor R.J.C. Atkinson. If you wish to study the archaeology of Stonehenge for yourself, I can do no better than to recommend the Professor's book, entitled 'Stonehenge'. It is an excellent book where facts are concerned, but I don't really agree with his interpretations.

[*All figures relating to Stonehenge and quoted hereafter are from Prof Atkinson's book, I must acknowledge the part he unwittingly played in my endeavour. Without his dedicated work on the monument I would not have been able to write this present volume*.]

Alternatively, if you just need to know the general layout, you can always study the pictures and drawings in chapter eight of this book, figure 7 is a good guide to the ground plan, but since it is my own production, it will not serve to check or verify my findings. You need Professor Atkinson's book in order to do that.

Initial investigation.

I started this book by saying it is a treasure hunt, and so it is. The treasure we seek is the ancient antediluvian knowledge that I claim, hypothetically, exists in the ground plan of the 'migdal' of Babel, which I have tentatively identified with Stonehenge.

Stonehenge has been well studied by generations of archaeologists and scholars, and as far as I know, apart from the 'eclipse prediction' powers of the Aubrey circle, and the supposed (but false) solar alignment of the Heel stone, none have observed any significant astronomical implications in the ground-plan.

I do not intend to compete with the scholars, I am just going to raid their books for data, and ignore their opinions about how and why it was built. The scholars will no doubt question my methods, and my logic, because the end result will prove that all their scholarly beliefs are wrong, woefully wrong.

*

Access to Stonehenge is severely restricted, so a personal visit would not be very productive. Such a visit would not help much anyway, because we are interested in the ground-plan, which is not visible except from above, and even then the full details are obscured by neatly mown grass.

The only practical way to investigate is by consulting archaeological drawings of the monument. I managed to obtain some large scale plans, but at first they appeared to be rather useless because they contained a bit too much detail.

There is also a major complication that I had not fully anticipated.

I had not expected the monument to be in pristine condition, but Stonehenge is a derelict, a ruin, and very little is left to make sense of. When I first saw the plan, I was dismayed, and my enthusiasm became a little deflated.

Most of the published plans I have seen have been

cluttered up with all manner of unwanted objects, like fallen stones, and archaeological notes and annotations.

It is also complicated by features that have been added by later generations. People for centuries, thousands of years, after it was built, have been there to bury their dead, to worship, to hold ceremonies. Many of the stones have been moved, toppled and broken, or missing altogether.

It is in a truly lamentable state.

Fortunately, with the fruits of the labours of dedicated archaeologists, and a great deal of study, I was eventually able to make sense of it.

*

After my initial confusion and disappointment, the details slowly began to emerge from the mess.

My first step was to take a drawing and erase from it the surplus minutiae that archaeologists seem obliged to put in, and the bits that represented fallen stones. Where possible, and with careful use of archaeological data, I put some of the missing and toppled stones back where they came from (on the drawing, not for real).

The result of this was something approaching the original ground-plan, or so I hoped.

*

If you read the archaeology books, there is always mention of the various stages of construction, which I tend to ignore, because if it is in fact Babel, there was only one stage of construction.

Having said that, it is clear that the construction of the

monument would have taken some considerable time, and would have required the expenditure of a great deal of effort; some of the trilithon stones weigh fifty tons, and the uprights of the Sarsen circle weigh about twenty-six tons each. If you add up all the Sarsen stones including the lintels the total weight comes to about one thousand five hundred tons of huge stone blocks. ('Sarsen' is the name given to a type of local sandstone.)

These had to be hauled from a place about twenty-four miles away, across country, by manpower, (or animal power?) then bashed into shape by hand with primitive hammer-stone tools, and stood on end in holes cut in the chalk, again, by manpower.

In addition, apparently, there are several tons of a different kind of stone, known as bluestones, which were transported all the way from South Wales.

All this effort would not have been expended without good reason, and I suggest to you that the 'good reason' is to pass important information down through the millennia.

*

The monument consists of a number of circles of holes in the ground, which are visible on drawings, but not in reality. Most of the holes in the outer monument are now filled in and grassed over, but their positions have been recorded by archaeologists.

The outermost of these is a circle of 144 feet in radius, marked by 56 evenly spaced holes, known as the 'Aubrey' circle. It is these that are claimed to be used for predicting eclipses.

Outside these and surrounding the monument are

circular bank and ditch features, the so-called Slaughter stone, and an 'avenue' feature leading away.

Inward, toward the centre, is a ring of holes that archaeologists call the 'Y' holes, and inward again, another ring called the 'Z' holes.

Then we have the main Sarsen stone circle, which is a very prominent feature. The inner faces of these stones are set fairly accurately tangent to a circle about 48.5 feet in radius.

Within the Sarsen circle, and in sequence towards the middle, are the 'Q' and 'R' holes with the bluestone circle, the set of five trilithons, the bluestone horseshoe, the 'back-sight' holes (see below) and finally the Altar stone. There is no marked centre to the monument.

This description will not help you in the least, but it does demonstrate how complex the monument ground-plan is. There is plenty of scope for hiding secret knowledge, but it is also very confusing.

I was stumped for a long time, because I had some preconceived notion that even if I found anything there, it would be in a rather simple form. You see, I suffered from the same ailment that afflicts many archaeologists, namely, 'if it is old, it is primitive'.

I was expecting to find some sort of relationship with the stars, or the constellations, perhaps the zodiac, but I could not find anything.

If I were writing a longer book, I would here recount all the failed attempts to find a connection with the heavens. I will spare you the tedium. All attempts to relate the ground plan to the stars failed miserably.

I had to do these checks, but the roughly circular form of the monument strongly suggested the orbits of the

Plate 1 Reproduced with permission, English Heritage.

planets might be involved, and I decided to spend my greatest efforts on examining that possibility.

So, after wasting just a little time on stars and constellations, I eventually tried the planets.

Investigating Planets

One of the aspects of Stonehenge that I learned from the archaeologists was the fact that it had an 'axis of symmetry' running down the middle of it. This is not a physical feature; it is a theoretical, geometric concept that is often drawn-in on plans of the monument. This theoretical axis has the advantage, from my viewpoint, of passing through all the major features of the monument, such that it could be used as one axis of a graph.

My method was to draw a graph of the Stonehenge

features, using the position where they came on the axis line, plotted against the orbits of the planets.

Once again I was expecting a simple relationship, if any, so I only used the first five planets, which were known to our own 'modern' ancients.

The procedure I adopted was very basic, and would probably make a scientist wince. I took one of the large scale archaeological drawings of the monument plan, one where I had erased all the extraneous marks and fallen stones. Taking data from Professor Atkinson's book, I then carefully checked the locations where I had reconstructed the missing features.

Once I was happy with it, I obtained a supply of photocopies of the modified drawing.

I then cut a strip of paper from the middle that included a narrow portion either side of the axis line, and which showed the main features.

I glued this strip onto the left hand side of a sheet of graph paper, such that it would serve as the 'y' axis of a graph, with the features already on it. (Note, 'Y' circle is not to be confused with 'y' axis, they are not the same.)

Next I drew up a list of astronomical orbital data from an astronomy book, (Norton's Star Atlas) and plotted them on the graph paper 'x' axis against the monument features.

I didn't bother with a central point; I did 'floating graphs'. The purpose of these was just to show if there was a relationship or not, identifying the exact nature of the relationship, if there was one, would come later.

I had to engage in a little manipulation of the monument strip, because the central area did not align with the outer area. It appears on drawings as 'upside down'. I later realised that this would provide for two graphs not one, but I am getting ahead of myself.

I proceeded to graph the stones and holes against the planetary orbits, starting with the innermost stone, the Altar stone, graphed against the planet Mercury, which is the innermost planet, and working outward from there. The next feature out, the bluestone horseshoe, was graphed against Venus, and skipping Earth, I moved on to Mars, and so on.

Nothing I tried worked; I got no result worth mentioning.

*

I could have given up, I came close to giving up, and I grew more and more depressed by the day. Silly to get so depressed over such a pointless thing.

I struggled to sustain my interest, until one day while reading Professor Atkinson's book I came across a statement that I had not noticed before.

The statement is on page 212 of the above mentioned book, in an appendix, and it says that a new hole, or pair of holes, had been found just behind the altar stone, one either side of the axis.

These were suggested as being socket holes for a pair of stones that would function as a 'back-sight' for observing the midsummer sunrise. This contradicted his earlier statement that the sunrise observation was "a popular and persistent misconception", (page 30 of 'Stonehenge').

An oversight that we are all guilty of, I expect a similar criticism can be levelled at any author, including this one.

There were no details about the exact position of these holes, but they broke my depression, and later proved to be one of the keys to the unravelling of the secret.

*

I repeated my above graphs, this time including the two new holes to represent Earth, and still I failed to get any sort of meaningful result.

The procedure met with no success, and again I was on the verge of accepting that there was no relationship when I made an unbelievable discovery.

All my difficulties had stemmed from my assumption that the monument would be primitive. I had approached the whole project with a kind of half-hearted attitude, and this was itself the result of the mental preconditioning we are all subjected to throughout our lives.

I had not looked for anything intellectual, because I had been pre-programmed to think 'old is ignorant'.

Once I started to think clearly, and adjust my mind to reject all the assumptions and premises of science and the media, I was able to examine the matter objectively, and started to make real progress. Soon the monument began to reveal itself for what it truly is.

I already knew that the planets do not orbit in circles, they have elliptical orbits. This means that as they orbit the sun, sometimes they are closer to the sun than at other times. The difference is not great; in fact some planets like Earth and Venus have very nearly circular orbits, while others, like Mercury and Mars, are slightly more elliptical.

The closest distance a planet gets to the sun is called the 'perihelion', and the furthest distance away from the sun is called the 'aphelion'.

These two distances can be averaged to give the 'mean' distance. The mean orbital distance is the one usually quoted when talking about orbits, but the perihelion and aphelion distances are just as valid.

There are lists of the perihelion and aphelion figures in astronomy books, (see table 1 in this book) so it was an easy step to graph the figures against the monument features, and suddenly, I started to get a result.

It was an almost instant success, when I plotted the perihelion and aphelion figures against the inner and outer edges of the Stonehenge features, I began to get a result that looked meaningful.

*

After a few tentative starts, and some more careful re-checks, I obtained a significant curve.

I was astonished, because if it was right then it meant that the builders of the monument knew more about the orbits of the planets than any primitive Neolithic had any right to know.

I took the perihelion and aphelion figures for Mercury and Mars, while Venus and Earth, being close to circular orbits, were represented by their mean orbit.

The figures for Mercury were plotted against the inner and outer edges of the Altar stone, Venus against the guessed at position of the 'back-sight', Earth against the bluestone horseshoe curve, and Mars against the central Trilithon, inner and outer edges.

The procedure actually seemed to work, and was a promising start, but after that it all fell to bits again. However, I had learned from the experience, and the lesson I had learned was 'Think sophisticated'.

*

My rather strange project made progress after that realisation, coupled with a statement made in the Professor's book. He referred to the different stages of build, implying that there was an 'inner' stage to the monument and the 'outer' stage to the monument, and although he did not use those words, and I am sure these are not his official designations, the notion gave me an idea.

Just looking at the plan confirms the notional distinction. I was aware that astronomers make the same distinction with regard to the Solar System. The 'inner' planets are Mercury, Venus, Earth and Mars. The outer are all the rest, Jupiter, Saturn, Uranus, Neptune and Pluto.

I had already obtained a partial result. I had a good graph for the inner System plotted against the inner monument, but continuing the plot wouldn't work. I tried a new plot, a separate plot, this time I graphed the outer orbits against the outer features of the monument.

Jupiter's perihelion and aphelion gave a very poor match with the inner and outer faces of the great Sarsen circle lintel, while Saturn and Uranus did the same for the 'Z' and 'Y' holes respectively.

Suddenly I had two graphs to look at and wonder at, and ponder the meaning of. They provided me with plenty of food for thought.

After thinking about it for a while, I tried to involve the enigmatic 'Q' & 'R' holes, along with the Bluestone Circle, but it didn't take me long to realise that these features fell between the Trilithons and the Sarsen Circle. I had already assigned the Trilithons to Mars and the Sarsen Circle to Jupiter, so it followed that the confusion of holes and stones that came between them could well be an attempt by the builders to represent the Asteroid belt, which falls between those two planets.

*

I ran out of features then. The Aubrey circle matched with Pluto aphelion, but Neptune and Pluto perihelion were missing.

I remembered that the monument was not finished; "they left off the building of it".

Another thought occurred to me at that time, and I feel I should mention it. The way the monument features are currently distributed in their dilapidated condition effectively prevents the drawing of a single graph, and forces the investigator to draw two separate graphs, one for the inner System and another for the outer System. At first I took this to be simply a result of the dilapidated state of the monument, but much later, when I had learned a lot more about these matters, I began to wonder if it might not have been built that way deliberately.

*

At this point I would like to inject a little technical note about the use of 'floating' graphs. They produce three kinds of results, and it is possible to estimate what kind of relationship is present, depending on the resulting shape of the graph line.

If there is no relationship, the resulting line is invariably a jagged staircase, like an ascending zigzag line.

If the result approximates to a straight line, there is a possibility of a linear one-to-one relationship.

If the line approaches a smooth curve, then the suggestion is that there is an 'exponential' relationship.

I had obtained two floating graphs that appeared to my eye to be reasonably good exponential curves, one for the inner features plotted against the inner planets, and the same for the outer. This raised my eyebrows a little. I was astonished. I call them 'crude' and 'inaccurate' just to be scientifically correct, but for an ancient and dilapidated Neolithic monument, they were incredible, miraculously good.

These original crude graphs can be seen in fig 8a.

Exponential math is not something Neolithic peoples would be expected to know about. If there was a relationship of any kind it would be just an ordinary miracle, but an exponential one would be quite a remarkable phenomenon. Indeed, it would be seen as impossible; but that is what I obtained, not just the one, but two.

This was my first glimpse of the 'treasure' that I was seeking. Not much, but enough to say there was something to be found.

It was a little like believing there was a chest of pirate gold buried on a desert island, and on a first survey, finding a few stray doubloons loose in the sand.

*

It was my first substantive clue, and it was enough to keep me wide-awake most of that night.

As I lay in bed staring up at the ceiling the graphs kept

whirling round and round in my head. They were real, but totally unexpected, and I could not quite grasp the full significance.

Surely they were far too advanced to be Neolithic, and could only mean that my previous deductions about Noah and Babel had been correct. That in turn would mean that the flood had been real.

I didn't know what to make of it, because I had discovered the impossible.

In total, spread over two very crude and rudimentary graphs, I had obtained eleven points of rough correspondence and one arbitrary (Venus, because I had to guess at where the 'back-sight' feature was.)

I still needed to confirm that it was a genuine relationship, but in my long years of work I had experienced many exponential curves, and just by looking at these two I judged them to be extremely close to representing valid mathematics.

This meant four things:-

1) Although the graphs I had obtained were clearly inaccurate, they were good enough to convince me that I was on to something.
2) The use of perihelion and aphelion distances of planets out as far as Uranus demonstrated that the designer of the monument knew a lot more about the planets than any Neolithic could possibly have known.
3) The curves demonstrated that exponential equations were involved, so again the designer knew a lot more than a Neolithic could possibly have known.

4) It demonstrated that there may well be some truth to the Babel story, and hence the story of Noah and the flood.

One thought that kept coming back to me was the question of why I had assumed it would be simply a matter of a primitive alignment. I had not expected this degree of sophistication, whatever else I might have imagined I might find.

I realised that my assumption was coloured by the prevailing paradigm, the attitude of just about everyone in the world, that there was no antediluvian race, that it was all a myth with no substance, and that ancient peoples were really stupid.

The thoughts and questions came and went in a swirl. Was I sure it was real? What else was there? Could I find the equations of the curves? How could these things possibly be true?

Eventually I fell into a restless sleep, only to awake early next morning, with yet more questions on my mind.

*

All representations of archaeological drawings of the Stonehenge ground plan in this chapter are derived from and traceable to National Monuments Record – English Heritage archive drawing reference number MP/STO0084.

Plates 2 & 3 Stonehenge aspects.

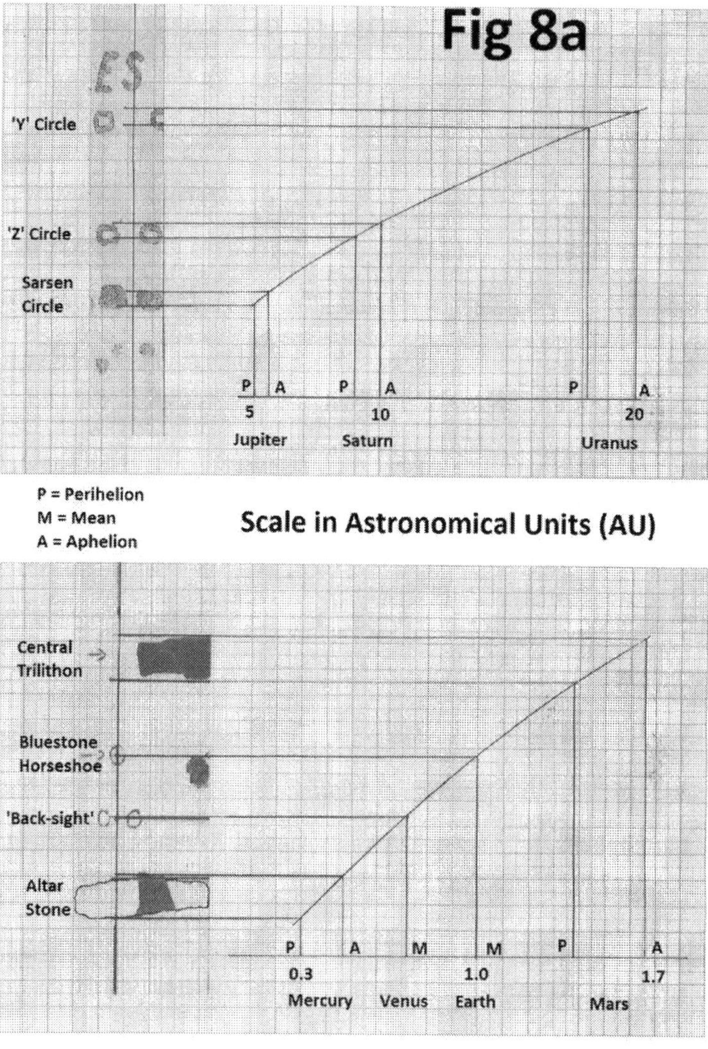

After a thoughtful breakfast I spent a long while sitting quietly with a cup of tea, dunking a digestive biscuit now and then, to help my thinking process while I tried to fathom out what my graphs meant.

The rough preliminary investigation had convinced me that there was indeed a relationship between the ground plan and the 'heavens'.

This changed my attitude towards the 'myth' of Babel, permanently. The two graphs, crude though they might be, could not be ascribed to chance. The graphs demonstrated that I could well have been right about Babel, and it followed that I was looking at the work of an antediluvian man.

All the calculations and claims in this book can be checked by experts if they are willing, and these two graphs are no exception. I have demonstrated how I obtained these graphs, so my findings can be checked. They are not a cheat. I acknowledge they are not perfect, but they are too good to be due to chance.

None of this was much help when it came to formalising the discovery.

It was real, it was fairly convincing, but it was what scientists would call 'suggestive' if they bothered with it at all.

*

The information I had obtained was very 'suggestive', and very encouraging, but not good enough to be convincing for science. I had to try harder.

One of the problems was the somewhat rough and ready nature of the monument features. There was not much regularity in the placing of the features, especially the 'Z' and 'Y' holes; they wandered about in an odd manner.

You can skip over this paragraph if you don't understand it, it isn't particularly important...

I had obtained curves that demonstrated a relationship of an exponential kind. So I repeated the exercise on semi-log paper and obtained two straight line graphs as a result. They were straight enough to confirm that the relationship was real and genuinely exponential, and allowed me to estimate the slopes, which gave me approximations for the values of the exponents, but they were not anywhere near precise enough to determine any definitive equations. Definitive equations would be needed to convince scientists.

*

We are not at the end of our treasure hunt yet, in fact we are nowhere near the end, there is still a long way to go, but it is worth pausing a while to consider the few scraps of information we have gleaned so far.

The builders of Stonehenge knew about Uranus, they knew the perihelion and aphelion distances of all the planets out as far as Uranus. They knew how to do exponential mathematics. It is fairly obvious that the builders were not Neolithic, and the structure is not therefore a Neolithic monument.

I am proposing that Stonehenge is in fact that ancient mythological structure known in the Bible as the 'Tower' of Babel. I say this because it is obvious (to me) that the builders were from an advanced civilization, they were certainly not Neolithic.

It is self-evident that the said civilization no longer exists, and must therefore have been destroyed, and we can only assume that the agent of destruction was the mythical flood.

Nobody would believe it, which is why I have included details of my methods and my results in this book, so that critics can check for themselves.

*

It was at this point, I seem to remember, when things began to get decidedly worse.

It was ancient knowledge, there was no doubt about that, but it seemed to me that just demonstrating that the designers knew a bit of astronomy and a bit of maths was not enough to justify building such a massive monument, nor was it enough to justify the Mighty Ones getting so cross about it.

It came to my mind that there must be more to it than just two curves. The curves may well be regarded as sophisticated by comparison to Neolithic standards, but were otherwise a bit of an anti-climax. I just knew there must be more.

I needed more accurate figures, and I needed to dig deeper, so I fell back to my old habit of reasoning from pure logic and a lot of guesswork.

I believed that my crude graphs were telling me the truth; they were too good to be not real, they could not be dismissed as chance.

If that was so, then it was clear to me that I was dealing with a very clever and intelligent designer. The person who designed this thing knew about Uranus, which was not discovered by us until 1781, and by this little fact I knew for sure that I was confronted by the prospect that the designer was from a highly advanced civilization.

It follows that if the designer was really as clever as he seemed, then he would have anticipated that his 'migdal' would fall into a state of disrepair, and he might well have included in the design a means to get around that problem.

I reasoned further, that if this intelligent antediluvian wanted his design to be understood, then he would have made it in such a way that it could be deciphered.

After all, he went to all the trouble of building the thing from fifty-ton blocks of stone, so that it would last for thousands of years, he simply must have included a way to make it readable. That is what I would have done, anyway.

*

I resumed my examination of the ground plan, looking for another clue, anything, that would allow me to read the antediluvian's mind.

What I was looking at was an exponential scale mathematical model of the orbits of the Solar System, without any doubt whatsoever, but that was not enough to justify the building of it. There had to be more to it, there simply had to be. The thought kept going round and round in my head, and wouldn't leave me alone.

The monument seemed like something strange to our world, but a little itch at the back of my brain told me that it was a resolvable puzzle, that there was a solution.

I just had to think like the designer.

I tried to imagine myself in his position, designing something that would have to last for thousands of years, and be read by...who?

The designer had no idea how smart or ignorant we

would be; we could all be as clever as Einstein or as stupid as a politician, so if I was in his position, I would have included something really simple to help in the deciphering.

I would have provided a 'dumb-person's key'.

I must be really dumb, I told myself, because I can't see it.

And then, like magic, I did.

I saw it literally. On the wall of the room I was sitting in, which was my lounge, there was an artwork, bought from a charity jumble sale. It was a peg-and-string pattern, made with pins and different coloured threads, in the form of a star.

It was a 'Eureka!' moment. I looked at the Stonehenge drawing once more, and all became clear.

The ground plan of the monument represented a pattern that could be reproduced accurately with the peg-and-string method!

If that were to work, then distances could be calculated from trigonometry, and so they would be highly accurate, accurate enough to produce graphs that would in turn yield equations.

*

I had to kick myself a few times for being so stupid. It was obvious the builders had used a peg-and-string method to lay out the plan; there was nothing else for them to use!

It was as if I had been straining my brain for something that was really simple and obvious.

If a Neolithic, or antediluvian using Neolithic methods, wanted to draw a circle, he had no other choice but to use a peg and string.

Just how he was supposed to divide that circle into fifty-six equal segments is another question, a question that archaeologists never seem to ask, but again, all he had to do it with were pegs and string.

Oh! And a stick; we will allow that they used a stick for rudimentary measuring purposes.

There was also the question of the thirty radials; they had to be done with peg and string as well, and that was another question that archaeologists never seem to ask.

I became a little excited, believing that I had cracked the problem, and I had, almost. It would only get me half way, but I didn't know that at the time.

Pegs and String

We have progressed from the Creation, to the Flood and Noah; from Noah to the Tower of Babel; from Babel to Stonehenge, where I obtained two rough graphs.

Now, I would very much like to introduce you to the peg-and-string model of the Stonehenge ground plan.

This is necessary in order to be able to refine the two crude graphs enough to produce equations.

*

I went out shopping, and brought home a large batch of clean white drawing paper to represent a grassy field, some rudimentary drawing implements consisting of a compass, pen and pencil, a very big eraser, and a straight edge to simulate pegs and string.

I also provided myself with a modern scientific calculator to check the accuracy of any geometry I might be able to come up with.

I then sat staring at a blank sheet of paper for quite a long while, thinking about how to begin. I tried to imagine myself as the designer, trying to design a ground plan that could be marked out in a field with minimal primitive tools.

After several more cups of tea and a whole packet of digestives, I was ready to make a start on a peg-and-string model.

*

It took me a while to work out how to produce fifty-six segments on a circle just using pegs and string and a stick, but I managed it in the end.

I also managed to convert those fifty-six pegged segments into thirty radials, and place all the features of the monument accurately.

If you think it cannot be done, think again. It turned out to be fairly straightforward, but rather long and repetitious, so I have decided to present the details separately. These details are to be found in chapter 8 of this book.

*

The peg-and-string method works. It works so well that I can reproduce the whole pattern of the monument, and reproduce all the planetary orbits, including Pluto and Neptune, with it.

I can even reproduce the mistakes the builders made, mistakes that I now believe to be deliberate, because they are the dumb-clue that gave me the dumb-key to unravel the secret. See fig 12. What I take to be deliberate 'mistakes' are shown in the disrupted area to the right.

Science would not be interested or convinced, and I can understand why. There is no natural law to derive the pattern from. It is an ad-hoc pattern, and the only way I can reproduce it is by taking my guide from the remains of a derelict monument.

In short, it is a wholly artificial pattern, a contrived pattern. It is like a knitting pattern, you need the list of instructions to produce the end result. Knit one, pearl two, etc.

The peg-and-string procedure is not derived from nature, and the fact that it works would not make any difference to a scientist.

The other problem with it is that it is very repetitive. Obviously I do not actually use pegs and string; I use pencil lines on paper, but the builders could have used wooden pegs and long lengths of whatever passed for string in those days, marking the ground with scratches or powdered chalk.

It would have been possible for three men, following written instructions, or knowing what they were doing, and working together, to produce the complete ground plan in a few days.

After that it's just a matter of digging the holes and deciding what to put in them.

*

It took a lot longer than it takes to type a description of it.

It also took lots of cups of tea, and loads of biscuits, but I finally managed to complete the design, and convinced myself that it was in fact the exact same design that the builders used.

I could say this because I could compare the product of my drawing with the archaeological details of the actual monument, and found that in many areas they were identical. I could explain and/or simulate the errors made by the builders. This peg and string method of constructing the ground plan is described in detail in part two, in chapter eight, where instructions are given to enable you to reproduce the monument ground plan for yourself.

Critics are also most welcome to follow the directions, and ask themselves if it is the sort of geometry that would be expected from a Neolithic person.

Calculating the Equations

Having finally cracked the peg-and-string drawing problem, I was in a position to calculate features fairly accurately from the chord lines of the model, using simple trigonometry. In this way I obtained figures that I could then graph against the astronomical data in the hope of obtaining results accurate enough to formulate equations for the curves.

It was a very boring and monotonous process to reproduce the monument and calculate all the distances, and I am not going to do it again here, (Instructions and drawings are in part two of this book) I will simply report that I obtained two accurate semi-log plots, from which I obtained two not-quite precise equations that involved all the planets out as far as Pluto.

I would like to draw your close attention to the words I have just written; I obtained valid equations from a

Neolithic monument that involved all the planets, including Pluto. Pluto was not discovered in modern times until 1930.

To me this was incredible, and represented conclusive proof that I was dealing with something antediluvian. It was advanced knowledge, and no mistake. It was only a very small fraction of the total knowledge that was to be revealed, but I didn't know that at the time.

If you want a sneak peek at the calculated results, the correspondence between the monument and the planets, take a look at figure 8.

The two exponents I obtained the hard way, from semi-log graphs, were 0.72 for the inner system and 0.48 for the outer. One thing I noticed straight away was that they were related, the one is 1.5 times the other.

I knew at the time that these could really only be approximations, but they were useful as interim exponents, and I was eventually able to refine them.

The final form of the exponents, given below, did not come until later; the way I settled on these is described in part two.

The equations I found are:-

For the inner system: $\mathbf{Si = Ki(AUi)^{(9/4\pi)}}$

And for the outer: $\mathbf{So= Ko(AUo)^{(3/2\pi)}}$

('i' signifies 'inner' and 'o' signifies 'outer')

'S' signifies monument distances.

'K' is linear scale factor.

'AU' is orbital data in Astronomical Units.

Please don't worry if you don't understand them, it really isn't necessary. They will be explained in part two. They are fairly simple really.

Fig 8b shows the graphs produced with these exponents, they are both straight-line graphs; compare Fig 8b with Fig 8a.

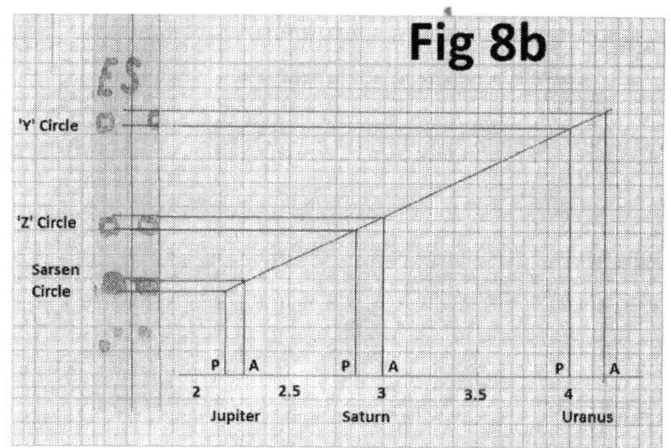

Scale in AU raised to power of $(3/2\pi)$

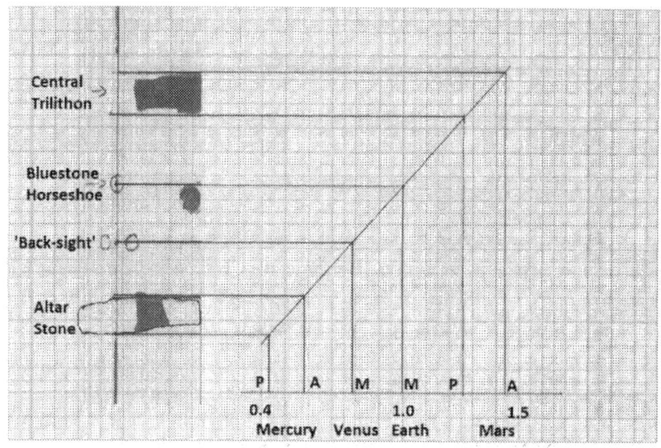

Scale in AU raised to power of $(9/4\pi)$

In brief, when the orbital figures for the planets are raised to one of these exponents, the numbers change, such that they no longer graph against the monument features as curves, instead they graph as straight lines. (See Fig 8b)

You may still be a little puzzled about why I went to so much trouble to determine these exponents and to check them. The reason is simple enough, the original curves looked as though they were exponential, but there was always the possibility that they could be due to chance. Sometimes things can look related when they are not.

Since this is now a serious project, it became necessary for me to eliminate chance, and this is what the two exponents do. It is no longer possible for a critic to justify any allegation that the relationship is due to chance. The exponents are a close fit to the monument, and what is more, the two exponents are very clearly related to each other, and as if that were not enough, they both embody the functioning of the astronomical rule known as 'Kepler's third law'.

These two graphs confirm that Stonehenge ground-plan is actually an exponential mathematical model of the Solar System planetary orbits, but of course, even with what I consider to be unassailable mathematical proof, nobody is going to believe it.

It is difficult to appreciate the truth of this relationship, just by looking at the monument, but it is mathematically valid.

It gets worse, because this claim is fully justified by the astronomical calculations in chapter ten, which are derived from the monument but are independent of it.

It follows that all the requirements are now met to pronounce that the monument is identical to the Biblical description of Babel, but nobody is going to believe *that* either.

This is by no means the end of our treasure hunt; it is

just another clue, another step along the way.

*

With the benefit of hindsight I can now say that the ground plan of the actual monument was never intended to be precise. It was a kind of reasonably accurate rough sketch to demonstrate how to proceed; not an end in itself.

It was a little like an engineering sketch pencilled onto the back of an envelope, showing how to do something, how to calculate something.

Reason dictates that the builders could not hope for the exactness and precision that would be needed to satisfy a modern scientist, not when they had to work with fifty-ton blocks of stone and primitive stone tools.

They concentrated on providing a method to enable the reconstruction of the message they desired to send down the millennia.

The monument is not precise, as a casual glance will show, but it is close enough to be described as 'accurate', and it is close enough to get the message across. What message? We will get there eventually.

*

At this stage, after a lot of trigonometric calculations, graph drawing on semi-log paper, and rather a lot of tea and head scratching, I had managed to formulate the equations of the two curves.

I now had two fairly satisfactory exponential equations that summed up the relationship between the monument and the orbits of the planets of the solar system, as far as Pluto.

This was astonishing, but it was still not enough.

Because I had obtained them from a peg and string method, no scientist in his right mind would pay any attention whatsoever.

Nobody is going to believe it possible to draw a fairly accurate exponential mathematical representation of the entire Solar System with a peg-and-string model. That is what the ground plan of Stonehenge is.

Proof is in part two of this book.

Proof or not, scientists will say I am a crank, a loony and such like and so forth. Well, to be blunt, I am finding it more and more difficult to care what scientists think.

Please stay with me for just a little longer; we are nearly at the end of this chapter.

The Combined Equation

I had found two closely related exponential astronomical equations in an ancient monument, and I had been able to represent all of the planetary orbits of the Solar System with a peg and string model. As if all that wasn't bad enough; things were about to get considerably worse.

At this stage I felt I was making slow but genuine progress, I had finished the peg-and-string model of the ground plan, and I had obtained two exponential equations that worked very well to relate the orbits of the Solar System to the monument features.

I knew there must be more; the two equations I had obtained were a shocking discovery, completely unbelievable, but two equations did not justify building such a monument.

All it tells us is that the designer knew an awful lot

about the Solar System and that he was certainly from an advanced culture.

It can even be argued that it tells us quite a lot about the nature of the antediluvian civilization immediately prior to the flood.

In order to be able to produce a design like that the designer would have needed access to astronomical observatory data, which means high power telescopes and the ability to measure orbital parameters. The exponential nature of the graphs implies that they had calculators, because it is virtually impossible to do complex exponential calculations without one. That alone implies that antediluvian society was based on an infrastructure of an advanced scientific nature.

We may accept that it tells us we were right about the Tower of Babel, but it still does not provide us with all the knowledge that remained encoded in the monument.

There must be more, because we have two equations. We might illustrate the thought by asking the question; why two?

It was while I was staring at the ground-plan yet again, thinking about this question of two graphs, that it occurred to me that the monument ground plan was itself a kind of graph.

This is evident from the details of the peg-and-string model. The inner monument is designed on the same peg-and-string template as the outer. The only difference between the two templates is one of scale.

It looked to me that the inner monument template was equivalent to the 'y' axis of a modern graph, and the outer template would then be the equivalent of the 'x' axis.

*

It was a graph of circular format, while we are accustomed to a rectangular format. A circular format looks very alien to our eyes, but it seemed to me that the ground plan really was a graph.

In order to see this, it is necessary to adjust our thinking and our prejudices. This graph, if that is indeed what it is, originated from the antediluvian world, which must have been totally different from ours in many ways, not least in the way they portrayed graphs.

The mathematical 'language' was surprisingly the same as ours, but the way they presented it was a little difficult to grasp at first.

The monument was a graph, and it graphed itself against itself.

The inner monument was apparently graphed against the outer monument, but in an unfamiliar circular sort of way.

Well, I spent a while toying with the notion, and then the penny dropped, suddenly a light came on in my head and I understood what the monument was all about.

If the monument was related to the orbits via my two equations, and if the monument was graphed against itself, then surely that meant I should graph my two equations one against the other?

*

I had the two equations shown above (and repeated here); these relate the monument feature to the orbits:

For the inner features: Si = Ki $\mathbf{(AUi)}^{(9/4\pi)}$

And for the outer features: So= Ko $\mathbf{(AUo)}^{(3/2\pi)}$

Of these two expressions the 'S' just represents the Stonehenge distances in 'sticks', and the 'K' is a constant of linear proportionality. Both these factors can be ignored, they are not important.

The important bits are the bits in brackets.

The monument appeared to be suggesting that the inner orbits should be equated to the outer orbits so that the combined equation would appear something like this:

$$\mathbf{(AUi)}^{(9/4\pi)} \quad \text{<---->} \quad \mathbf{(AUo)}^{(3/2\pi)}$$

Obviously for this to work there would need to be some kind of relationship function to go in place of the double-headed arrow, and this would need a bit of mental effort.

I had nothing to lose by trying it, so that is what I did. I drew a graph of these two functions, plotting one against the other, and the result so impressed me that I decided it was time to give up on the tea and try something stronger.

*

My dog and I went out for the evening, down to the pub to meditate on my discovery, with a glass or three of Glenfiddich.

Sitting in the inglenook next to the log fire, dog at my feet, glass in hand, I closed my eyes and tried to take on board the significance of what I had found.

At that stage I had not worked out all the details, but I intuitively knew that the details would not be long in coming. I had discovered the reason the antediluvians built the monument. I had discovered the reason why the Elohim would want to stop the work, or so I told myself.

I understood the message, it was genuine ancient knowledge that modern science and the general public are blissfully unaware of; the equation related the outer orbits to the inner orbits.

My hand shook as I sipped my warm malt whisky, not knowing that there was a bigger shock to come.

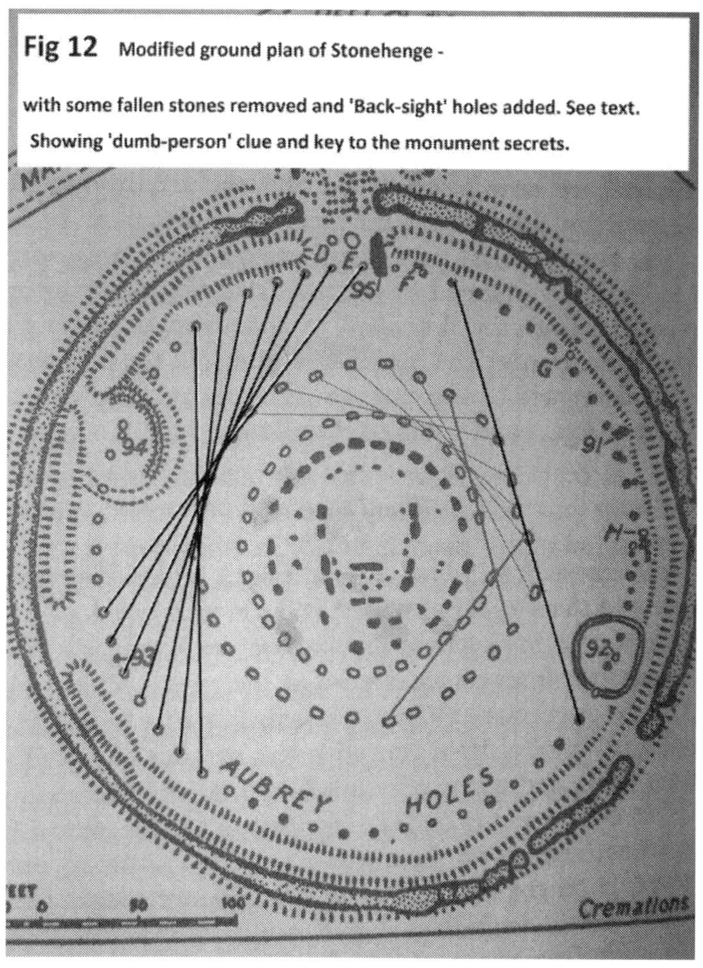

Fig 12 Modified ground plan of Stonehenge - with some fallen stones removed and 'Back-sight' holes added. See text. Showing 'dumb-person' clue and key to the monument secrets.

The next day, after an evening of celebrating my success, I had a bit of a headache, probably as a result of all that thinking.

I knew it was highly likely that I had not exhausted all the secrets hidden in the monument, but what I had discovered was more than enough for me at that time. It made my brain hurt almost as bad as a hangover.

The new equation was a combination of the two previous ones, and when I drew the combined graph on paper, relating the orbits of the inner system to the orbits of the outer system, it gave me a sense of satisfaction. It made me think that I had solved the riddle. I was right, but I was only half right.

It soon got a bit worse.

Once my headache had cleared I returned to the task with renewed enthusiasm. The new equation had fired my zeal, and whetted my appetite, I became hungry for more.

I started work on the new equation to figure out the constants, to try to constitute the graph in a presentable manner. In order to do this I had to consult the monument in detail.

Before long, without me even realising it, I had a whole wealth of new knowledge about the Solar System pouring out of the monument.

It was new knowledge, but at the same time it was ancient knowledge that is independently verifiable, and found to be true. (Technical details are in part two of this book, in chapters 9 & 10 and figures 9 & 10.)

The equation that I had newly obtained by graphing the inner orbits against the outer orbits was a 'stand-alone' formula; an astronomical equation that once found no longer depended on Stonehenge. It depends only on itself, and can be checked and verified with astronomical figures taken from a modern astronomy book.

The finished combined graph, and the equation that describes it, are very clearly a modern world's version of the monument ground-plan, in Cartesian format instead of the antediluvian circular format.

Everything, the ground plan, the peg-and-string, the equations, the graphs, are all mathematically the same thing. They are all the same mathematical representation of the Solar System of planetary orbits, just presented in different formats.

This may be hard for you to see, but you may take my word for that.

A brief tea break.

Once I got into the details of the monument, it was like getting inside the designers head. The monument ground plan is nothing less than an exponential mathematical model of the Solar System, produced by the peg-and-string method; that reveals an equation that has Earth-shattering implications.

You will of course understand that 'Earth-shattering' depends on it being accepted by those who rule the world. As yet, the Earth has definitely not shattered.

To give you an idea of just how exciting this was for me, perhaps I can tell you that I have done quite a few exciting things in my life. It has not been all tea and biscuits. Opening the door to two elderly ladies was not the first time something scary has happened to me.

I have been diving, naked, in the South China Sea, with sharks, and that was quite exciting. I have been lost alone in the Malayan Jungle and that was interesting. I have jumped out of aeroplanes; I have been down an abandoned mine and crawled along dark tunnels full of bats and spiders; I have been thrown out of a brothel in

Thailand at gunpoint. I have even tried to catch black cobras with a forked stick, just for a bet. I have been in down-town Chicago during a shoot-out between cops and crooks.

I have done all these things and much more.

I tell you these things not to boast, I am aware that many people have done much more exciting things than I have, and women who have babies must find the experience pretty exhilarating. I only mention these things to let you know that I have been 'around the block' a few times.

Quite a lot of thrilling and scary things have happened in my life, but none of them compare, none of them were as disturbing and as frightening as discovering this equation.

The math shown on fig 10, and its ramifications, was the single most electrifying and fearsome thing that has ever confronted me and challenged me. It is necessary to understand it, or you will not appreciate what I am saying. A professional astronomer who gives it his full attention should find that his blood runs ice-cold, chilled in his veins, if it doesn't actually freeze solid.

End of tea break.

Our brief intrusion into archaeology is over. Now we will leave Stonehenge to the archaeologists. Let them continue with their scratching and digging for shards of old pottery, blissfully unaware that we have been trespassing on their territory.

We will leave the archaeology, leave the antediluvian world and have a closer look at the new combined equation.

It may be that there are a few more trinkets of knowledge to be gained from the monument, there are areas I have not studied, like the Heel Stone and its possible astronomical significance. The Heel Stone was obviously important to the builders, and it seems that the trilithon side arms are aimed at it. I do not know what it signifies, it could mean anything. It could represent a dark star (that some call Nibiru), far beyond the Oort cloud, on its way to destroy the Earth again, or perhaps it isn't.

The 'Station Stones' appear to have been a later addition to the monument, and for that reason I have ignored them, but they might have some significance. I am happy to leave such matters to others.

I have my treasure of ancient knowledge, and that is more than enough for me.

I would like to share the treasure I have found with you, and I hope to do so in the following chapters, and of course many more details are available in part two of this little book.

*

I am worried that you might be one of those people who do not like mathematics.

I would like to show you the equation, and the graph, and I warn you that when you turn to the next chapter you will see the equation, and the simplified graph.

But there is no need to worry. I just want you to see them, there is no need to fear them; they do not bite. They are just black squiggly marks on paper, and that is all. There is no punishment if you do not understand them.

I am not intending to launch into a lengthy series of calculations, and I am not going to give you a math lesson, this is not the place for that.

I just want you to look at them.

It is like saying, “Here, come and look at my lovely scorpion, see the sharp little sting in its tail.” But you don’t have to come close.

Will you come with me? I will try not to get too technical.

Chapter Four

Ordered orbits

This chapter is going to be even more difficult than the last. All the more so because I have promised you that I would not get too technical.

This chapter is about the astronomical equation that was the final outcome of my work on Stonehenge. It is a very powerful equation, a very meaningful equation, and it changes rather a lot of the things we once thought we knew.

It tells us unbelievable things about our origins, and about the Solar System, and it does so with verifiable mathematics.

Talking of origins reminds me that many people do not appear to have any interest in their cosmic surroundings; their minds are fixed firmly on local matters. We are all educated from childhood to 'fit in' with the rest of society. We all tend to become unconsciously indoctrinated with the views held by the majority.

This indoctrination includes the unquestioning belief that the world's professional academics know everything there is to know about the Solar System. As a result, even those who consider themselves to be free thinkers can hold to their deeply rooted understanding of the cosmos.

The equation derived from Stonehenge changes our view of the Solar System, to such an extent that most people will find it difficult to take seriously. It doesn't simply make us look at the old view in a different way, it changes the entire system.

The planets stay in their same old familiar orbits, nothing physical changes, but the equation turns everything we supposed to be true on its head.

It is as though the familiar traditional Solar System of astronomers has been discarded and replaced with something totally different.

*

This is what people will find difficult to accept. It is very hard to change our deep-rooted convictions, even when confronted by the mathematical facts.

I have become fully convinced of the reality of new Solar System because I have been involved in the calculations for quite a while, not only during my researches but again more recently in having the need to ensure that the mathematics was all correct before writing this book. Because of this close connection, I no longer have any trouble accepting the new Solar System, but I am aware that the situation is different for you, my reader.

The only way to adjust the mind to a novel situation is to practice. That means to check the calculations, go through them, examine them, and then think about the implications.

This is too much to ask of most people, so an acceptable alternative would be for you to ask a mathematician to verify the calculations for you.

*

In the last chapter we found two exponential

equations, each of which related part of the Solar System of planets to part of the Stonehenge monument features. At first these two equations looked like ancient knowledge, and I thought perhaps that was the end of the road, but the equations were just another clue, pointing to the combined equation.

I realised that the first two equations could be joined, to form a 'master' equation, which would be independent of the monument. This master equation would join the one group of planets to the other group of planets, without the mediation of the monument.

It was easy to produce the general formula for the new master equation, but it took a little while and a fair amount of button pushing to finalise the details. The end result was an equation which forms the basis of this book.

This is a treasure as good as any I could hope to find, but it also turned out to be another clue, another step on the way. It is a golden key that allows us to open an even greater treasure chest.

*

Before I start on describing the actual equation, I would like to remind us both, yet again, of the path our researches have followed.

We have pursued clues from the Bible story of the Elohim and Creation, to the global Flood and Noah; from Noah to the Tower of Babel; from Babel to Stonehenge, where I obtained two rough graphs.

From there we used a peg-and-string model of the monument ground-plan. From this I was able to formulate two exponential equations relating the planets to the monument features.

Most recently we have joined those two equations to form one new equation, which applies directly to the Solar System.

Through this chain we can see a link back to the story in Genesis, even though we are about to take a trip into space.

Through all our previous exploration we have been confined to the Earth, or have had at least one foot on the ground, but now we take to the heavens, we leave the Earth and everything in it, and explore the Solar System, which is the third principal theme of this book, and is where we unlock the greatest treasure.

We can do this with the aid of the final equation, which describes the relationship between the orbits of the planets, without the need for further reference to earthly things.

So now we leave the Earth, we leave Stonehenge with its pegs and string, we leave Babel, and Noah, and the Flood, and fly into space, into the realm of the Mighty Ones, to see what they are up to.

A Valid Equation

I could have gone into a great deal more detail during our researches in the last few chapters, discussing things that I came across along the way, like C14 dates for Stonehenge, which I found to be saying more about the level at which the samples were buried than they were about dates. I will mention this dating method in more detail in a later chapter. I chose not to do so now because I did not wish to divert your attention from the central theme.

Things like C14 dating will be used to try to debunk the

equation. Science will try to show that I made a mistake in my analysis of Stonehenge, or in my analysis of the Bible. They will try their best to find some way to ignore my finding.

One thing they cannot do is to claim that the equation is not valid. In the years since I discovered it I have had it checked and rechecked a hundred times.

There is no mistake. The equation is valid.

The equation is also a little like a message in a bottle. Once the message has been removed from the bottle, the bottle can be discarded.

Stonehenge/Babel was such a bottle, a bottle adrift on the seas of time, waiting for someone to extract the message.

The final equation which you will soon see below is a stand-alone formulation that no longer requires the Monument to support it.

There is no further need for Stonehenge, or Babel, so if scientists try to challenge my analysis, hoping to throw out the baby with the bath-water, they will be wasting their time. We can dispose of the monument now, because we have extracted the information that Noah encoded into the ground plan.

The equation has no further need of Stonehenge, and nor do we, except and unless we are interested in other aspects of that old monument.

*

If we spend a few minutes thinking about it, we can say that the equation validates the link back to the Genesis story, but nobody is going to believe that until they fully understand the mathematics of the equation, and confirm for themselves that it is valid.

Scientists might claim that I invented the equation myself, so that they might avoid accepting the reality of the Genesis story and an ancient antediluvian civilization.

I would be flattered, but such a thing would be beyond my capabilities, I am no Einstein.

In any case, why would I lie about the origins?

If I had in fact invented the equation myself, surely I would claim the credit for myself, rather than give the credit to a long-dead mythological figure?

I am telling you this, because as my last reader, you might abandon me if you hear such tales, and I would not wish you to do that. Not yet, because I have more to tell you.

Please understand and accept that the equation is not my own, I did not invent it. The equation really did originate in that ancient ruined monument we know as Stonehenge; that was once known as the Tower of Babel.

Now we will spend a while looking at the equation, if you don't mind.

The Equation

The mathematics referred to in this section is included in part two in much greater detail, so if you really want to get deeply involved, then please keep reading as far as chapters 9 & 10 in part two. It is also summed up on graphs 9 and 10, which are also in part two.

The first thing I wish to point out is that although we have left Stonehenge behind, the people who lived before the flood must have known all that is in this chapter, and more.

They must have known this equation…

$$\mathbf{(AUi)^{(9/4\pi)}.ln30 - F = (AUo)^{(3/2\pi)}}\text{.....Equation 1}$$

This is the equation that I finally obtained from the monument; this is the first part of our treasure of ancient knowledge, but the meaning of it needs explaining.

If you just look at the form of it you will see that it is made up of parts of the single equations I showed you earlier, in the last chapter.

Those two single equations that related the orbits to the monument have here been combined.

*

I can imagine you staring at it and thinking ‘What!!?’, and I don’t blame you, it seems a little incomprehensible, and without an explanation of what it does you will not appreciate its value.

In a nutshell, it demonstrates that the Solar System is neatly ordered.

*

I would like to say something now that I can only say because it is not my equation, it came from Stonehenge. I am not bragging, I am just stating a fact. To put the equation into perspective, it has the potential to change the world.

This is why God stopped the building of Babel. This is what the builders of the monument worked so hard to preserve, to pass down the generations.

The builders of the monument, survivors of the flood, were desperate that this knowledge would be passed on to future generations, and it is our job to try to understand why that would be.

These are subjects we can discuss in more detail later, for now I need to explain briefly what the equation means, and why it is so important. This is going to be difficult without coming over all mathematical, but I will try.

*

If you look at the equation you might notice that it is rather simple, by which I mean that it is not long and complicated. It is short, and in comparison to a lot of other mathematical equations, it is very simple.

Because it is so short and so simple it is easy to check, and it has been checked over and over again. It is valid.

What the equation actually does is described in detail in part two, but for now we may just accept that it demonstrates a neat kind of order in the Solar System, order that should not be there.

This is a very significant fact. According to science there cannot be such order in the system of planets.

*

Later on I was told by an expert that I was not being very professional in my presentation, which is not a surprise because I am using a format learned from the antediluvian monument. The way I express it is in the form in which I found it, and the way I am accustomed to using it. While it is in this form it also allows us to look at various different aspects that do not show up when it is expressed in more professional formats.

*

The graph in Fig 11 (below) is a ***very*** simplified representation of the workings of the equation. It is the same thing as the equation, showing how it relates the planetary orbits.

It is a true representation of the Solar System, and at one and the same time, it has a direct linear correspondence with the ground plan of Stonehenge, and the peg-and-string pattern.

The equation and the graph are not arbitrary. They are definitely not numerology.

The equation is elegant and meaningful, and applies to all of the known planetary orbits of the Solar System. In fact it also applies to the empty spaces in between, but not many people would care about that.

What it does is to relate inner planets to outer planets, such that if you know the mean orbital distance or period of any planet, you can calculate the mean orbital distance or period of another one.

If you know the simple rules that apply, it is possible to calculate all the orbits or periods of all the planets, from any two.

It does much more than just to demonstrate a simple linear relationship.

*

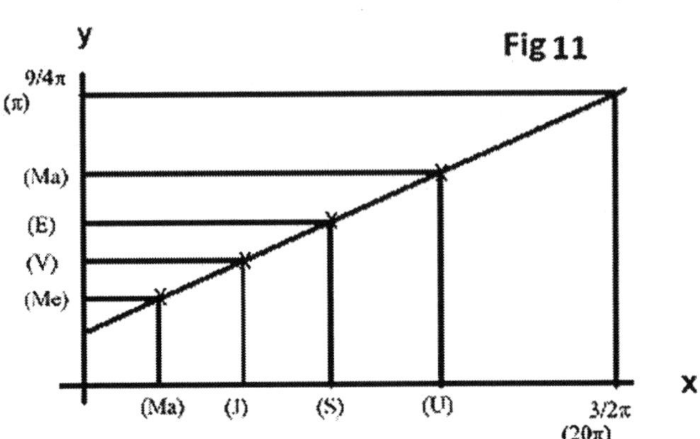

If you were to consult the technical details in part two of this book, you would soon realise that the Solar System is in fact ordered in a variety of different ways all at once.

Even before the equation is applied, it is evident that the exponents are related to each other; and that they are simply the radius and area of a circle of circumference three.

After the exponents have been applied the outer planets are seen to be in a linear relationship to the inner, (simplified in fig 11 above), and the whole system can be represented by an artificial peg and string pattern.

There are more relationships that I discuss in detail in the technical section, showing that the Solar System is indeed ordered.

*

This ability to calculate 'orbital-mean' and orbital periods of planets from other planets may not sound like much, but it is something that astronomers have not yet been able to do (unless they have read this book), and they would not expect to be able to do it, because it is contrary to all their theories of our origins.

While I had the equation in the above format I asked a friendly mathematician from my local university if he would check it for me.

He did, and found nothing wrong, (except for my unprofessional presentation) but in checking he did a statistical breakdown, calculating a 'best fit' equation from the main four data points.

His conclusion was that my equation, that is the one obtained from Stonehenge, was a better 'fit' than the 'best fit' equation his methodology produced.

*

The conclusion was that the equation is real, and it functions accurately, in a way that is not predicted by science, or even known to science.

Usually, we would expect equations to do something. ***This equation proves that the planetary orbits of the Solar System are neatly ordered.***

Once it has done that, it seems to have no physical function, but that doesn't mean it is not important. It is really, very, very, important, and I hope to make you understand just how important it is before you throw the book away. The figure I have just shown you, (fig 11), is a very simplified version. For the full details please see chapter 10 in part two.

It is possible to have a lot of fun with the equation, if you have the mathematical skills to enjoy it. It is great fun using a calculator to 'planet hop' around the Solar System, but there are also some very serious aspects.

For example, and this is quite important, the equation works without any references to gravity or mass.

Newton's gravitational laws of motion are not involved.

This means, quite simply, that we cannot use gravity to explain the order in the Solar System.

Another oddity that is really important is that it works with AU as a distance measure. This means that all the planetary orbits are ordered relative to one AU, which is the mean orbit of planet Earth.

In other words, the planets are ordered relative to the Earth.

*

So, I repeat myself for your benefit; if you are still a little baffled by the equation, and not sure what it does, there is no need to worry. All it does is what is already done. It demonstrates that the supposedly random Solar System is in fact neatly ordered in a number of different ways all at once.

Once we know that, there is no use for it other than as a study tool.

It may seem that it is rather marvellous that such an equation could be produced by an antediluvian civilization, but so what?

Why did they go to all that trouble to tell us about it?

Well, it gets worse.

In fact, it gets a ***lot*** worse, but you really need the mathematical skills to understand just how bad it gets (see chapter 10 of this book.)

For now, we will continue with our treasure hunt using just words.

*

According to astronomers, our Solar System formed from the effect of gravity on a huge disc, or cloud, of dust and small stones that was trapped in orbit around the sun.

This is called the nebular hypothesis.

It is a hypothesis, which is a little less meaningful than a theory, it is certainly not a fact, but it is treated as a fact by astronomers.

Under the terms of this concept, the planets slowly grew by a process of accretion, as dust and meteors were dragged down by gravity to add their bulk to the growing planet.

In the case of the outer planets, which are apparently made up of gas, it was a slightly different process but still involved gravity.

The general rule is that the planets came into being by the action of gravity, and nothing else.

There was nothing to guide planets into specific orbits except gravity.

This means that the orbits should be essentially random, and no mathematical equation should ever be able to fully relate to a random assemblage of nine planets.

The equation we have under our consideration not only relates the planets, it does so in a number of different ways, all at once, and very accurately as well.

So it would appear that we are faced with the choice, either the equation is wrong, or scientists are wrong.

There is a compromise possible, which we will discuss later, but from the scientific viewpoint, for scientists, all is lost.

This is where the simplicity of the equation becomes important. You might not understand it, it might seem complex to you, but for a scientist, for an astronomer, it is the very essence of simplicity.

The equation is simple, it is easy to check, and it is right.

There can be little in the way of argument or dispute; there is no wriggle room for science. The system is ordered.

It gets worse.

*

About the time of Darwin, there was a man called Lyell, and another man called Laplace.

(I paraphrase this story just a little.)

Before Darwin published his 'Origin of Species' the world lived in the darkness of ignorance, the only light was the wrecker's lamp of the Church.

Darwin said, *"I can explain the origin of man from apes, but I need lots of time for life to evolve, and God will not let me have so much time."*

Lyell, who was a geologist, replied, *"I can give you as much time as you like, under my principle of uniformitarianism, but I need a very old Solar System, and God will not let me have an old Solar System."*

Then Laplace, who was an astronomer, piped up, *"I can create a very old Solar System from a cloud of dust, and I don't need a God to do it."*

So Laplace showed how to randomly accrete a Solar System from a random cloud of dust, without asking for God to help.

When his process of random accretion was complete, he proclaimed the finished Solar System to be extremely old, and gave Lyell what he wanted, a very old Solar System, made without a God.

Once Lyell had his very old Solar System, his principle of uniformitarianism would work just fine, so he was able to present Darwin with a very old Earth.

In this way Darwin found himself with the very old Earth he needed, with lots and lots of time for life to evolve, and man's ape ancestors soon came swinging down from the trees.

So, everyone was happy, and people realised they didn't need a God to explain things. Children were educated to appreciate the new scientific way of understanding our origins, which ultimately was based on Laplace's theory.

Gradually over the last hundred and fifty years or so, the modern world of secular reasoning and atheistic science has come about.

The problem is that the combined equation, which came from a Neolithic monument, ruins all that.

The equation proves that our Solar System is not random. It looks like Laplace was wrong.

If Laplace was wrong, then his theory would fail to support Lyell, and without the support of Laplace, Lyell's principle of uniformitarianism would falter and fail.

In turn, without the support of Laplace and Lyell, Darwin's theory of evolution has nothing to support it, so Darwin would also fall.

They topple like dominoes.

So where does that leave science?

Without foundation, that is where science finds itself if the Babel equation is real, and it is.

It means that Darwin's theory of evolution no longer has a leg to stand on.

It gets worse.

*

The problems that emerge if this equation is recognised are far reaching and profound. It would have a grave effect on many disciplines of science, quite apart from the theory of evolution.

All our understanding of human history would need to be changed drastically. As things stand it is believed that human history stretches back into the mists of time for millions of years. It is a story of slow and gradual progression from ape to modern man, and there is no room for a highly advanced technological civilization along the way, other than our own.

If the equation is valid, and it is, and if it was obtained from Stonehenge, as it was, then the builders of Stonehenge simply must have come from an advanced civilization that has now vanished.

If all trace of an advanced culture has vanished from the Earth, then there must have been a global disaster like the flood.

The flood ruins everything, not just the landscape, but all scientific theories that ignore it, including palaeoanthropology.

A global flood would have wiped out the civilization, but it would also have totally changed the topography and geology of the Earth. Our understanding of past geological events would be wiped out by the recognition that there was, had to have been, a global flood.

Earth sciences founded on Lyell's assumptions fail.

Sediments did not all accumulate over eons; many were deposited in a very short time-scale during the flood, as was believed for thousands of years before Lyell, Laplace, and Darwin came along.

Even the science of plate tectonics might need revision. What effect would a sudden massive increase in the volume of water have on the ocean floor? How would drastic isostatic adjustment affect plate movements? How quickly could it happen?

The equation efficiently describes order in the Solar System, and does so without the need for gravity. Our views on the origins of the Solar System would need to be changed.

Astronomers have been studying and measuring the Solar System for a century or more, yet they have failed to notice the simple fact of order.

If astronomers cannot account for the origin of the Solar System; which is its own back-yard, why should anyone listen when they pontificate about the origin of the entire universe?

It gets worse, in fact, it gets really bad.

Ordered Orbits

It is at this point in the narrative when I must get very serious. This is not a joke.

One of the things that derive from a study of the equation is the grid of ugly black lines on graph fig.10.

This grid is arranged in accordance with the rule of Pythagoras.

It is imperative that you understand the mathematics in chapter 10, and the details of the derivation of the Pythagorean grid on graph fig. 10.

If you do not understand the use of the grid then that might be a major obstacle to your understanding. An obstacle, but not an incurable problem, for you can always get someone else to explain and verify the calculations.

As long as you understand that this is real and not some kind of bad joke you might be able to accept what I say in this section and the next. You might also be able to find someone to explain the inescapable implications.

If you cannot accommodate the mathematics of the Pythagorean grid on fig 10, then what follows from it will obviously be meaningless for you. I am not saying it is your fault, not at all; it is just the way things are sometimes. My old mum used to tell me “There is no shame in not understanding, the shame is in not trying.”

So, I can only suggest that if you really want to know, you should ask a mathematics teacher, or someone with mathematical abilities, to explain it to you.

Pythagoras

The Pythagorean grid on fig 10 is derived from the main equation (Equation 1), which you have seen already, and represents the ultimate in ancient knowledge. It is the golden treasure of all ancient knowledge. It is what this book is all about.

It will be worth your while to try very hard to understand it.

I will have to explain the implications, what it means, and take the risk, or simply stop writing.

*

There is no way of putting this gently, or letting it sneak up on you quietly. If it has to be said, I might as well throw it straight at you and say it plainly. Let me get it over with.

The order in the orbits is artificial.

The equation is artificial. It is wholly artificial. It owes nothing to any law of nature.

It came from an artificial, man-made, stone monument which in turn can be reproduced by a simple peg-and-string pattern.

There can be no doubt that the equation is utterly artificial.

If the Solar System is in close accord with the requirements of an artificially contrived equation, then what are we to say about the Solar System?

The order in the orbits of the Solar System is also artificial.

We can imagine that the antediluvians contrived the

equation, but they must have obtained it from observation of the solar system. The antediluvians did not put the planets in artificial order; they did not make the planets orbit in accord with an artificial equation, all they did was notice, and pass it on to us.

It gets worse still.

We can be fairly sure that the planets did not arrange themselves into such an intelligently contrived artificial pattern without help. Since gravity is not involved in the equation, it would not be possible to invoke gravitational forces.

The artificiality of the ordered orbits is emphasised by the number of different ways in which they are related. It is simply not possible to justify any claim that the order is natural. For precise details, calculated with nine decimal places over nine planets, see chapter 10, in part two.

There is no conventional explanation for it.

We may think to invoke the operation of 'chance'.

We might say that the planets became ordered like they are by the operation of blind chance.

Well, fair enough, but it is possible to apply a little mathematics and actually calculate the probability that the Solar System could have become ordered by chance alone.

I am not going to go into the calculation here, because I promised you I would try to keep things interesting, but the calculation results in a figure that is so huge it is difficult to write down.

There is one chance in 10 with seventy '0's after it.

To give an idea of how huge that it, the number

exceeds the estimated number of stars in the known visible universe, squared.

This means that if the order in the Solar System is due to chance, then our Solar System is unique. Our Solar System would be the only one of its kind ever to exist in the entire Universe.

What are the odds that intelligent life would evolve on a planet that is part of the only ordered Solar System ever to exist?

I think we can rule out chance.

It gets even worse.

I am open to other suggestions, but it seems to me that the only possible explanation is that ***the Solar System was put in artificial order relative to the Earth, by some powerful intelligent entity.***

Let me say that again so that there is no mistake about what I am saying.

The mathematical and astronomical facts insist that -

In the beginning, some unknown intelligent power put the Solar System in order relative to the Earth.

*

So we see, when we started this chapter we all lived in a natural Solar System, and now, a few pages later, we live in an artificial one.

Obviously, this is a bit much for anyone to swallow without lots of proof. Well, the proof is in your hands. It is in part two of this book, in detail. If you do not understand it yourself, all you need to do is take it to a mathematics teacher and ask him to check it out for you.

Tea break

It is now time for you and me to sit down with a nice cup of hot tea, and a biscuit, and have a little friendly chat.

I started this book with a promise that it was not a religious book; I said it was not a devious trick to get you to engage in Bible study.

Now you must be thinking I lied, because I appear to be saying that there is a 'God' after all. Well, not so!

I am saying that the orbits of the Solar System must have been ordered by an intelligent entity. That is not the same as saying 'God'.

It is true the entity is obviously a very powerful one, but it is most probably not just one. It is almost certainly many powerful ones, or mighty ones. We could call them 'Elohim' for want of a better word, and unless someone can show otherwise, we can assume these powerful entities are physical, not supernatural.

There is nothing supernatural about the order in the orbits. Whatever is going on, it is very real and very physical; it is not some theological invention.

I do not need to go to church and kneel and pray for a divine vision, I can calculate it all on my calculator.

It is possible that the early scribes knew this, but that later pious theologians changed things to suit their own views.

It is something we might like to look into a little more closely, but it is certainly not an attempt at Bible thumping.

We will have some more tea and biscuits in the next chapter.

End of tea break.

<u>Summary</u>

We started in the Biblical book of Genesis, discussing the Elohim and the Creation and the flood and Noah.

We progressed from Noah to Babel; and from Babel to the ground-plan of Stonehenge. We deduced that Stonehenge ground-plan was plotted on the ground with a peg-and-string method.

From this we were able to obtain two exponential equations that related the planetary orbits to the monument.

When we combined these two equations we produced a master equation that took us out into space.

This combined equation demonstrates that there is order in the orbits. The order in the orbits is so multi-layered that it cannot be due to chance or natural causes.

Our firm conclusion is that the order in the Solar System is artificial, and that the orbits have been deliberately arranged to accord with a simple equation, and the principle of Pythagoras (Described later, in part 2).

It follows that some unknown intelligent power put the

orbits into such a neat Pythagorean order.

Now you might like to take a brief holiday, study the math in Chapter 10, and fig 10, and when you are satisfied that you understand it, and that it is genuine, then you are welcome to come back here and join me again as I return to Genesis, and have another look at what the Elohim are up to.

Chapter Five

Of Gods and Men

In the beginning, Mighty Ones put the planets in order, relative to the Earth. (Genesis chp.1 v.1, my translation.)

*

I find myself in the position of a 'postman', the man who delivers letters, you know, the guy who the dog tries to bite.

I mean that I find myself in a situation where I am carrying a big bag full of information, and I feel that I am under some obligation to pass it on.

I do not claim that I have any part to play in the origin of these things, only that I stumbled across them whilst at cynical play.

Now I am trying to deliver the message to the right address, and that is all. I just hope the dogs don't get rabid and savage me.

*

It may be thought that the suggestion that the Solar System is artificially ordered is so outrageous that it cannot possibly be true, and must consequently be demoted to the status of 'opinion'.

Unfortunately it is a verifiable mathematical fact. One of the reasons I have included detailed descriptions of my methodology is so that others can replicate my procedures, and will no doubt obtain the same results, unless they deliberately misrepresent them.

Leaving aside the question of 'artificial' for a moment, there can be no question that the orbits are ordered, and the simple fact that the mathematics was obtained from an ancient monument is enough to cast doubt on the established understanding of history and reality.

The main equation, which is used to generate fig. 9, is enough to demonstrate that there is something seriously wrong with the established view, but the 'Equation for Venus' (in chapter 10) and the Pythagorean relationships of fig.10 prove beyond doubt that the order is not natural.

*

I have demonstrated these things, I have established that the planetary orbits of the Solar System are neatly ordered, and I have included the necessary mathematics to prove the case in part two of this book. If anyone doubts my claims, which I admit seem to be rather extreme, they should kindly first obtain a full understanding of the math before rejecting my words.

I just want to be clear that you understand what I am saying. This is not theory, not a joke, nor is it a mistake.

I speak the truth, I lie not, when I state that the order we observe is artificial. Again I say; the orbits of the Solar System are in an artificial order. If critics, or scientists, would be so kind as to check the mathematics!

This is not some fictional Solar System, not some hypothetical set of planets; this is the real one, the real Solar System we are living in right now.

Time for another little tea break I think.

All the Stonehenge stuff is just the road we followed to get here; it is true, but it is not very important. The mathematics in Chapter ten of this book, and the graph on fig 10, are the heart of the matter.

I have provided the mathematics, but there is nothing I can say or do to help you to understand. No harm will befall you if you do not understand the math, this is not an exam or a test of some kind, you don't get graded, but you will not fully appreciate the significance without that understanding.

So if you cannot grasp the meaning of all the squiggly bits, there is no need to worry. It will all become clear in the fullness of time.

On the other hand, if you really want to understand, then there are one or two things you could do to obtain guidance.

If you are still at school, then you are in the perfect place to get assistance, you just need to get hold of your math teacher privately and politely ask him or her to explain. Start with a simple part, and build up from there.

Believe it or not, you will find that mathematics teachers actually like to talk about mathematics.

If you are no longer at school, there are plenty of mathematics teachers in the world, there must be one in your area willing to help.

Alternatively, there will be others in your position that have read this book, and may be able to assist you in understanding it; all you need to do is find them.

I want you to understand the math, because in the coming chapters I wish to discuss the implications, and without that understanding you will think that everything that follows from it is just a fantasy, a fairy tale, or science fiction.

You may think to take my words on trust, or on faith, but I do not really recommend that, I would rather you checked the calculations if at all possible, or get them checked by someone else.

It is blind faith, belief without understanding; that has caused many of the world's problems.

I do not recommend faith, not at all.

Assume I am wrong, assume I am a liar, assume I am mistaken, assume I am a confidence trickster, you can assume anything you like but please do not take these things on faith.

Mathematics on its own is interesting, but it is even more interesting if it means something, so now we should look at some of the implications of living on a planet in an artificially ordered Solar System.

End of tea break.

We have discovered an equation, and we know that it means the orbits are artificially ordered. Now we have the opportunity to examine what the implications are. We might use this knowledge to throw some new light on the earlier verses of the scripture.

For example, we may reasonably ask if all this represents a good enough reason to justify the survivors of a global disaster building a massive stone monument?

The answer has to be an emphatic 'yes', the information fully justifies the building of such a monument.

If the orbits of the Solar System are neatly and artificially ordered, then it follows that there is **something greater and more powerful than man**. It also follows that this 'something greater than man' was at some time here in this Solar System, because they put the System in order.

This is not theory, this is a fact.

We note that in the Biblical narrative 'that which is greater and more powerful than man' is already accepted and referred to as 'Elohim'.

This thought produces a circular situation. Our original contention was that the monument was built by antediluvians who had survived a flood, and they wanted to pass on information.

These same antediluvians were responsible for the claims and statements in Genesis that the Mighty Ones existed.

We have to conclude that the builders of the monument were trying to tell us, not about some other unknown power, but about the power they were already familiar with, the Mighty Ones, or Elohim.

By building the monument, they are letting us know that the Elohim are not a theological fiction, they are a real physical force to be reckoned with.

The monument message is not simply a statement; it carries inescapable mathematical proof along with it.

"The Elohim are real, and they are powerful enough to put the orbits of the planets in order", that is the message from the 'tower' of Babel, Stonehenge, and the mathematics included with the message invite us to 'go look' and check for ourselves.

This I have done, it is true, and the proofs are in part two, and I say the same thing to you; 'go look', check for yourself.

It follows from this that at least some of the statements made in the Biblical book of Genesis are true.

It gets worse.

*

There are a great many questions that arise from the observation that we live in an artificially ordered Solar System, and even more questions develop from the necessary reality of the power that created that order.

For example, we may wonder what these Elohim are like and where they possibly came from, and here we encounter a major difficulty.

I ran into this problem when I tried to tell a Creationist Christian what I had discovered. His reaction was one that I had not anticipated. He became quite agitated, angry with me for suggesting that I might have evidence that God is a reality.

He informed me that the existence of God cannot be proved or disproved, and that this was an article of faith held by Christians everywhere.

*

I confess I didn't understand it, but it would seem that the Elohim of the Bible, the power that ordered the orbits, cannot therefore be the Spiritual God of Christianity.

This raises major problems, because if the order in the orbits was not the work of God, then it is evidently the work of someone else.

In order to please the Creationist Christians I would have to assume that the power that ordered the orbits was not the Creator of the Universe, but some hitherto unknown power that is also called 'Elohim'.

If the Elohim are not the Creator God, then what are they?

If the Elohim are not God, then where is God in the Bible?

The Christian view leaves me no choice but to proceed on the basis that the Elohim of the Bible are physical beings.

I would suggest to Creationist Christians, and others, that if you believe in God's salvation then surely the power of God to save does not depend on proof, or lack of proof, but rather it depends on what is in your heart?

Is that not so?

*

I do not like to upset Christians, who for the most part are good people, so I will not continue to insist that the Christian Creator God is real.

I will continue this narrative on the basis that the Elohim are physical, if only to please Christians.

If you, my only reader, would make up your own mind about the power that ordered the System, then I will continue on the advice of the Christians, and assume that it is physical.

If anyone objects to this then they must take the matter up with the Christian Church. They are more qualified than I am to comment on the nature of God, and of course they are at liberty to write and publish a book to correct the content of this one.

*

It is also advisable to be minimalist, by which I mean that we take the lowest and simplest proposition. This is also known as the principle of Ockham's razor. To give an example, we do not need to assume that these putative Elohim actually ‘created’ the planets, to be more reasonable we would take the minimal view and say that they could have moved pre-existing random planets, and put them into mathematical order.

As a working hypothesis we will accept that physical beings could have the power to move planets. We suggest they could do this by the use of advanced technology and access to vast amounts of energy, possibly by directly tapping into the nuclear reactions and power output of the Sun.

If this proposal is considered to be anything like valid, then it is reasonable to conjecture that they did not originate here in this System.

It follows that they came from somewhere else, and the only other ‘place’ they could have come from is the stars.

They must have had a reason for coming here, and we might like to wonder what that reason could be.

It is clear that they did not come here to conquer and pillage.

Clones

The Biblical narrative has proved to be correct in the case of Noah and Babel, or at least, assuming the truth of those stories has yielded real equations, so it is not unreasonable to place a small amount of confidence in the other stories in the same book, but we must always keep in mind that when we read the Bible we are not necessarily reading a record of facts. We are reading the words of a scribe; we are reading a record of what the scribe *believed to be* facts.

If we read the first few chapters of the creation story, we may note that the creation of human beings is given a prominent position.

There are elements of the story that appear to be pure fantasy, like trees with magic fruit, and talking snakes, but if we read between the lines, another story emerges.

It was one of the stated intentions of the Elohim to create man ***in their own image.***

Genesis 1

26 And God said; Let us make man in our image, (1) after our likeness (2)

27 So God created man in his own image (3), in the image of God (4) created he him; male and female created he them.

Four times in two adjacent verses the statement is made that men are created in the image of the Mighty Ones, after their likeness.

Our modern human scientists could make the same declaration, the same stated intention, and if our modern scientists had made that stated intention, we would say that they intended to clone themselves.

It is against international convention and international laws for scientists to clone a man in their own image. They could do it, but they are banned from doing it.

The Elohim were not answerable to human laws and so if they were flesh and blood, and wanted to clone themselves, and make man in their own image, there would be nothing to prevent them from doing so.

The scripture also says that the monotheistic God made man out of dust.

*

I suppose it is up to you what you want to believe, but I think that the Biblical story of creation reads like a garbled account of interstellar colonisation.

The whole thing makes a great deal of sense if we assume that the Elohim came to the Solar System in the first place because they *wanted to start a colony of cloned copies of themselves*.

This would seem silly but for our new understanding that we live in an artificially ordered Solar System, and that the Elohim, or whatever they call themselves, must really exist.

Of course, if there is any justification for the assertion that the Elohim made clones of themselves then it must follow that the Elohim are also flesh and blood. A spirit God could not make a clone of Himself nor make man in any physical image of Himself at all.

Clones, as we know them, start life in a helpless embryonic state in a laboratory somewhere, and grow to be babies in a crèche, before developing into children and then full adults.

If we are to follow through with the thought that the first humans started as slightly imperfect cloned copies of the Elohim, then we must also accept that in the early days, as children, they would need protecting. Even as young adults, in a new and unfamiliar world with no knowledge or history to guide them, as innocents, the new humans would need protection, education, and guidance.

So we might expect that the clones would be placed in a protected environment, just as modern scientists would put captive-bred animals in a 'halfway house' to accustom them to self-sufficiency, before finally releasing them into the wild.

The 'Garden of Eden' served that function.

*

The young humans were raised in the protected area of the Garden of Eden under the watchful eye of the Elohim.

We can guess there were more than just two youngsters, for Adam just means 'man' or 'mankind', and Eve means 'living'. It is reasonable to expect that more than just two were created. Later on, after the eviction, Cain finds himself a wife, so there must have been more than just the traditional pair.

In chapter 2 of Genesis, Eve is just called 'Woman'. Gen 2 v 23 ***'she shall be called Woman.'*** ('ishshah = 'woman')
Man and woman, male and female, created he them.

No matter how many there were, or were not, when the young humans reached the age of puberty, and became conscious of their sexuality, the Elohim recognised that they were almost ready to be released.

But how would the Elohim know if the young humans were able to think for themselves? How would the Elohim know that the humans were capable of making independent decisions?

One way would be to give them an order, and see if the humans disobeyed.

A clone that disobeys its master is acting autonomously, thinking for itself, making a decision and taking control of its own destiny; ready and able to make its own way in the world.

Genesis Chp. 2.

16 ....And the LORD God commanded the man, saying, Of every tree of the garden thou mayest freely eat:

17....But of the tree of the knowledge of good and evil, thou shalt not eat of it: for in the day that thou eatest thereof thou shalt surely die.

We all know what happened next; they disobeyed, and ate of the fruit, which was so tempting. Even under the threat of death, the young humans decided they wanted to eat that fruit.

Having disobeyed, the humans proved they were capable of exercising free will; taking responsibility for their own decisions. They had demonstrated independence, and shown that they were as the Elohim, sentient beings, knowing good and evil, or in modern terminology, able to think for themselves.

Genesis Chp 3..

22....And the LORD God said, Behold, the man is become as one of us, to know good and evil:

The release from the protected area has been dressed up as an eviction, but the end result is the same, the new humans were not to be allowed to return to the Garden, they were faced with making a living in the wild.

*

In Genesis 2 vs. 19 & 20 we see a somewhat confused account of what could have been a survival course. Man is introduced to the animals, to name them, but he also thereby had the opportunity to learn to recognise them, and to learn some of the characteristics of those animals, which would be useful after being released from the garden into the barren and dangerous wilderness.

'You have named this a sheep, you can eat a sheep'.

'You have named this a lion; you should not eat a lion'.

At the last moment before the young clones were evicted, the Elohim minders demonstrated how to kill and skin animals, to make warm and protective clothing (Gen 3 v. 21). We may deduce from this that the youngsters were being given another lesson in survival, they would need it because they were about to leave the protection of the Elohim in the Garden, and had to learn how to fend for themselves.

Even after the colonists were released into the wild, the Elohim kept a friendly eye on them, visiting now and again to check on progress (Genesis Chp. 4).

And so the age of the antediluvians began.

*

One other interesting point that comes from verse 22 is this:-

Chp 3 v 22 ...and now, lest he put forth his hand, and take also of the tree of life, and eat, and live for ever:

A barrier was placed at the garden gate, cherubim, (machines?) with flaming swords, to bar the way to the tree of life.

If man was supposed to be like the Elohim, but not quite, then we can see that the Elohim quite probably live for ever. (This may sound strange, but if we cannot accept the concept of immortality, then we can substitute the notion of indefinite life, wherein cells are regenerated, illness cured, damage repaired, and say that they lived for tens of thousands of years.)

In order to prevent mankind from living forever, he was prohibited from eating of the 'tree of life', whatever that means.

Although mankind was cloned from the Elohim, he differed from his Creator in that one respect. Man was not to live forever.

Mankind might not have eaten of the tree of life, but still the antediluvian humans claimed to have a life expectation of nearly a thousand years. It is no surprise that they grew in power and knowledge. It would be possible to learn a lot and accomplish a lot if we could look forward to nine-hundred years of life.

Somehow someone from the dim and distant reaches of pre-history managed to learn an awful lot about the Solar System, things that modern science is unaware of. If antediluvians were gifted with such longevity, then they would be more than capable of designing and building Stonehenge.

The only conclusion I can come to, considering the facts, is that there really was an ancient and long-lived race of people who we may call antediluvians.

It gets worse.

*

It would seem that everything progressed nicely until we get to Genesis chapter six, when something very strange happened.

Genesis 6:

1 And it came to pass, when men began to multiply on the face of the earth, and daughters were born unto them,

2 That the sons of God saw the daughters of men that they were fair; and they took them wives of all which they chose.

3 And the LORD said, My spirit shall not always strive with man, for that ***he also is flesh****: yet his days shall be an hundred and twenty years.*

4 There were giants in the earth in those days; and also after that, when the sons of God came in unto the daughters of men, and they bare children to them, the same became mighty men which were of old, men of renown.

5 And GOD saw that the wickedness of man was great in the earth, and that every imagination of the thoughts of his heart was only evil continually.

6 And it repented the LORD that he had made man on the earth, and it grieved him at his heart.

7 And the LORD said, I will destroy man whom I have created from the face of the earth; both man, and beast, and the creeping thing, and the fowls of the air; for it repenteth me that I have made them.

8 But Noah found grace in the eyes of the LORD.

These verses are very difficult to understand in the classic monotheistic religion.

They are difficult to believe in this present analysis, but in keeping with the assertion that humans are clones of the Elohim.

The sons of God, literally the Sons of the Elohim, were just Elohim, in the same way that the 'sons of men' are just men.

The Elohim were clearly capable of interbreeding with human women.

*

If we look a little closer at verse 3, we see a rather enigmatic statement, and I quote *"My spirit shall not always strive with man, for that* ***he also is flesh****."*

'Spirit' is 'ruwach', which has been translated as so many things. Literally it means 'wind' or 'breath', but when the 'spirit strives' it means 'patience' (according to Strong's). The particular four words that drew my attention are those I have put in bold. Why the 'also'?

"I am losing patience with man, because **he also is flesh**".

Here is another example of variable translation; the concordance gives the word for 'flesh' as ***'basar',*** which can mean many things, amongst them being 'Family or blood relation'.

Nobody needs to be an expert in Hebrew to understand that any uncertain translation needs to be understood in context, and the context here is one in which there are 'marriages' taking place between

Elohim men and human women. Is the scribe here trying to tell us we are 'blood-relations' to the Elohim?

*

If we are to take this literally, and at face value, then this passage demonstrates that the scribe believed that the antediluvian humans were a closely related species to the Elohim.

So what is going on here?

To be honest, I do not know, but it is possible that this was an attempt to modify the human gene pool.

"There were giants," says the scripture, and nowadays we recognise gigantism as being 'excessive growth due to overproduction of growth hormone by the pituitary gland before the end of adolescence,' and it could also be a genetic defect.

So perhaps something was going wrong with the cloned race of sub-Elohim humans, and the Elohim were trying to correct this problem by adding more of their own genetic makeup to the human gene pool.

An alternative understanding is to say that the anecdote was added to the scrolls by a scribe to convey the information that the Elohim were the same species as men. To say they could interbreed is to say that they are the same flesh and blood as we are.

Explicitly; we are clones.

*

After the cross-breeding, the result was the appearance of mighty men, men of renown:

"..also after that, when the sons of God came in unto the daughters of men, and they bare children to them, the same became mighty men which were of old, men

of renown."

I suspect it might have been an attempt to correct a genetic defect, an attempt that had catastrophic results.

*

As a hypothesis, we could say that the Elohim had revealed themselves to men in their true colours, and from then on the relationship between gods and men collapsed.

Men realised they were not in control of their own lives; they lost the confidence that comes with freedom and self-determination; they became hedonists, giving themselves over to pleasure and abandonment.

The damage was done, and could not be repaired, the colony was in terminal moral decline, and so the Elohim must have realised that there was no future for the antediluvian population.

6 And it repented the LORD that he had made man on the earth, and it grieved him at his heart.

It seems the Elohim finally lost patience with man, and found no alternative but to scrap the lot, and start again.

The Elohim had made a mistake, and admitted to having made it, thus proving that the Elohim of the Bible are not the omnipotent and omniscient infallible God of the Church, who would not make such a mistake. It is worthy of note that it was antediluvian mankind that shouldered the blame.

*

Some humans were chosen who were considered to be suitable breeding stock to start the colony afresh, these were instructed in the means of survival, and a flood was brought upon the Earth to eradicate everyone else.

The cross-breeding had an effect on later generations, as the genealogies demonstrate. After the flood the lives of successive generations became shorter and shorter, decreasing in a natural looking manner, until the life expectation was the standard threescore years and ten that we know today; plus or minus a few.

*

It is now possible to see why Noah built the monument, incorporating an exponential mathematical model of the Solar System. He wanted future generations to know what he knew, but he forgot to get the consent of the Elohim.

The Elohim did not want mankind to know the whole truth, not at that time, because the truth is something that the antediluvians had found unacceptable, and perhaps, we modern humans might also find it equally unacceptable.

There was also the suggestion that there were other things that the Elohim wished to hide. Not only did they stop the building of Babel, they also prevented other things from being revealed.

Gen 11, v 6 ...and now nothing will be restrained from them, which they have imagined to do...

However, there is no cause to think that we are permanently banned from knowing the truth. Had a permanent ban been required, Noah's monument would have been obliterated. It was left where it was, in an unfinished state, so we may assume that the Elohim intended that one day, mankind would again have access to that knowledge.

*

And so we may reasonably conclude that we are not evolved from apes, we are third generation descendants of the Elohim.

Generation one were the Elohim themselves, who, for reasons they never explained, wished to create mankind in their own image, clones of themselves, rather than biological children produced in the normal way.

Generation two were the first clones, the antediluvians, these were made to have shorter lives than the Elohim. They were told to go forth and multiply, so they could colonise the Earth in the name of the Elohim.

I am suggesting that something went wrong with the first colony, but I am not sure what. Perhaps they had a defect in their genetic makeup, that could not be remedied, and so they were destroyed.

The third generation is alive and thriving on Earth today, but they do not know of their origins.

We are that third generation.

It gets worse.

*

Why did the Elohim put the Solar System in order, when they could have made it truly random?

The Solar System appears to be random normally, before the exponents are applied. When the exponents are applied the order is revealed, but it could have been made truly random, it would still have provided a home for an Elohim colony.

The only reason I can think of is the same as the reason

I ascribed to Noah, the Solar System is also a 'message in a bottle'.

The Solar System is the same as Babel, the same as Stonehenge; it carries within it a message for us, if only we would read it.

When Noah built Stonehenge/Babel, he was doing on a small scale exactly what the Elohim had already done on an astronomical scale.

Where Noah had used rocks to encode the equation, the Elohim had used planets. That is the only difference, except that the Elohim did not apply the exponents first.

*

The message in the Solar System is the same equation as we found in Stonehenge, we learned of its existence from Stonehenge, but why is it in the Solar System in the first place? And we might well ask, why that particular equation?

We could answer the second question first.

The particular form of equation was used because it enables the orbits of all the planets to be related in so many different and clearly artificial ways that it is ***impossible to claim that the system is natural.***

It would always be possible for scientists to dismiss one form of order as being due to chance, but the system is ordered in about eight different artificial ways all at once (See part two).

Scientists cannot possibly deny it is artificial.

The Elohim put the system in order, and in such a way that it is impossible to claim that it is natural.

In so doing they are proving to us that they exist.

So that answers the first question as well. ***The Elohim want us to know they exist.***

*

The equation does not appear to actually do anything physical. It is not required to produce stability in the orbits, or anything like that. It seems to serve no function other than to act as a message of some kind.

It was put into the orbits before humans were created, but it needs an intelligent mind to read it. It would mean nothing to dinosaurs or chimps.

The fact that the order exists can only mean that the Elohim had every intention that the Earth would be populated by intelligent creatures one day.

Are we to suppose that they would wait around for billions of years on the off-chance that Darwinian evolution would produce humans?

I answer that question with a clear 'No!' From the very beginning their intention was to populate the Earth with cloned copies of themselves. Their intention was to start a colony. We were not an afterthought, we were their primary purpose.

That is why they came here, and that is why they put the order into the orbits. The order in the orbits is a message for us.

The equation in the Solar System has been there from before humanity came into being in the Garden of Eden, but it is not necessary to assume it has always been that way.

I mentioned the possibility of a compromise with the scientific viewpoint earlier, and it is possible to generate a compromise without changing the current discovery at all.

We may speculate that originally, when the Elohim first came to this System, they found a planet that was suitable for colonisation, but was already infested with all manner of fierce carnivorous beasts that would eat up the first clones as soon as they were released.

Clearly the dinosaurs and similar problematic creatures would have to go.

As it so happened, the Elohim wanted to re-arrange the planets into a specific order, the order we find today, so it would be no trouble to them if the dinosaurs were destroyed in the process.

The sequence of events would then be;-

First, a random Solar System existed that theologians could claim was created by the One True God. The system obeyed all the rules of science. People like Laplace would have liked it. Scientists would be very happy with it; it could have been billions of years old.

[Unfortunately for scientists if the System was ever random like they want it to be, they can no longer prove it. The system is artificially ordered now. We researchers may speculate that it was once random, but scientists are no longer able to demonstrate their case.]

At that time, before the Elohim came, the Earth existed but it was not in the same orbit as it is today, it might have been in accord with the theories of Lyell and life might have evolved according to Darwin.

The Earth may well have been a little closer to the sun,

hot and humid and covered in life, including dinosaurs and trilobites. From time to time fossils may have been formed, as required by science.

Second, relatively recently the Elohim arrive. They find a Solar System that is not in any kind of order. It is random, as required by science, and it is billions of years old, as required by science.

The Earth is there, and it is old, and its rocks and strata contain fossils, as required by science.

The Elohim survey the entire system, and see that the Earth is suitable for a new colony. It is the right size, made of the right material, and it has the right gravity. It already has an oxygen atmosphere, and plenty of water. It also has a convenient magnetic shield to protect from solar radiation.

The Earth is selected as the right place for the new colony.

Third, they decide to start work.

The energies expended in rearranging the planets are beyond our comprehension, but it was done. The fact is that the Solar System is currently in an artificial order, the evidence is in part two of this book.

Unless scientists want to claim that the System was created in that ordered state, they will have to accept that at some time, primal chaos was changed to a very neat and clearly artificial order – and that cannot happen without invoking the Elohim.

The Elohim rearrange the planet's orbits to conform to

the equation, and in the process of moving the planets the Earth may well have been blasted by all manner of high energy radiation, and most of the life that was on Earth got destroyed.

The dinosaurs were no longer a problem; they were buried, along with any fossil remains. Whatever life was on Earth before the move would also have been buried along with the dinosaurs. Much of the life may have been roasted and turned into coal and oil, to become our fossil fuel reserves.

Fourth, having got the Earth into the desired position, they had to terraform it. The surface would have been completely devastated by the energies needed to move it. Terraforming a planet is something that our human scientists have seriously considered doing to Mars. If humans can consider doing it, the Elohim would find it no problem at all.

Eventually the skies cleared of dust, the sun shone again, and the new Earth was born.

Having arranged for dry land to re-emerge from the sea, complete with its thick layers of sediment and fossil bearing strata, they set about producing fresh life.

Using technology, not magic, they created all manner of new life on Earth, and also perhaps bred from selected species saved from the previous world.

That is not so difficult, seeding life. Our modern human scientists could do it as well, if they really wanted to. They store plant seeds, and frozen gametes, and embryos of endangered species for future breeding.

Our scientists can genetically engineer life.

If we can do it, so could the Mighty Ones.

The stratigraphic situation is further complicated by the later devastation of Noah's flood, which would have been minor in comparison, but still capable of introducing geological confusion. The end result would be the world we see today, with scientists measuring ages in millions of years, and creationists crying 'No! No! It is recent!'

Scientists find old bones and produce a theory of evolution, not knowing that the Earth was wiped clean in comparatively recent times and life regenerated.

*

Having restored stability to the Earth, and established a viable ecosystem, a planet covered in vegetation and mammals and things, the gods set about creating humanity, in their own image, in their own likeness, as clones of themselves. Of course, in order to make clones, they had to be physical creatures themselves, made of the same flesh and blood, the same cells and tissues and DNA that we were to become.

The clones were placed in a protected area, and so the story started, and were it not for science and the modern Church, we would have understood it all along.

*

It is worth noting at this juncture that all of the above accomplishments allocated to the Elohim could be carried out on a much smaller scale by modern human scientists. Our scientists can travel in space, move small asteroids if they wished, terraform a planet, clone themselves, spread preserved life, genetically engineer life, engineer an ecosystem. None of the things allocated to Elohim are physical impossibilities, just rather difficult for us humans given the scale of the challenge.

But none of this explains why the Elohim wanted to put the equation into the Solar System in the first place.

Why the Equation?

It is a matter of simple common sense to say that the Mighty Ones would not do something to no purpose. They must have had a good reason for encoding such an artificial equation into the System.

It must be something to do with us, because there is nobody else around to read it.

If we conclude that it is a message for us, a message that we should be able to read when we are sufficiently developed in intelligence, then we should also be able to hazard some kind of guess as to what it might mean.

The equation constitutes a real message from the Elohim to mankind, and I have included enough information in this book for the most sceptical of critics to be able to check and verify the equation and everything else that is relevant.

The order in the orbits is real, the equation is real. It follows that the Elohim are real, and that their message to us is real.

The message is in the equation, in the undeniable fact that the orbits are artificially ordered,

The message says, ***"Hi!"***

It says, ***"We are here!"***

It says, ***"We are very powerful, we moved Jupiter, we moved Saturn, we put the Solar System into order."***

It says, ***"We created you, and stocked your world with all manner of minerals and fuels, so that you could grow and develop."***

It says, ***"We mean you no harm, we are your parents."***

It also says ***"<u>We want you to know about us.</u>"***

In effect, it is a 'first contact' message.

The message has been there since before we were created, waiting for us to find it, and recognise it.

They are introducing themselves gradually and gently, they are making us aware of them, and when we are ready, it will be up to us to decide when that will be; we will be able to meet with them openly.

Then they can tell us what it is *really* all about.

*

I have included the comment "We mean you no harm" despite the fact that they destroyed the entire antediluvian population of the planet, and wiped out Sodom with all its inhabitants.

They are our ancestral parents, and they have been with us for thousands of years, and apart from the destruction of Sodom they have not done us any direct harm that I know of.

They could have done, at any time. They could have destroyed us, or ruled over us by force. They could have enslaved us, but have chosen not to, and they have kept to their decision for all those thousands of years.

It is clear to me that the antediluvians were aware of the message, but something went wrong, as discussed earlier. Exactly what went wrong we will never know for sure; but it is plain that the first attempt at contact failed to achieve a satisfactory outcome.

*

There are other possible reasons for putting the order into the system, reasons which do not exclude the 'first contact' message, but are additional to it.

The equation might also be a kind of signature, or a warning, so that 'others' might know that this is an Elohim system, spoken for, and defended. (It is just a thought; it is equally possible that there are no 'others' to worry about.)

And in truth, we are defended, for the Elohim are our guardian angels.

There can be no science-fiction invasion of aliens, intent on taking over the world. The Mighty Ones have gone to such a lot of trouble to create us; they would not stand idly by and watch while we are destroyed by others.

So the equation could be both a first-contact message for us, and a 'no trespassing sign' for others, if any others exist, which is unlikely.

*

It gets just a little bit worse.

When we talk about 'first-contact' it sounds like we are expecting to meet with aliens and that would not be quite right.

The Elohim are not aliens, exactly. To call them aliens would not be pedantically true. They are our progenitors, our long-ago ancestral parent.

We could think of them as being 'our fathers in heaven' if we were not concerned about offending the Church.

*

So where are they, where are the Elohim?

How can we contact them if we do not know where they are?

There are many imaginary answers that are just barely possible, but they hardly merit considering.

They could be inside the moon, hiding from us, but living without sunshine and fresh grass and clean air.

They could be living tedious lives in caves on Mars.

They could have gone home, wherever that might be, or moved on to the next Solar System scheduled for the establishment of a colony.

It is possible that they are living in a cloaked 'mother-ship' somewhere in space outside the Solar System, perhaps they are the occupants of the many UFO's that are claimed to be in our skies, but I think a more mundane answer is the most likely.

We can answer the question 'Where are the Elohim?' if we continue with the process of giving the scripture the benefit of the doubt.

In Genesis chapter 3;

8 And they heard the voice of the LORD God walking in the garden in the cool of the day: and Adam and his wife hid themselves from the presence of the LORD God amongst the trees of the garden.

I would remind you that this is what the scribe understood as an actual event. The scribe saw nothing wrong with the Chief of the Elohim walking about in the garden, talking to himself.

We can dismiss this as a primitive fancy, as the Church must do, or we can accept it as a description of what was believed in the days of the scribe who wrote the words.

Or we can say that every word is inspired by God, who was, of course, that very same person who was walking in the garden in the cool of the day.

If we were to continue to read the rest of the Bible, we would find a great many instances where God is seen to be appearing as a man.

In a later story, Abraham provides another example. He encountered three men who were sent to destroy Sodom. One of these men was addressed by Abraham as the LORD God. (Genesis 18 vs. 20, 21) Only two of them actually turned up in Sodom, where they were described as angels by the scribe, but taken to be ordinary, rather handsome men by the citizens, who wished to 'know' them.

And later still;-

Exodus 33

11 And the LORD spake unto Moses face to face, as a man speaketh unto his friend.

Just a couple of examples; you might like to search for others.

*

Of course there will be any number of theologians and religious experts who will be eager to find fanciful explanations for verses such as this, but we are free to give the scribe the benefit of the doubt, and say that he was telling the truth.

In other words, the best place to look for the Elohim is here on Earth.

*

They needed some form of transport to get here, all those millennia ago, and they needed the tools and the cosmic planet-shifters to get the job done, but once all has been accomplished, they would like to enjoy life.

They like to walk in the ‘cool of the day’, so it would follow that they might well enjoy other aspects of life on Earth, like music, wine and fine food, or perhaps even art and other forms of entertainment.

They look like us and we look like them, so how would we know them?

The man sitting behind you on a bus could be an Elohim, how would you know?

They could live and enjoy the rain and the roses and the sunshine, and walk among us, and we need never know.

It gets a little worse.

Chapter Six

Cargo Cult

A cargo cult is a kind of Melanesian millenarian movement encompassing a diverse range of practices and occurring in the wake of contact with the commercial networks of colonizing societies. The name derives from the apparent belief that various ritualistic acts will lead to a bestowing of material wealth ("cargo").

From Wikipedia, the free encyclopedia

*

It would appear that when isolated indigenous island peoples make contact with a superior culture the brief meeting may result in religious or quasi-religious worship. This is apparently a well-established phenomenon.

The same principles can be applied to the ancient antediluvian peoples who had contact with the Elohim. There are only two minor differences.

1/ the humans were not indigenous to this isolated island-planet called 'Earth'; they were created by the superior visitors, according to the Biblical narrative.

2/ the 'cargo' was not material objects, rather it was the hinted-at possibility of eternal life.

We can reasonably expect that the superior beings would be worshipped as gods by the human race that they created, and that because of the continuing but infrequent contacts between human and Elohim, this worship would be extended throughout history, and may even be prolonged into the present day.

If we care to look, we would find that just about every culture that has ever existed has practiced some kind of worship of superior beings, usually in exchange for some form of benefit, including the forgiving of sins and the bestowal of eternal life.

From antediluvian times, through to the Chaldean, Babylonian, Persian, Egyptian, Greek, Roman, Israelite, all the way through history to the modern world, we humans have engaged in an elaborate version of a Cargo Cult.

The Cargo Cult that we first see in Genesis has been global, and very long lasting.

*

Psychiatrists have a word for people who want to be worshipped. I do not know what the word is, but it is not very flattering.

There is nothing I can find in the early chapters of Genesis that suggest that the Mighty Ones want to be worshipped. They do not mention any desire to be followed around by a congregation of obsequious sycophants.

So this book is most certainly not an attempt to start a new religion.

*

The Elohim, the Mighty Ones, that others call 'God', are in fact physical flesh and blood, our long-ago ancestors.

From the words in the Bible, as far as I am aware, what the Elohim desire most is to be respected, accepted, and understood.

'Worship' is an obsessive, exaggerated and ritualised substitute for genuine respect. We should respect the

Elohim as we might respect our own human parents, but not worship them.

They want us to know and accept that they exist; and that we are their descendants; and that is why they put the orbits in order.

*

This book is not about worship, it is not about religion, it is simply about ancient knowledge. I would rather that religion was not involved, I would rather just talk about mathematics, but the original clues are inextricably linked with the book that has been hijacked by worshippers. Religious people of all denominations demand a monopoly on the Bible, and demand the right to dictate what it means.

My own view is that the Bible is for anyone, even atheists, and it is not about religion, it is not about worship, it is about the fate of humanity.

If we extrapolate current trends it is not difficult to see that if nothing changes, mankind has no future at all.

We are overpopulated, running out of food and energy and living space.

As I write, the estimated population of the world is seven billion. In a few decades it will be fourteen billion. The increase is exponential.

The authorities are going to find it harder and harder to stay in control; violence will spread along with starvation and disease. The only end for an overpopulated world is disaster, where the land is turned into a desert littered with corpses.

You and I might ask ourselves if the Elohim would want that.

The answer has to be ‘no’.

But now we need to ask what they really want.

Why did they create us? The answer is surely not to die of starvation on an overpopulated planet?

They created us to be like them, or so it says; “Let us make man in our own image.”

*

It gets worse.

Let us not forget that the Elohim did not originate on Earth. They came here from elsewhere. If we ask where they came from, there are not many answers to choose between. Simple logic dictates that they came from the stars.

There are a great many statements from various scribes to the effect that the Elohim (God) rule in the heavens.

Psalms 103

19 The LORD hath prepared his throne in the heavens; and his kingdom ruleth over all.

This is just one example, but it seems to be common knowledge in the scripture that the Elohim rule the heavens.

It has always been believed that they have a ‘Kingdom of Heaven’ or in more modern terminology, a Galactic Empire.

To put the whole story into an ultra-modern perspective, we might imagine this Kingdom of Heaven, this Galactic Empire, as consisting of thousands of stellar systems where the Mighty Ones hold sway.

The empire grows, not by conquest, not by violence,

but by **colonisation**.

They search the Galaxy looking for solar systems with suitable worlds and having found one, like the Earth, they start work. They call in the planetary engineers and rearrange the system to encode their signature, the equation, in the orbits of the planets; in the process they destroy any previously existing life.

They terraform the planet, then they start a colony of clones.

I use the word 'clone' for want of a better, I do not wish to sound offensive to men or Elohim, but 'clone' is the word that best describes the creation of men.

The men they create are 'in their own image' according to Genesis chapter one.

27 ***"..So God created man in his own image, in the image of God created he him; male and female created he them..."***

The assertion that we are in the image of the Elohim is emphasised by repetition. It is clear that if we are to take this as the inspired word of God, and if we are to accept that it is literally true, and give it the benefit of the doubt, then we simply must accept that we are 'clones' of the Mighty Ones.

As the clones (us) develop and become civilized, thousands of years may pass, but eventually they reach the stage where they learn astronomy and mathematics and inevitably, sooner or later, they must discover the equation, the first-contact message, encoded in their system.

The clones then learn that they are not alone in the universe, and if they accept their situation they go on to make contact, and at the end, they must become fully fledged Elohim in their own right, and join the ever growing empire.

*

As an aside, we can see a possible way of distinguishing between physical Elohim and the Monotheistic Infinite Spirit God of the church.

We may ask a question of the Infinite God, 'Why would He put the orbits into a clearly artificial order, what purpose would it serve an Infinite Almighty Spirit God?'

I cannot answer for such a God, nor can I answer for the Church, but it seems to me that the Almighty Infinite Spirit God of the Church would have no reason whatever for putting a secret message into the orbits.

What would it achieve?

If it is a first-contact message from the physical Elohim for their offspring, as a prelude to the offspring joining the Galactic Empire, it makes sense.

*

All this sounds like a mixture of blasphemy and science fiction, but it is what you get if you consider the reality of an ordered Solar System, and the implications of Babel/Stonehenge, and base an understanding of the Bible on pragmatism.

In the fullness of time we would develop to the point where we can meet with the Elohim, communicate with them, share their technology and scientific knowledge.

Perhaps, when the time is right, some of us might be shown the supreme secret, the focus of all the Cargo Cults on earth, the much desired gift of immortality, or we might be taken to join the Elohim, as was claimed happened to Enoch in Genesis chapter 5.

24 ***And Enoch walked with God: and he was not; for God took him.***

*

'Life after death' or 'eternal life' seems to be part of the human psyche, and is found in every culture on the planet. It is always accepted as a kind of mythological hope more than a scientific fact, and the notion pervades the whole of human history. Immortality is the 'Cargo' that the Cargo Cults thrive on.

If we accept that the Elohim are physical and from the stars then it follows that they must live for an extremely long time, or they would never have got here, and could not have ordered the Solar System.

Immortality, or eternal life, would probably be a more acceptable idea to us if we substituted the term 'indefinite life', meaning that we just keep on living without growing old and deteriorating.

Throughout the whole of time, religion has always aspired to conquer death, and living forever has been a dream of men all down the ages. This is no doubt because we have noticed that death has a tendency to spoil things.

Death is something that tends to stop people acquiring huge amounts of knowledge and understanding. We do not have time to read all the books that have ever been written. One of the problems with learning is that no matter how intelligent we are we do not have enough time to learn much before we are dead.

Scientists divide up their abilities into different disciplines, because none of them have the time to study everything.

Death also tends to take the shine off of our personal achievements. It puts a damper on our long-term ambitions.

We cannot plan to colonise the universe, because we would be dead before we learned the technology of interstellar travel.

We do not live long enough to make the journey to a distant star system.

We are like mice in a laboratory cage trying to understand the human world; hamsters trying to figure out what jumbo jets and nuclear bombs are for.

We are in this position of eternal ignorance because we have this annoying habit of dying.

Imagine what we could do if we lived for ever?

In just a few thousand years of learning, as individuals we could become very powerful, we would know an awful lot about everything; in short, we would be Elohim.

Scientists are working to understand the processes of aging, and claim to be making some progress, but some would hope they do not succeed in making themselves immortal. They would claim that scientists have done enough damage to the world already.

*

There is also the matter of the 'tree of life', which, according to the scribe who first penned the words, was growing in the Garden of Eden, and from which we can no longer eat. This is the root, the origin and the source of all modern Cargo Cults.

Apparently, according to the myth, we are like the Elohim in all respects except that we do not live forever. If we ate of that tree of life and lived forever, we would actually be Elohim ourselves.

It is probably not a literal tree with magic fruit. If there were to be any truth in the story I would expect the description is just a metaphor. It would be a poetic way of portraying a process that would enable us to stay alive indefinitely. It is a process, a secret that only the Elohim know.

We ordinary humans die for a number of different reasons, and if all these causes of death could be fixed, by science not magic, we could continue to live without growing old and feeble minded.

Changes to our genetic code could prolong our natural lives without end, but even so there would still be other causes of deterioration and death.

With sufficient scientific knowledge fatal illnesses could be cured or even prevented. Accidental injury and tissue damage could be repaired. Old age could be banished by cellular regeneration.

It is not an impossible scenario; it is just not within the reach of our current medical science.

One side-effect of extremely long life would be overpopulation. Our present population growth is slowed because individuals die, but if we didn't die we would be packed together shoulder to shoulder by now.

If there is a race of 'immortals' like the Elohim, then they must either give up reproducing or they must expand their territory. If they wish to continue to breed then they would be evermore on the lookout for new worlds and more living space.

The notion that the Elohim have indefinite life

expectation is consistent with the notion of an expanding Galactic Empire, and interstellar travel.

There is a 'dream-vision' in Daniel chapter 7 that portrays one as the *'Ancient of Days'*, which is a clear verbal picture of someone very elderly indeed. The vision is not real, but it does reflect the fact that the scribe understands that the ruler of the Elohim is extremely old.

*

If we accept, just for the sake of argument, that the Elohim know of a process whereby ordinary humans might become like one of them; then it is surely evident that from time to time they would use it.

The possibility of such a procedure existing is implied in Genesis, but much more positively stated in the Christian literature.

There is no hard evidence of the reality of such a method, but it is worth considering the implications if it were a possibility.

Consider what we could be like if we could live forever?

But also, consider what we would be like if we lived forever and were like Hitler? Or mass murderers, or paedophiles?

In Genesis, according to the words of the scribe, the way to the tree of life is guarded, so we might assume that means we cannot ever find the secret for ourselves.

If immortality is ever granted to men, it will be on a selective basis, an individual basis. The Mighty Ones would not give immortality to the likes of Hitler, we would hope. If they gave anyone this great gift, they would have to make very sure they gave it to the right person.

It is possible that part of the plans and intentions of the Mighty Ones is that you, if found worthy, could be subjected to this process and thereby become one of their number. Space travel gives them plenty of room to expand their population, by biology or by cloning, there would be no limitations. The population of Elohim in the universe would be constantly growing, and the empire or 'Kingdom' of heaven would be constantly expanding.

If this were happening, would we know about it? People would vanish, never to be seen again, like Enoch, or Elijah, who was taken up in a whirlwind accompanied by a chariot of fire. (2nd Kings 2 v 11)

The scripture clearly and unambiguously suggests that some people in the past may well have been selected to join the Elohim.

I cannot say if this is a valid observation or not, but it would explain a great deal; and it is logical. If a person knows full well that the Elohim are real, and accepts that the Elohim are in charge, and if the Elohim think that person is a good candidate, and worthy, why not?

That is after all why they came here, it is the reason given in Genesis; it is the only sensible reason for the ordered Solar System. It is the reason for everything.

It is also something that can be observed in the distorted teachings of the Church, and the reason why so many wars have been fought. Soldiers in many ages and many lands have gone to war on the promise of eternal life if they get killed.

When we die and are buried, the priest intones words

to the effect that we will be resurrected and our immortal souls go to 'heaven' and we will live forever.

The search for a way to conquer death is as old as religion, but it is possible that the answer has been with us all the time.

The elderly ladies who stood on my doorstep had the answer; they said the story was literally true. Maybe it is. Quite a lot of it is, anyway.

*

But these are selfish thoughts. What about mankind as a whole?

It seems to be fairly evident that the antediluvians were the ones intended to be promoted to the rank of Elohim. Enoch was one of them.

It is also clear that the Elohim were known to the antediluvians, because Noah obviously knew about the equation, and we can only suppose that his fellows before the flood also knew.

Something went wrong. I am not sure exactly what went wrong; I have done my best to figure it out. The best I can come up with is a genetic failure, or a psychological failure. It might even have been a genuine accident. In the end, the intentions of the Elohim failed, and the antediluvians were all destroyed bar eight.

But their loss is our gain, or could be. The Elohim have clearly not given up on their ambitions.

If humanity in general, world-wide, were to accept the reality of the Elohim, and accept that the Elohim know best, and if humanity were to do their bidding, then the current bleak outlook for the future might become more one of hope.

The Elohim know the answers to human problems, but they can do nothing to help until humanity recognises their reality, and accepts them.

If humanity would but recognise and respect the Mighty Ones, and follow their lead, the world would benefit, the world would prosper.

*

Unfortunately this is not likely to happen, the powers-that-be, the governments and politicians, and the most vehement opposition of all, the religious authorities, will never accept these things. Even if the Elohim were to land a huge spacecraft on the White House lawn, I doubt that they would be accepted.

It is not just religion that would reject the Elohim, there is also a campaign being run by evolutionist scientists to elevate Darwin to the rank of a demigod. The people that wish to deify Darwin maintain that belief in a supernatural God is delusional.

This is the kind of smug conviction that assumes there is no power greater than man, no mind greater in capacity than the infinite mind of humanity. I wonder what supporters of the God Delusion idea will make of the math in my chapter ten? The implications cannot be dismissed as delusional, and the consequences for Darwin are just as disastrous.

*

I have intimated that the Elohim could still be with us, living amongst us, and this could be true. Indeed if we are to contact them, it simply must be true, for if they have all departed and left us on our own, if they have all gone on to another system, we cannot contact them.

We are limited to the use of radio waves, and the electromagnetic spectrum is limited to the speed of light.

If we wanted to contact the Elohim while they are away, it would take decades or centuries for our signal to reach them, if ever.

Again, if we consult scriptures beyond Genesis, the scribes tell us that the Elohim have a way of being around without us knowing. It may be technology, or some understanding of physics that we are ignorant of, but according to the scribes, the Elohim have a way of knowing what is going on.

Even if the main party left us thousands of years ago, some remained, for according to the scripture we are being constantly watched and monitored.

So it may not be so difficult to contact them after all. A simple message on the TV might do the trick.

Someone is going to ask why they don't just simply tell us that they exist, and stop playing hide and seek.

Well, it doesn't really work like that.

What they want to end up with is free-minded willing equals, not indoctrinated psycho-slaves. They may have revealed themselves to our human ancestors, and tried to educate them, but they could not forcefully indoctrinate them, they would not get what they want and need if they did that.

We must go to them, not them to us.

They have actually dropped an awful lot of hints over the ages, but as 'rational' humans we have ignored the clues and transformed them into fable.

As 'religious' people we humans have interpreted and distorted the ancient testimony so that it is now barely recognisable. Where 'rational' people have dismissed it all as mythology, religion has transformed a story of interstellar colonisation into a theological fantasy.

*

If the Elohim revealed themselves today, in modern times, and tried to announce their presence before we were ready, how would we react?

Our politicians would no doubt regard them as cranks or lunatics, and they would be politely invited to have a chat with a psychiatrist:

"Oh, so you are a space traveller are you? Tell me all about your childhood."

If they tried to prove themselves with a display of power, we might assume they were invaders and assail them with nuclear weapons, which would be our mistake.

They can move planets; they could easily reduce ours to a glowing cinder, or hurl it into the sun.

It would be best not to treat them as our enemy.

Such talk of violence and rebellion is always a human failing, and our undoing.

We will have no more of it.

*

Death, in general understanding, is something that all men are subject to, but if some of the stories in Genesis have turned out to be true, then surely it is reasonable to suppose that some of the other claims the scribe makes may also be true?

If the Bible tells a tale of interstellar colonisation, and

terraforming, and the careful raising of cloned offspring in a protected area; and if Babel is true, and if the Elohim really exist, and if the Solar System really is ordered; if all these things are true, then the 'Tree of Life' may also have some truth to it.

Death, as an end to everything, really does have a tendency to take the fun out of life.

Time is a similar problem.

Death and time are the two enemies of true progress, not just as individuals but as a species. Immortality has freed the Mighty Ones from these constraints but they still apply to us.

If the Elohim decide that mankind is not ready, then they will treat this book as they treated Noah's efforts. It will not be published, it will be prohibited.

So, if you are reading these words, you will at least know more than I do at this moment. You may also be reading the next chapter, and I haven't even written it yet.

Time is a funny thing.

If you have questions that you want answered, you may think to ask me, but here is the rub; by the time you read these words I could be dead and buried.

You will need to ask someone else, or find the answer for yourself.

Or I might like to take my turn, and ask *you* a few questions.

For example, I would like to know; did the Elohim allow me to publish?

Perhaps you could tell me if the book is selling well?

Alas! You cannot answer, and I could not hear your

answer if you did, because, as stated above, I am probably dead.

From these little observations it becomes obvious that there are distinct advantages to being immortal.

*

As a matter of interest, immortality is very likely to be possible in scientific theory. Scientists have demonstrated that the cause of death is genetic. We are 'designed' to die. Designed by evolution, science would say, or designed by the Mighty Ones, it makes no difference. Death is a product of genetics, and so immortality must also be a product of genetics.

Common sense tells us this. Giant tortoises of the Galapagos Islands can live for a hundred years or more; as can some parrots, horses about thirty, dogs live about fourteen years, hamsters about three, and humans about seventy.

The differences are not about size, but about species, which is all down to genetics.

If someone clever enough, someone like the Mighty Ones, were able and willing to somehow change our genetics, we could live for ever, unless we got run over by a bus. Gene therapy is something that mankind has only recently discovered, but we can be sure that the Elohim will have full mastery of its potential.

So, the claim that immortality is an option is not just pure fantasy, it is a scientific possibility, and a religious tenet of faith. So when the scribe tells us that there was such a thing as the tree of life, which would enable us to live for ever, it is not such an outrageous fantasy as we might at first think.

*

Religious people would object to this, it is only natural for them to do so. I have heard a lay preacher claim that immortality is only to be obtained through faith in Jesus Christ, who is, he claimed, the spiritual 'tree of life'.

According to Genesis (Chp. 3 vs. 22-24) we are barred from the tree of life, but pious individuals do not appear to take that into account.

I would ask the Church to explain what exactly is meant by the word 'spiritual', but I do not anticipate a rational reply.

I could even point out that Jesus was also subjected to 'voluntary abduction' (Book of Acts of the Apostles, verse 9).

9 And when he had spoken these things, while they beheld, he was taken up; and a cloud received him out of their sight.

10 And while they looked stedfastly toward heaven as he went up, behold, two men stood by them in white apparel;

11 Which also said, Ye men of Galilee, why stand ye gazing up into heaven? this same Jesus, which is taken up from you into heaven, shall so come in like manner as ye have seen him go into heaven.

People stood watching as he went up; their eyes followed Jesus as he went up into a cloud. Two mystery 'men' appeared beside them and spoke, informing the observers that Jesus will one day come back down again.

Were these mystery men Elohim? The scribe would want us to think so, who else could they be? If they were Angels or Elohim then they were indistinguishable from ordinary men, apart from the white clothing.

Here we also see what 'heaven' means; it means the sky, the clouds, it means 'up there'; it does not mean an alternative dimension.

In fact it would seem that Jesus knew beforehand that he would be levitated up into the sky, and from this we can deduce that the event was planned in advance. If this one thing was planned, then so was the rest. We must conclude that the whole of the story of Jesus was planned by somebody powerful operating in secret. (See part 4 of this book; page 431)

John 6 v. 62 ... What and if ye shall see the Son of man ascend up where he was before?

John 20 v. 17 ... Jesus saith unto her, Touch me not; for I am not yet ascended to my Father: but go to my brethren, and say unto them, I ascend unto my Father, and your Father; and to my God, and your God.

The Church refers to this event as the 'Ascension' and has made it a major part of their ritualised belief system, despite claiming that 'heaven' is a 'spiritual dimension'.

Jesus supposedly had a 'resurrected' re-vitalized body, and a rational man would ask a few pointed questions, such as "Where did he go?"

The only answer a cleric could give to such a question is to say that the physical body of Jesus went up into the sky, into a cloud. All I can say is that I agree; that is exactly what happened, but, what happened next?

Reason is not part of ecclesiastical doctrine, though they have been heard to claim that they base their faith on 'reasoning on the scripture'.

*

In the early pages of this book I mentioned that the content would be rejected by both science and religion, even though the basis for what I say is demonstrated to be undeniably true in part two of this same book.

The problem arises because both science and religion have one thing in common. Both hold positions of power over the minds of men, and the future of mankind.

I do have some respect for religious people, especially the two elderly ladies who called at my door. At least they had the courage to go out and talk to total strangers about their beliefs.

To be honest most of my respect is limited to those virtuous and devout monks and scribes who devoted their lives to preserving the scriptures during the dark ages of history, and to some extent to those who spent their energies translating from the original texts.

It is mainly the ecclesiastical monopoly on the interpretation of the words of the Bible that I object to, and the historical and modern abuse of that power.

Religion has always been used to control men, in the past and in the present.

It has started and engaged in a great many wars in the past, and inflamed and encouraged others. Even today it continues, venturing into terrorism and many other brutal acts of aggression. Even while religion is engaged in waging war it presents its Janus face of peace and love.

Yet religion has had a positive influence, so my criticism is muted, if only out of respect for my two silver-haired ladies. (I am sure if they read this book they will be very pleased with my progress.)

Religion, all the sectarian divisions of Christianity, is governed by a group of pious individuals who exercise authority on the basis of their claim to know what God requires of men.

These people are called by different titles depending on the sect, and all preach the various 'right ways' to worship the One True God. They all exercise power by claiming to know what God wants, and by passing on the commands of God to their respective congregations.

What God wants is simply stated in scripture.

Micah 6, v. 8 ..He hath shewed thee, O man, what is good; and what doth the LORD require of thee, but to do justly, and to love mercy, and to walk humbly with thy God?

To do justly, love mercy, and walk humbly with thy Elohim. That is all that God or Elohim require of us. That is all. So who invents all the rest?

*

If the content of part two of this present book is true, as it is in every major respect, then the teachings of these divine ecclesiastical persons are shown to be false, and hence their powerbase is removed.

Consequently, there is little point in asking a theologian or religious leader, or any 'man of the cloth' to give his opinion of this work. He will not accept it. He cannot accept it.

He will say it is the work of Satan, or something along those lines.

*

The same stricture applies to science in many of its disciplines.

Science is like religion; it wields power over the minds of men, and by that power supports religion, the two join forces and use their combined power to structure and control the world.

I have earlier stated that I have a respect for science, and so I do, for without the efforts of many men of science I would have had no knowledge of the orbits of the planets, no knowledge of Stonehenge, nor any figures to guide me, and no calculator, nor a computer to write on.

Archaeologists have done sterling work in unearthing the details of what remains of Stonehenge, and I especially respect and admire the work of Professor R.J.C.Atkinson; and highly recommend his book.

Mathematicians of all kinds are important, because without them I would not have had the geometry or the algebra to formulate the equation.

Science and technology have been a great boon to mankind, and to the writing of this book.

My only criticism of science is that it does not seek truth, it seeks 'an acceptable theory'; acceptable to the establishment, that is.

The science of Archaeology must interpret its findings to conform to the accepted paradigm, and therefore cannot accept that Stonehenge has a geometric integrated ground plan, or that it was built in a relatively short time by a small group of highly intelligent people from an advanced culture.

The science of palaeoanthropology cannot accept that there was an advanced civilization on Earth; the science of geology cannot accept that there ever was a global flood.

The science of astronomy cannot accept that the Solar System is neatly ordered, or that planets can be moved to create such an order.

No scientist, no high priest of science will ever be able to accept the content of this little book.

The only way to answer the problems this book presents is for both science and religion to ignore it, or ridicule it, or attack it in every unscrupulous way possible.

Astronomers have already demoted the status of Pluto, from planet to something else. Pluto is represented in Stonehenge, (Vernier Circle) it is in the math, and it is in the Solar System.

Pluto does not care what scientists call it. As Shakespeare puts it in Romeo and Juliet, “What's in a name? That which we call a rose
by any other name would smell as sweet.”

So it is with Pluto, it remains in its orbit; it remains where it has always been, and it doesn’t matter one little bit if scientists call it a planet or a rock.

The facts remain facts.

Scientists will not accept the findings of this work, not under any circumstances, so there is no point in asking them for their opinion.

There is also nothing to be gained by me pandering to their demands that data should be presented in acceptable form. Acceptable to whom? One might well ask.

To return to the theme of this chapter, if science and

religion both find it impossible to accept some simple geometry, and some very simple maths, how could they possibly accept the reasoning that leads to the conclusions in these pages?

How can religion accept a multiple god, and a physical one at that, after so many generations of monotheism? How can they accept the suggestion that they are worshipping their own ancestors in an elaborate form of Cargo Cult?

Theological books speak of monotheism as if it is something really fabulous, as if it was some kind of great leap forwards in religious thinking. Monotheism is surely something that is a matter of revelation, not religious thinking? Theologians speak of monotheism as if it were an invention of Moses, a fiction of pious believers. They should really make up their minds. Is monotheism real or not? Perhaps they want it both ways, when they stand on shifting sands they feel they are on safe ground.

Is it not the case that theologians have decided that it is not possible to prove or disprove the existence of the monotheistic One True Supreme Being?

If that be true, then what have I uncovered? The powerful beings that put the Solar System in order are proven to exist with the mathematics in my chapter ten. These are Mighty Ones, Elohim, and by the argument of the theologians they cannot be the Supreme Being, so must be something else.

There are a great many instances in the Bible, too many to mention, where the expression 'living God' is used. In the Hebrew, according to Strong's concordance, this is *'chay Elohim'* which quite literally means 'Living Mighty Ones' and here the word *'chay'* is the same word for 'living' that is used for plants, men and animals, and running water. It is also the word for 'life' in 'tree of life'.

There may well really be an Omniscient and Omnipotent Infinite Spirit God, Creator of the entire Universe, as described in monotheistic philosophy, I have no evidence to the contrary, but that does not necessarily mean that the Bible is talking about the Supreme Being when it says 'Living Elohim'.

I refuse to accept that such an Infinite Spirit God would kill and skin an animal and use the skins to make clothing for a naked man and woman. I refuse to accept that an Infinite Spirit God would talk to a desert nomad face to face, as a man talks to a friend, or fly around the wilderness in something resembling a very noisy helicopter. But a physical Living Elohim could do all these things and more.

If it is so difficult for science and religion to accept simple mathematics, and they won't even look at it, how much harder will it be to accept the logic and reasoning that follows inexorably from those same calculations?

How can they accept that the Solar System is artificially ordered, that the Elohim are real, and that we are not evolved from chimps? How can they even think that we humans are directly descended from the gods?

Furthermore, we may reasonably hold the ambition that one day, these Elohim may grant us the privilege of eating of the fruit of the fabled 'tree of life', and so we may be invited to join their ranks.

How could science or religion possibly even consider such a statement, not even for one minute?

*

In my introduction to this book I said this:-

'The trail that leads us to the treasure is obscured by prejudice and overgrown by the long ages of history. The clues we must follow are hidden beneath layers of legend, and camouflaged by a thick crust of tradition.'

I could have added that the facts are obscured by a patina of piety and deliberate obfuscation.

The ignorance of modern science and religion are just two facets of a common malaise, they **do not want** to know. They are willingly and wilfully ignorant of the facts of history.

There is a pertinent observation in the Bible that sums up what I have been trying to say in this chapter:-

2 Peter 3

5 For this they willingly are ignorant of, that by the word of God the heavens were of old, and the earth standing out of the water and in the water:

6 Whereby the world that then was, being overflowed with water, perished:

Those words were written just two thousand years ago, and since then a lot has changed in the world, but the simple mathematical facts that underlie our history have not changed at all.

They have been obscured, buried in ignorance and superstition, but they remain, as solid as the rocks of Stonehenge and as permanent and as visible as the planets in their orbits.

*

In summary, modern religions all conform to the definition of a cargo cult, as described by Wikipedia at the start of this chapter.

They have charismatic leaders and engage in a variety of ritual practices in the hope of obtaining gifts from a superior being, not just material gain, but forgiveness of sins and eternal life by way of reward for their observances.

These practices were initiated by sporadic contact between humanity and the Elohim in the distant past.

*

If you have not yet thrown this book out with the garbage, then I offer you my thanks.

In fact, rather than consign it to the local land-fill site, it would be better if you give the book to a charity shop; in that way someone else might buy it, and a needy person may benefit from the proceeds.

There is only one more chapter to go before we hit the technical details in part two, and I hope you can stay with me, or I will be wasting my time writing it.

Chapter Seven

The Unction of Sanctity

Some time ago, I discussed the subject matter of this book with a friend. He said that if it were to be published it would "Plunge the world back into the dark ages of religious intolerance!"

I dispute this, but even were it to be the case, I would still publish if I were able.

I would advocate that the world should return to Genesis, and I do so with the best of all possible intentions. I want mankind to survive, and the only way we are going to survive is to ask for the help of the Elohim.

As previously stated, I do not suggest a new religion, nor am I trying to suggest that we abandon technology and all the benefit it brings.

I am trying to suggest that people, all over the world, might start to discard both religion and the theory of origins that science insists on, and try the third way.

The Elohim are real, they are not imaginary.

Somebody put the equation into the Solar System, and it sure as hell wasn't me.

It would be nice to think that people would take the matter seriously, but they won't, of course they won't.

*

At the moment there are just the two of us, you and me, and it will take more than two to convince the

Elohim that they should come out of hiding.

Scientists will not even look at the equation, and if they did they would dismiss it out of hand, like they dismiss everything else that does not fit their 'standard model'. Why upset the applecart for one simple equation?

"If that is true, it will overturn everything we have ever believed!" is the cry I have often heard. It follows from this rather stupid statement that scientists cannot ever make a mistake; it seems that science regards itself as infallible, like the Pope.

Science sometimes appears to be structured a little like established orthodox religion in that it is founded on power, and faith in its own inventions. Nothing is allowed to change; nothing is allowed to challenge their convictions, not ever.

Many who believe in the Bible are fervently in favour of a literal understanding, believing that every word printed in every version of the Bible is literally true, but they deny their own creed by refusing to accept the literal meaning of it.

Creationists always want the Creation to mean the entire universe; they hardly ever consider alternative meanings.

Where the English says 'created' in verse one, Strong's concordance gives ***'bara'*** as the Hebrew which can mean to create, shape, form, or fashion.

In fact, it is more commonly used in the context of creating order, rather than creating out of nothing. In most places the meaning of a word is chosen to conform to the context, but we need to be very careful to identify where the meaning of a word actually changes the context.

'Heaven' or 'shamayim' simply means the sky, the stars, the planets, or basically anything 'up there'. The scripture doesn't use it to describe the universe, in fact the word 'universe' doesn't get a mention in the Bible, or at least, I can't find it.

I point this out simply to show that there are alternative meanings to the one chosen by the theologians. Someone long ago chose to translate the words as meaning 'create', and then theological experts added the inference of 'universal' creation 'ex nihilo'.

I prefer to say it means to create order, to fashion, shape, or create form.

The translation I gave earlier, "In the beginning, Mighty Ones put the planets in order, relative to the Earth." is an alternative meaning that is fully in accord with the wording and context of the first verse of the Bible.

A slightly more clumsy but accurate version would be "In the beginning some Mighty Ones created order in the Planets, relative to the Earth."

Who is right? Obviously for the religious people in the world, tradition is right.

Ever since I gained my understanding of the math in chapter ten of this book, the meaning of Genesis 1 v. 1 has become 'Created Order' and I cannot see it any other way.

*

A huge proportion of the population of planet Earth already languishes in poverty and despair, and has little or no education.

While people are dying without hope, those who could

make a difference spend endless ages arguing about who is right, each takes his own entrenched view. Neither atheistic science nor establishment religion would ever consider the third option, that neither is right, that both are equally wrong.

How can we hope to draw the attention of the Elohim to our plight, if the world doesn't want to know?

*

But the Elohim are already aware of our plight. They watch us constantly. Of course they know, but they do nothing, because if they act, they will be destroying the very thing they want to obtain.

The only way forward is for mankind to humbly recognise the Mighty Ones, and to ask politely for their help.

Is that going to happen? Never in a million years, but I have to try. To know what I know and to refuse to even try to communicate it to others would be criminally irresponsible. So I must try.

I must publish this book as a first step.

*

Let me assume, just for the sake of argument that the content of this book were to be taken seriously by the leaders of this world, what changes may we expect to see in the world as a result?

To begin with, I would hope that the work described in this book would be evaluated and critically examined. This is not likely to happen, but one can always hope. If it is found to be of no worth then it should be ignored, and rightly so, but, on the other hand, if it is found to be valid, as I know it is, then I would hope the authorities of this world would accept it, and react accordingly.

If it is found to be valid then I would hope that efforts would be made to educate the world about the order in the Solar System and the artificial nature of that order.

As a result of confirmation of the work in part two of this book, I would hope and expect that, first and foremost, the multitude of different religious organisations would all drop their animosity one towards another and join forces to recognise the sorry state the world is in, and decide with one voice what they are going to do about it.

There is a lot of work to be done if the world is to be saved, and time is short.

I would hope that the energies of scientists the world over would be directed towards helping humanity overcome and survive all the problems it faces, rather than spend all of its time and effort on furthering Darwin's imagined story of origins.

All hypothetical work about Earth's origins and history would be abandoned, and research directed to finding evidence of what really happened.

Money spent on space research is actually wasted. The antediluvians knew more than we do, and their knowledge of space didn't help them one little bit.

The Elohim could wipe us out with a thought, so weapons research and manufacture are of no use. Weapons are useless except when they are turned against our own selves in wars which were, are, and always will be, the produce of insanity.

Efforts should be made by the UN and other world

authorities to try to make contact with the Elohim, to ask for their help.

It is not much to ask, but I do not believe it will ever happen.

*

I have previously mentioned that the Mighty Ones are watching over us, like they were guardian angels. This is probably true in the sweeping sense that humanity is of great interest to them, but it does not mean that they are going to correct our personal mistakes.

In mentioning angels, I should point out that the angels are the same thing as the Elohim. The word 'angel of God' simply means 'messenger of the Mighty Ones', and it follows that a messenger of the Mighty Ones is himself a Mighty One. I would also like to point out that throughout scripture, the angels look like us. There is no mention of angels having wings. Cherubim (machines?) have wings, but not angels.

There is a rather dramatic and picturesque description of an Elohim and a cherub in 2 Samuel 22....

10 He bowed the heavens also, and came down; and darkness was under his feet.

11 And he rode upon a cherub, and did fly: and he was seen upon the wings of the wind.

12 And he made darkness pavilions round about him, dark waters, and thick clouds of the skies.

An even better description of a cherub is given in Ezekiel Chp. 10, but it is too long to discuss here.

Suffice it to say that a cherub has all the characteristics of a machine, most commonly a flying machine.

There are three kinds of angels in the Bible,

1) Real ones that I call Elohim, these look and behave just like men.

2) Visionary ones that look and behave just like we would expect a technological projection to be like.

3) Dreamed angels, seen in mental visions.

If I say that angels permeated the Biblical narrative right up to and including the time of the early Christian church, I would be referring to those that are described by the scribes as being real, and I would be saying that the Elohim took a direct interest in humanity up to and including that time.

The other two categories of Elohim may be of some minor interest, but do not carry the same significance for me as the reported real ones.

Since the days of mass communication and scientific secularism they seem to have decided to take a back seat.

*

In the scriptures beyond Genesis there are a great many instances where the Mighty Ones are mentioned as being in over-all supervision of the Earth, and the kingdoms of men. It is worth noting that in most, if not all, of these cases the Elohim are reported to have guided, rather than compelled, a certain course of action.

Having said that, there are also times when they have shown a total disregard for what we humans think.

They destroyed the antediluvian world with a flood, and they did not hesitate to disperse the builders of Babel and confuse their languages, for daring to try to publish the very thing I wish to publish in this book.

As mentioned elsewhere, according to the scribe, three men, one of whom was 'God', came to visit Abraham, and destroyed Sodom with fire and brimstone. (Gen Chp. 18 & 19)

*

The Biblical narrative of the Elohim did not end with Genesis; it continued on down through the ages. I toyed with the notion of writing a much longer book, but I didn't want to dilute the message of the equation with too many extraneous details.

There are many claims made in scripture that the Mighty Ones take an interest in the affairs of men, even in seemingly trivial circumstances. See, for example, the infamous flying machine in the first chapter of Ezekiel, and the fact that Ezekiel identified the 'pilot' as the God of Israel.

Ez 8 v 4 And, behold, the glory of the God of Israel was there, according to the vision that I saw in the plain.

Ezekiel was a devout man, a believer in God; he would not make up fiction, or tell lies. He reports what he saw, and his report is reliable, because Ezekiel believed in God.

In Ezekiel Chp. 10 he identifies this flying machine as a 'cherub'.

In passing, it is a conundrum for those who believe the words are the literal truth, the inspired word of God, because God is the man sitting in the pilot seat, several times identified by Ezekiel as being 'The God of Israel'.

Ez 1 v 26 and upon the likeness of the throne was the

likeness as the appearance of a man above upon it.

In general though, the Mighty Ones do seem to let us run our own affairs, but that might well be an illusion.

We are important to them, we are their young, their next generation, they have put a lot of time, work, and effort into producing us. From this it follows that they would not willingly stand by and do nothing while we destroy ourselves, but by the same token, we cannot rely on them stepping in to help either.

An examination of the entire scripture reveals that the Elohim run the world much like the proverbial shepherd tries to run an unruly flock.

For the most part they do not force action, they rather prod and steer, gently nudging the world of humanity in the desired direction.

We may also like to consider the many prophetic utterances in the scripture; predictions of the then future. With the benefit of hindsight, many of them appear to have been fulfilled.

One way the Elohim could ensure that a prophecy is fulfilled is to manipulate subsequent events in order to fulfil the prophecy themselves.

This is not the place to engage in a long discussion about how the Mighty Ones have been quietly guiding humanity from behind the scenery, but I would like to suggest that they are not of infinite power.

They achieve things in much the same way that we do, with hard work. The work they do may have appeared miraculous to earlier humans, or even to us, because of their greatly superior knowledge and abilities, but still things can go wrong.

One might suggest that Christianity was started as an attempt to put humanity back on track, but it failed. How many Christians would accept a pragmatic version of the Lord's Prayer?

Christianity has spread its influence all around the world, but if it results in sectarianism and violence, as it so often does, then it is not in accord with the intentions of the Elohim, as far as I understand those intentions.

The pervasive theme of Genesis and the entire scripture is one of 'righteousness' or rightness.

If we wanted a definition of 'righteous', we could consider what the scribe says; I quote again, repeating myself from earlier, it is required that we do justice, love mercy, and walk humbly with our Mighty Ones.

Violence and mass murder, from whatever source, do not match well with this requirement.

The situation humanity finds itself in is a simple one to understand. If we do not come up to scratch, the Elohim will allow us to destroy ourselves, and simply start again as they did in Noah's day.

They cannot force us to recognise them, we must do it ourselves.

The old maxim is true; the Lord helps them as helps themselves.

*

There are those men in high positions, men in power, who garb themselves in rich raiment and perfume themselves with the unction of sanctity. These walk amid idle luxury and uncounted wealth, their embroidered robes wafting through clouds of incense while they dally with rarefied theological propositions.

These are the men who have deceived humanity with garbled nonsense, dogma and doctrine that no man can understand except them themselves.

They disport themselves on high pulpits, enjoying the adoration of the congregation, spouting platitudes, and professing to speak the mind of the One True God.

They know only power, and they care nothing for the poor, the children who eke out a living on rubbish dumps while the high priest dines in opulent plenty.

They profess to be God's representatives on Earth, but they know nothing of God. If they knew of God, they would know the truth, and they would speak the truth and live the truth.

These are not ever going to accept the reality of the Elohim, nor would they be able to accept the work in this book, because this work puts the lie to their claims to know God.

We may question the assertion that they know God, or that they have an infallible insight into His divine mind, but we will get no answer from them.

They are the elite of the Earth, and will not stoop so low as to answer the critical questions of the common man.

But consider the future for these powerful teachers of nonsense if the Elohim are ever contacted. What would they have to say then? All their falsehoods and greed would be exposed; they would stand naked before their maker, without so much as a fig leaf with which to cover their deceptions.

No, they will never accept that Babel is real, nor will they accept the rest of this little book, and they will certainly not accept the equation.

*

A similar situation would prevail amongst scientists; there is a down side to everything.

I have suggested that we might continue with technology, which is the practical application of science, but that might not be possible.

Many of our great minds work on the trickier problems of the Universe. The top scientists in the world work in places like CERN in Switzerland, where they have built a huge particle accelerator, to search for the building blocks of matter, so they may better understand the origins of everything.

Scientists have spent a fortune and much effort on building powerful telescopes and rocket-shuttles to get them into space, the better to research the cosmos.

Thousands of our best brains work in scientific research seeking to solve the mysteries of nature.

What would be their future, if all they had to do was ask the nearest Elohim to give them the answers and explain everything to them?

Scientists of all disciplines might just as well give up, and the technological spin-off would cease.

We see that if the Elohim were ever to become generally known to humanity, the world as we know it would change dramatically, and this is possibly one of the reasons they have kept a low profile for the past two millennia.

*

There would be no more structured religion, with all its ritual and paraphernalia and intoned hokum. It would no longer be possible to sustain the argument that one particular way to worship the One True God was better than any other.

All the many and varied competing sects would falter in the presence of the very God they claim to worship.

There would no longer be any need for scientific research, and hence not much need for universities to teach science.

With the failure of the Church, and the closure of all our research establishments and space centres, industry and the economy would falter.

Some might suggest that these drastic changes should be seen as good reason for ***not*** revealing the Elohim to the world, that such a revelation would be a disaster for humanity. It would upset the status quo, and cause no end of trouble.

My own view is somewhat more positive.

Sometimes when I look at the world through the eyes of my TV set and see the terrible state the world is in, I feel a tinge of doubt about my conclusions.

The conclusions are not acceptable to most people, but cannot be avoided.

The stories in Genesis have been preserved for thousands of years when they could have easily been lost or destroyed. In particular, the story of Babel has been preserved for thousands of years, and come down to us, when it could easily have been lost or destroyed.

Stonehenge/Babel, that crumbling old monument, has

survived for thousands of years when it could easily have been destroyed. It is ancient and dilapidated but it is still possible to read the message it contains.

The order in the Solar System, the artificial equation, was put there before mankind was created, when there was no need for it. It is meant for us, we can know that because there is nobody else to read it.

All these things integrate, they combine to send us a clear message and the message is this...

We are not animals, we are not apes; we are gods.

If that is too grand for us, we can say we are embryo gods, infant gods, gods in waiting, starving gods, gods in agony, gods crawling in the dust, gods crying for lost loved ones, but we are gods nonetheless.

We are not evolved apes, we are gods. We cannot avoid our destiny by denying our heritage. We are gods.

The sooner men understand that slight difference, the better we will be able to face the future.

It is true that first contact may bring problems, and it is for this reason that the choice of when that first contact is made has been left up to us.

If governments were to take this seriously, they would be wise to prepare the general public in advance, prepare the world for a peaceful contact with our long-ago ancestor.

*

I stalled over writing some of these things, not because they are unbelievable, but because they are true, and because, if they become generally known to the wider public, great and unforeseeable changes might well sweep across the world.

I doubted, and could not come to a decision, but there is nothing to be gained by procrastination. It has to be said:

If this little book is ever published, then first-contact will have been initiated.

If you are reading this book, then you will know it has been published. After that, it is only a matter of time.

---------------------*---------------------

Well, that is just about all I wish to say on the matter of the Elohim, at least for a while. I thank you for your patience, and now it is time to venture into the mathematics that provides the substance for my outrageous claims.

We are about to enter that dark and terrible place where you learn that all I have said is true.

I fear that you may not survive the experience, and I would hate to lose you so soon, but it is an essential step on the road to understanding.

*

I start with the easy things, which are just instructions on how to draw all the planetary orbits of the Solar System to an exponential scale, using the peg and string method. This first section is not particularly technical, it is just drawing lines and circles, you might actually enjoy trying to follow the instructions and draw the ground plan of the migdal of Babel yourself.

Of course, this is actually the ground plan of Stonehenge, and we do not discover that it is the Solar System until later.

*

I hope you can stay with me, I will feel lost without you, but after the drawings comes the introduction to the astronomy and it gets a little bit more mathematical.

After the gentle introduction to the astronomy and a little math, you will be dropped in at the deep end with Pythagoras and some of my graphs. These chapters also present tables of data and a few demonstrations of the calculations, and the application of the equation.

One possible cause of confusion is the use in the math of the letter 'y' to represent astronomical values. This should not be confused with the archaeologist's use of this same letter on the Stonehenge plan, there is no connection.

You may or may not be aware of the fact that mathematics can be presented in a variety of different ways, without changing the meaning of it.

The graphs are all just diagrammatic representations of the workings of the equation. They are intended to illustrate, not confuse.

If you do not understand them, don't worry, just enjoy looking at them.

After the three technical chapters I review the situation, and then there are some chapters of chat.

Finally, as an appendix, there is a copy of an evaluation of my work written and presented in a manner that should be acceptable to a fully qualified professional mathematician. It is not the way I would choose to present it, and I do not care for it much. I was trying to please the scientists in those days. These days I don't care about pleasing them.

They've got it all wrong anyway.

*

There are two points that I would like to make, and I wish to stress these points and draw them to your attention.

1) I have no objection to scientists examining this work, but it was not written for scientists, it was written for you, my only reader. Scientists have been misleading the world for 150 years, and I am sure they are the last people to agree with this little book.

So if you wish to ask a scientist for his opinion, please do, but do not expect any great enthusiasm to be displayed.

2) **ALL** the graphs in part two are the same. They are all just different ways of presenting the same astronomy and mathematics. (Apart from the blank one, fig 10b). They all represent the order in the orbits of the planets, they are all the same. This includes the drawings of the Stonehenge peg-and-string model. Do not get confused.

One other point to make, the original Stonehenge ground plan, as built by the builders, is not precise. I have mentioned this before. It is not intended to be exact; it does not need to be perfect. All it needs to do is to be accurate enough to pass on the method used to derive the main equation, and it has achieved that objective.

I will have a few more comments to make here and there in part two, but by and large, this is the end of part one.

Again, I would like to thank you for staying with me, you helped a lot, if you can manage to struggle through part two, then that is more than I can reasonably expect.

If you cannot follow the calculation, you could always ask a friendly mathematician, or math teacher, to check the results for you.

There is no point in asking a scientist or a religious person, but mathematicians should not be biased. Most schools have a mathematics teacher, and it is not really very difficult math, it is just repetitive.

Or you could skip the maths, and meet me again in chapter eleven.

END of PART ONE

Ancient Knowledge.

Part Two

Technical Details

In which the Ancient Knowledge is described in mathematical detail, and the Order in the Orbits is demonstrated.

Ancient Knowledge

Part Two

Technical details - Author's Comments

I would like to say a few words to any scientist who may accidently find himself reading this book.

There are words used by scientists rather frequently. Words like 'ad hoc', 'arbitrary', and 'a priori'; words that scientists often use as some kind of evil incantation, a curse to consign undesirable scientific works to the bottomless pit of obscurity. I am aware of these words, and their meanings, so please bear this in mind if you continue reading.

I would like to repeat, in case it was missed the first time, that this is not a scientific work, it is a treasure hunt.

*

Stonehenge is the treasure chest, but we cannot open it with the keys provided by science. We need a 'dumb-key' to open it.

The dumb-key is found by asking ourselves what geometric drawing implements did the builders have? They must have marked the ground with some kind of plan or they would not have known where to dig the holes to place the stones.

The only geometric implements they would have had access to would be the basic ones that men living in the wild might find in the environment.

They would no doubt have a long straight pole or stick to use as a measure, and sharpened pegs to scratch lines in the turf, or to drive into the ground to mark places. They would have rope, or the ancient equivalent, made out of twisted fibres or knotted hide thongs. Pulled tight these would provide a straight line, which could be marked on the ground with chalk dust. (The monument stands on chalk bedrock)

These are the only implements they would have; pegs and string and a stick.

These are our dumb-keys; we must recreate the ground plan of the monument using just pegs, a stick, and string, or with pencil and paper.

As it happens, we will also be drawing an exponential graph or mathematical model of the Solar System, but that is on an 'a-priori' basis.

Some of what follows is ad hoc, and some is arbitrary, or appears to be at first glance, but it opens the treasure chest and gives us access to the content, so I don't really care much about a scientist's opprobrium.

Chapter Eight

Of Pegs and String

"There is no substitute for experience."

A true statement, so I hope you can actually get involved and draw the ground plan for yourself. It is tedious and repetitive, but as the end result is a model of the Solar System. You might find it worthwhile.

*

This is not intended to be an archaeology instruction book. The description of the main features of the monument are taken from a book by Professor R.J.C. Atkinson, entitled simply 'Stonehenge', which is an excellent book for those who wish to learn about the monument, and which I highly recommend to anyone who wishes to know the facts.

Astronomical data is from an old 17th edition of Norton's Star Atlas, but any modern and accurate astronomy book will do.

*

The details in this section assume that you are already familiar with the main features of the structure, and familiar with the details of the planetary orbits of the Solar System.

If not, then it is unfortunate, but not a great disaster; we are dealing with numbers for the most part, and I assure you I would not knowingly falsify numerical data.

We are about to draw the complex ground plan of a primitive Neolithic monument starting from scratch, so it would be well that you know what the features are, or you won't know what I am talking about.

(Note, we are only going to draw the features that led to the discovery of the equation, other features just clog up the drawing)

*

The peg-and-string method leads to a cluttered drawing when representing it on paper, because the construction lines and marks remain. In practice the monument builders would have simply marked the features they required with chalk dust, or scratches in the turf, and then moved on.

This method is also very repetitive and tedious, but not as tedious as moving a thousand tons of rock across twenty-six miles of country.

If I was one of the builders, I know which job I would have preferred.

There are two parts to the monument, the outer and the inner. The outer consists of all features that lie outside of the great Sarsen Circle. The inner consists of all those features that lie inside the Sarsen Circle.

The Sarsen Circle itself is part of both, but we will leave it until we do the inner monument.

Although there is good reason to suppose the actual builders started with the inner monument, we will draw the ground plan of the outer monument first.

The Outer Monument

Section one, the 56 Aubrey points in the outer circle.

One obvious question that nobody seems to ask is how primitive Neolithic peoples were supposed to divide a circle into 56 equally spaced points, without the aid of geometry? Apparently they chose the number 56 deliberately, in order to use it as an eclipse predictor, (G. S. Hawkins Stonehenge Decoded - Souvenir Press, London, 1965) so they must have had a reliable way of doing it.

It is impossible to do this simply by pacing it out, and if anyone doubts this, they need only try it for themselves to become convinced.

It is difficult enough even with the aid of modern drawing implements, so it should be impossible for a primitive man.

The geometry I devised and herein describe is a method that could be carried out by men living in a field under reduced circumstances, but they would need to know what to do.

*

It is necessary for the persons drawing the plan to obtain a straight and sturdy stick. I wanted to call this a rod or pole, but both of these terms are already in use and refer to fixed measures.

I shall call the monument measure a 'stick' for want of a better.

The 'stick' can be any convenient length. The length of the stick determines the final size of the monument.

There is no need for any calibration marks on the stick, it is just a stick.

Items required are the above mentioned stick, a long length of rope or the Neolithic equivalent, a lot of sharp wooden stakes and a bag of chalk dust for marking the ground in the appropriate places.

One of the sharp wooden stakes is to be used to scratch the ground; the others are to be driven into the ground to serve as pegs; so they would need a big stone to use as a hammer.

Clearly, it would be better to do this on paper, and so we shall, using modern drawing equipment like a pencil and an eraser.

You will need to select a 'stick' for yourself. The length of the stick will determine the finished size of the monument.

If drawing on A3 size paper a stick of one centimetre would be suitable, but the real outer monument plan was drawn using a stick of approximately 194 inches.

<u>To start the Construction of the plan</u>

<u>The 56 points of the Aubrey circle</u> (see fig 1).

Step 1) Draw a straight line up and down the centre of a large sheet of paper. In the real thing this would be a line on the grass pointing in a chosen direction. Call this line the 'axis'.

Step 2) Mark a point on the axis line to be used as a centre, (C) roughly in the middle of the page. In reality this would be a large sturdy peg stuck in the ground.

Step 3) Use the stick to produce a string of 10 sticks in length. Use the string, or a set of drawing compasses, to draw a circle of radius ten sticks centred on the chosen central point.

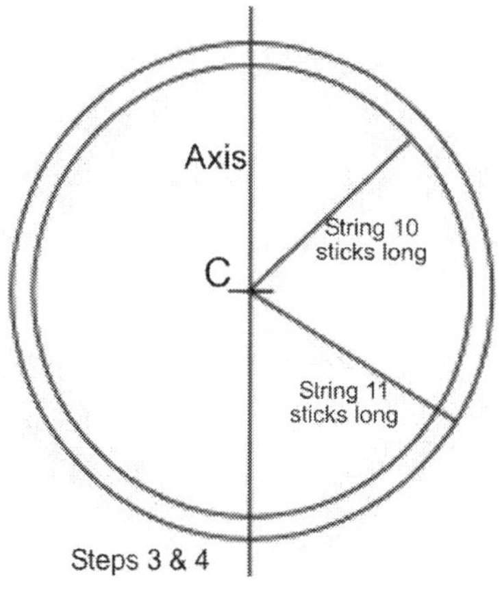

Step 4) Draw another circle 11 sticks in radius on the same centre, as in the small diagram on the left.

Step 5) Using a string 11 sticks long, draw a straight line 11 sticks long starting from any point on the outer circle such that it ends on the inner circle (step 3) and produces a chord on the inner circle.

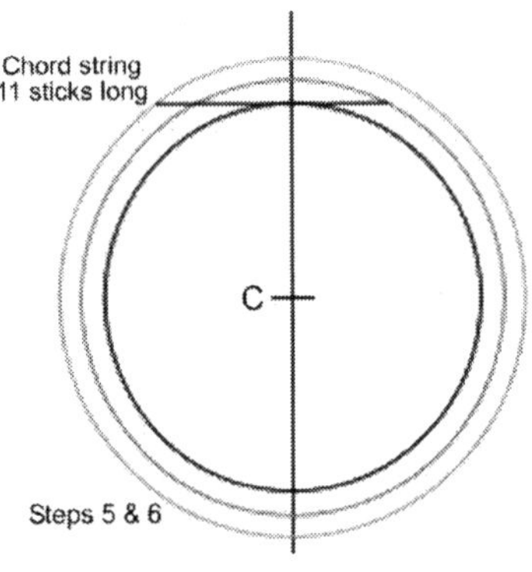

Step 6) Adjust a length of rope or string to draw a third circle from the same centre (C) such that the circumference is tangent to the line drawn in step 5, as in the small diagram on the left.

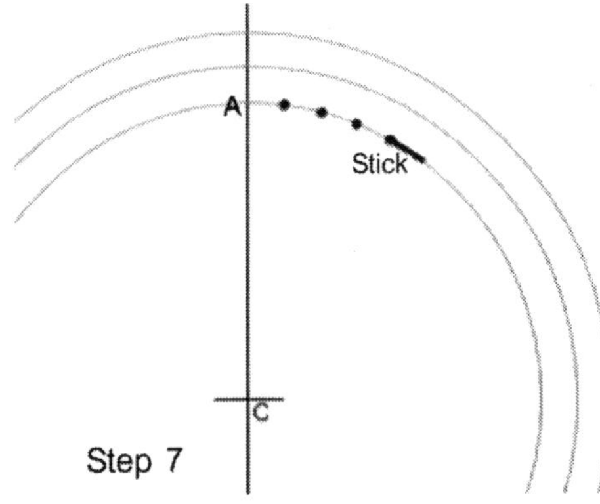

Step 7) Starting from a point where the final circle (step 6) crosses the axis line; you should use your stick as a tangent to this inner circle and work your way around the circle marking off successive stick lengths. This should be done as accurately as possible.

It can be calculated that on the full-size monument this procedure produces a circle of 56 equally spaced points, with 4 inches spare on the last point. On the scale of the full monument this is a negligible error, which would not be noticed. On smaller models it only shows up by calculation.

Scientists should not trouble to complain about this minute error, I will not take any notice.

We will refer to this circle as the Aubrey Circle (outer) and the points as Aubrey points.

Note. By calculation the 56 points will fit, but on a small scale it is very tricky to get the points evenly spaced, and it is possible to accumulate errors and get the wrong number of points. I can guarantee it is possible to get it right, and one of my large figures is done by my own hand, just to prove it. Obviously there will be small errors when it is done by hand, but these will not really matter much, just as long as you end up with 56 points evenly spaced.

*

If working in a field, drive sturdy wooden stakes into these points.

These stakes will be dug up later to leave the 56 Aubrey holes, but we will leave them in place until we have completed the ground plan.

If these steps are correctly followed, the result will be as shown on **fig 1.**

If you have successfully constructed this circle of 56 points, then it would be advisable to obtain a few photocopies, because they will be needed again later, and photocopies of the one you have will save doing it over again.

*

The circles of steps 3 & 4 can be used later by the builders as guide lines to correctly place the surrounding bank and ditch. The line in step 5 can now be erased.

It would be useful to number the Aubrey points from 1 to 56, working clockwise around the circle, starting with the first one to the right of the axis line. These numbers are for reference purposes only, and have no other significance.

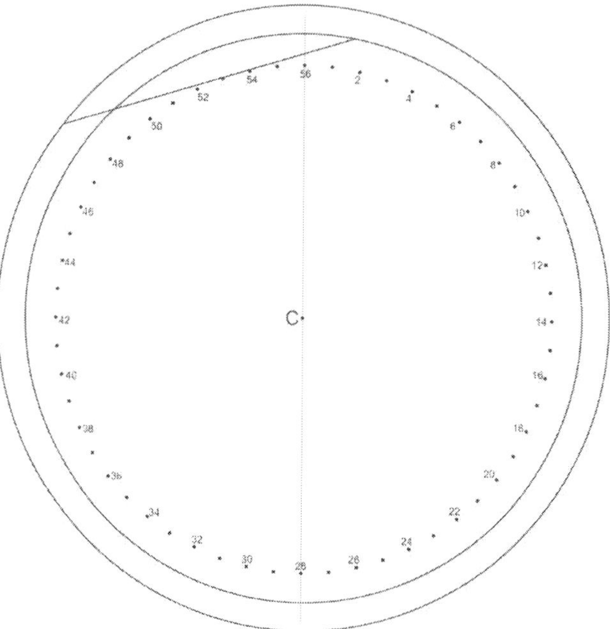

To start drawing the monument it is necessary to first construct the circle of 56 points, known as the Aubrey Circle.
It will be necessary to do this twice, once for the outer and once for the inner. Although these are to different scales it will be convenient if you photocopy your finished drawing, to save doing it again.

Fig 1 - Construct the Aubrey Circle (See main text)

Section two, the thirty radials. (see figs 2, 3 & 4)

Archaeologists have noted that one of the main features of the monument is the existence of thirty radials in the mid-section of the monument. The so-called 'Y' and 'Z' 'circles' of holes, and the main Sarsen Circle, all point to the construction of thirty radial lines. Archaeologists do not explain how this could be done by men living under primitive Neolithic conditions.

The method I have devised and outlined below, will work in a field, but could only have been known to someone with knowledge of geometry and mathematics.

There is archaeological evidence in Professor Atkinson's book, and on the site, to support the claim that this method was actually used.

*

To produce thirty radials from 56 outer points.

Step 8) Draw a chord across the circle from Aubrey point 2 to point 42 and make a mark where it crosses the axis line. As a check, repeat this for Aubrey point 54 and point 14.

Step 9) The distance between the point marked in step 8 and point 28 on the Aubrey circle is to be taken as the diameter of a new off-centre circle. It will be necessary to bisect this diameter to find a new centre (C2) and radius for this new circle. This can be done with a long length of string; find the radius and hence the centre by folding it in half, or use a compass.

Draw this new circle, on a new centre, but still on the axis line, such as the circumference is a complete circle that passes through the point described in step 8 and point 28 on the Aubrey circle. (As in fig 2).

This circle will be referred to as the 'vernier' circle.

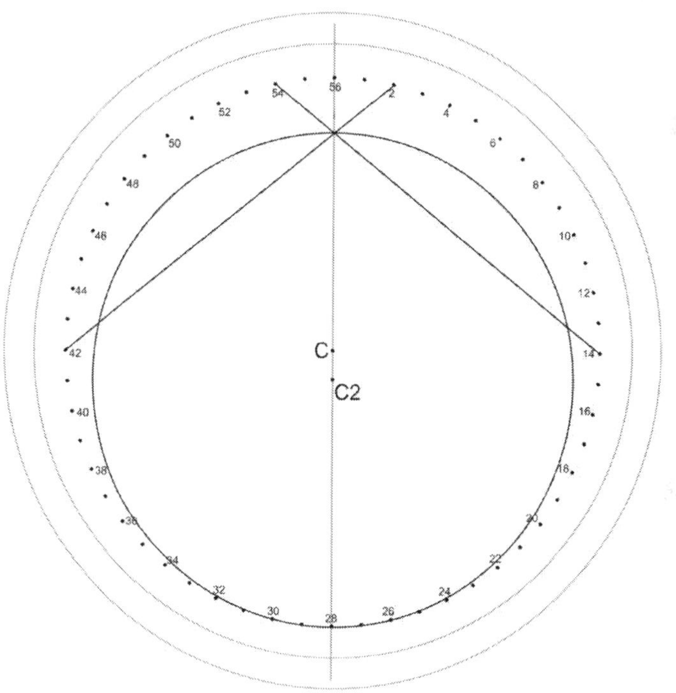

Steps 8 & 9

Fig 2 Construct Vernier Circle

Step 10) It is important that this step be understood.

Connect a line from Aubrey 55 to Aubrey 15. This is as a chord spanning 16 segments of the Aubrey Circle.

When I say 'from' I mean start at point 55 and mark the point on the vernier circle where this line first crosses it.

Also mark a section of the middle part of the line, or draw in the whole line as I have done on my figures.

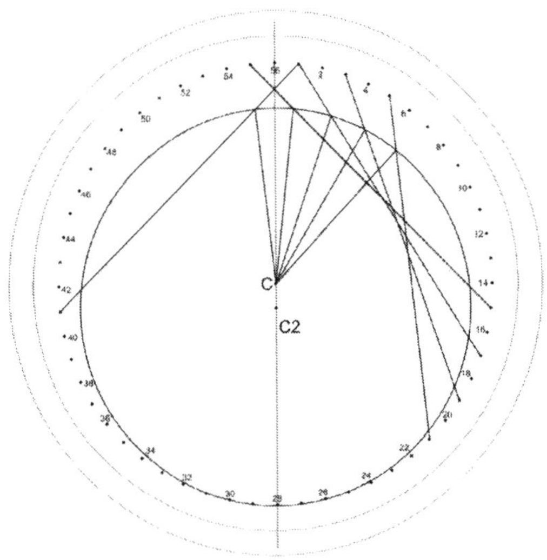

Steps 11 to 14

Fig 3 Start Producing the Thirty Radials

Step 11) Moving the chord line clockwise to Aubrey point 1, connect Aubrey 1 to Aubrey point 17, again spanning 16 Aubrey segments, and again mark where this line first crosses the vernier circle, and mark a section of the middle of the line, or draw in the whole line.

Step 12) Continue this process clockwise, skipping even-numbered Aubrey points. From successive odd numbered Aubrey points, draw chords spanning 16 Aubrey segments, marking only the **first** crossing of the vernier circle, and the central part of the line, until point 27 is reached as a start point.

Complete this chord, and then change to step 13.

Step 13) When Step 12 is complete, repeat the procedure in an anti-clockwise direction, starting with a chord line from Aubrey 1 to Aubrey 41, again spanning 16 Aubrey segments, and again marking where the line **first** crosses the vernier circle, and marking a section of the middle of the line. Continue in this manner, skipping even-numbered points, until Aubrey 29 is reached.

If this procedure was understood and followed accurately, you should end up with thirty points marked on the vernier circle.

Step 14) Connecting each of these 30 vernier points to the original centre, (C) with light lines, will present thirty radials. These should be numbered, for convenience, starting at the first one marked (step 10) to the right of the axis and numbering clockwise from 1 to 30.

Here we should note that if the vernier circle is not drawn accurately, if it is a little on the small side, an error will occur such as will spread the two radials (1 & 30) either side of the axis slightly further apart than the rest of them.

This is an actual feature of the monument, as reported by Professor Atkinson.

(page 38 of 'Stonehenge' the Professor notes that "the two uprights forming the entrance to the circle – no's 1 and 30 – have been deliberately spaced one foot wider than the rest, and the gaps between the adjacent pairs reduced correspondingly.")

I take this as evidence that this method was actually used, and the builders got the vernier circle just a little too small, either accidentally or deliberately.

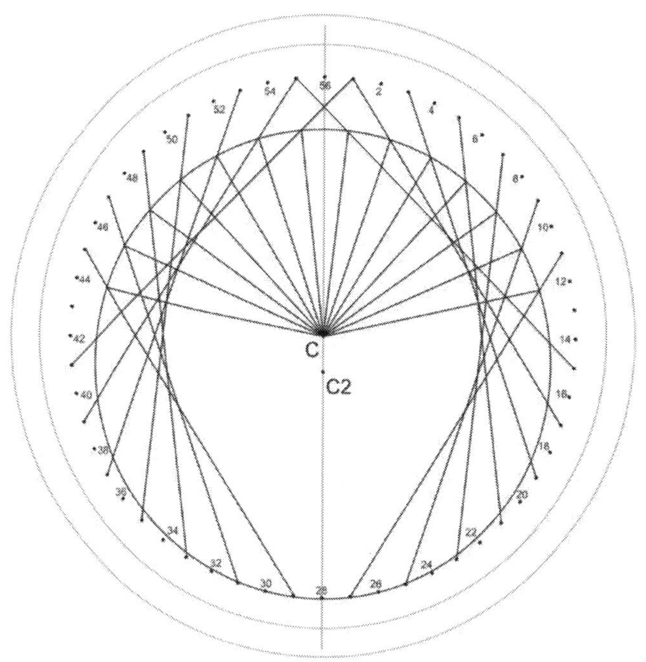

Fig 3a
Continue Fig 3 and steps 12 & 13
to complete the circle, and produce 30 radials.

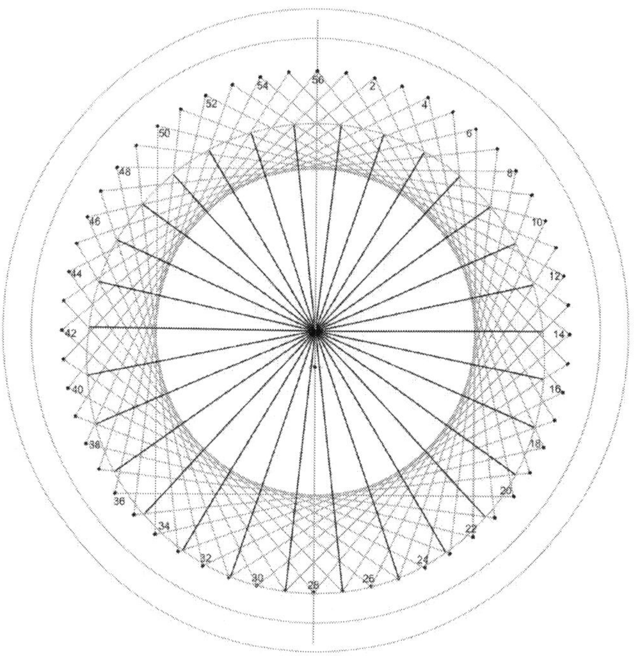

Fig 4 Thirty Radials and 'Y' circle Completed. Mark Where Radials Cross the 'Y' Circle.

The 'Y' circle.

As a result of this construction you should also have a network of crossing chord lines that produce a rough circle inside the vernier circle. This corresponds to the archaeological feature referred to as the 'Y' holes.

Step 15) This 'Y' feature may be completed and smoothed by connecting all the even-numbered Aubrey points, again spanning 16 Aubrey segments. These are the ones that we missed before. Mark the central part of these chord lines. The builders made a 'mistake' doing this; one of their chords spanned 17 segments instead of 16. (See fig 12) This was one of the clues that led me to consider the peg and string model. I think it was deliberate. It should be noted that this 'mistake' could easily be replicated by this method of producing the 'Y' circle.

Do not add any more radials, thirty is enough.

Step 16) Mark all the points where the thirty radials cross the rough circle delineated by the network of crossing chords. This is the foundation for the later digging of the 'Y' holes, but for now, we suggest that pegs were driven into the ground at these points. The appearance of the 'Y' circle as a by-product of this method of producing 30 radials is also powerful evidence that the method was actually used.

From this we may deduce that the builders were not primitive men.

They had advanced understanding of geometry.

The ‘Z’ circle.

Up until now all the geometry has been sequential, but here we come to a loose end.

The builders included the ‘Z’ circle, but there is no geometric need for such a circle, and apparently no way of determining its position or derivation. We should put it in, but if we do not yet know what it means we will need to guess, or copy the monument.

I have put it on my drawings by copying the method apparently used by the builders. The ‘Z’ feature could be placed in an arbitrary choice of chords drawn from the 30 ‘Y’ points (step 16). Inspecting the archaeological drawing suggests that this is what the builders appear to have done, spanning seven segments of the ‘Y’ feature, thus subtending an angle of 84 degrees at the centre. In doing this they made another apparent mistake, continuing to span seven segments of the ‘Y’ circuit, even through the disrupted area produced by their earlier ‘mistake’. (Fig 12)

It should be noted that this ‘mistake’ could easily be replicated by this method of producing the ‘Z’ circle.

This formed another of my ‘dumb-clues’.

Step 17) Draw chords across the ‘Y’ circle such that the chord lines span seven segments. Complete the full circuit in this manner to delineate a ‘Z’ circle feature. (fig 5)

Step 18) To finish the ‘Z’ feature we should mark in the points where the 30 radials cross the 'circle' delineated by the network of crossing lines. The result is called the ‘Z’ circle.

Note; I am aware that the actual monument presents large holes to represent the ‘Y’ and ‘Z’ features, and I intend to show the holes later. For now, let us please leave them as lines and points.

Step 19) Finally, we could draw a simple circle of radius 3 sticks centred on our original central point, although not shown on my figures this will help us place the inner monument when we have drawn its ground plan. It will fit neatly onto this circle.

This is the almost completed outer monument, (fig 5).

Please do not erase the chord lines.

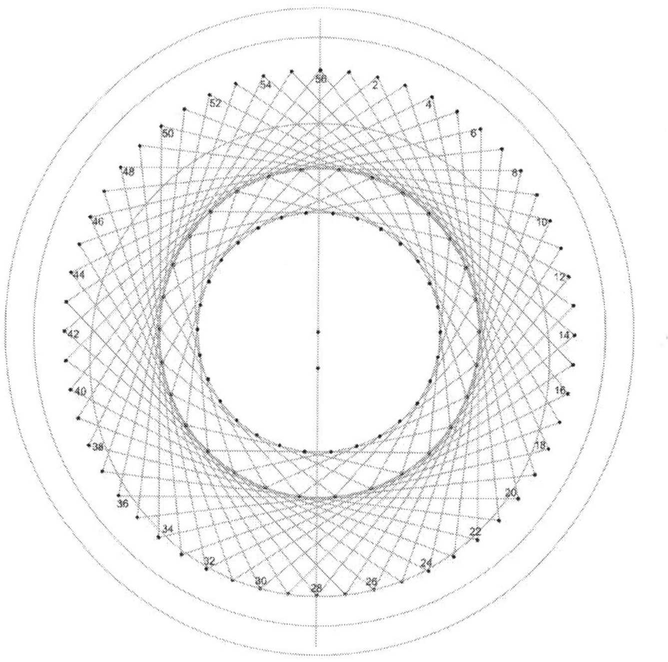

Fig 5 Almost Completed Outer Monument showing Aubrey circle, 'Y' Circle, 'Z' Circle and thirty radials, with bank & ditch guide lines.

We will now move on, to consider the inner monument.

The Inner Monument (See Fig 6)

The builders used a shorter stick length for the inner monument, 3 outer sticks are equal to 10 inner sticks.

Since the monument is ratiometric, and we are simply working on paper, it doesn't matter; we just continue, using the same stick as we used before, remembering that we are working to a different scale.

We start as we did with the outer monument, starting with a copy of the Aubrey circle. If you have a photocopy of figure 1, then go to step 21.

Step 20) It is necessary to draw the 56 points again, so if you do not have a photocopy please take a new piece of paper and repeat steps 1 to 7 to create a new one.

Step 21) We should now use this copy of the Aubrey circle to determine the locations of the inner features. This is not as easy as in the outer monument, because there is no geometric imperative to guide us.

It is here that the term 'ad-hoc' comes into its own. Scientists will object strongly to this, but it cannot be helped.

Step 22) Placing the Great Sarsen Circle. (See Figs 5, 6 & 7)

The circles of 10 and 11 sticks radius used to start off the drawing are here used to delineate the Sarsen Circle; the inner faces of the Sarsen Circle uprights are tangent to the circle of 10 sticks. Since 10 small sticks is the same as three long sticks, (step 19) it is easy to see how this connects the two monument structures. Please note that the thirty radials are already produced. I have introduced some random elements into my drawing of the stones, to simulate the dilapidated nature of the real thing.

Step 23) The Bluestone Circle.

There is a lot more to do, but when we have finished drawing the inner plan, the inner 56 point circle can be converted into the somewhat confused archaeology of the so-called 'Q' holes. The present bluestone circle is not where it was to start with. See Professor Atkinson's book, page 60. The 'Q' and 'R' holes underlie the current bluestone circle. The outermost of these rings, known as the 'Q' holes, are where the original circle of 56 pegs would have been.

Inner Features

Before we dig out the 56 inner pegs and replace them with bluestones to create a bluestone 'Q' circle we must now attempt to place the remaining structures, which are:-

a) The Trilithons
b) The bluestone horseshoe.
c) The 'back-sight' holes.
d) The 'altar stone'.

The Trilithons.

I tried long and hard to find a geometric necessity for these features and found none.

The Trilithons are not difficult to place, but they lack a

geometric reason for the placement.

The main verticals of the central trilithon lie between chords drawn from 'inner Aubrey' points 21-35 and 20-36. Other pairs of chord lines place the other stones, as shown on the drawings.

(It was at this point that the thought occurred to me that the stones had been placed to draw attention to the chord lines, the complete reverse of my previous working mind-set. From then on my attitude to the monument changed. I ceased trying to place the features with chord lines, and started trying to identify which chord lines were indicated by the features.)

The chord lines indicated by the remaining trilithon uprights are 31-48 and 30-49, 33-52 and 34-51. On the other arm of the 'U' the lines are 26-7, 25-8 and 23-4 with 22-5.

The trilithon uprights are placed between these pairs of lines. Since I now believed the stones were only put there to draw attention to the chord lines, the actual stones are not important. I have put some on the drawings to indicate roughly where they are.

Bluestone Horseshoe.

This feature is placed almost exactly corresponding to the same circuit as the 'Z' feature on the outer monument, suggesting that the original inner plan was identical to the outer. It can also be approximately placed by drawing chords from the inner Aubrey points spanning 19 segments.

On my drawings I have not troubled to complete the full 'U' shape, which is obtained simply by finding the desired chord lines.

'Back-Sight' holes.

The name is derived from a preconceived notion that these holes held stones that served a certain purpose. The name is unjustified, but we may as well use it.

Regrettably Professor Atkinson does not give much in the way of location data in his book, stating simply that they are behind the Altar stone. I place them (from astronomical data) where lines 17-38 and 18-39 cross the axis, one on either side of the axis.

Altar stone.

Another stone named by preconception. It has nothing to do with an altar.

The stone lies across the axis "about 15 feet" from the inner face of the main trilithon (Page 56 of 'Stonehenge'). Unfortunately the Professor fails to say if the 15 feet refers to one of the edges of the stone, or the centre.

Since his book is intended for general reading only, we cannot criticise him for this, but it does leave me with a minor difficulty.

In the end, after much consideration, I joined inner Aubrey point 40 to both 16 and 17, as shown on the figure. This placed the stone across the axis as near as possible to the Professor's description.

Since the stone is tapered and lies across the axis at a slight angle, it appears on archaeological drawings almost exactly as shown on my figure. This suggests that the Professor's suggestion (page 56-57 of 'Stonehenge') that it once stood erect is possibly erroneous, and that the builders actually aligned it with the same chords that I used.

It is possibly a coincidence, but the altar stone is approximately one ***outer*** stick long.

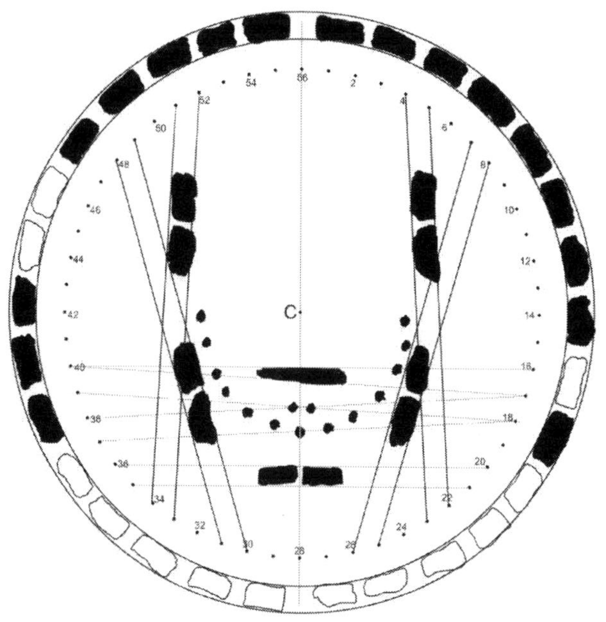

Fig 6 Inner monument plan produced with same template as outer monument.

Completed Plan (See fig 7)

The finished inner monument plan would have been drawn out full size on the ground before the outer was started. If we want to put the inner drawing that we have produced in its correct place, we would need to cheat a little and shrink our inner monument drawing to fit.

Using modern technology the inner drawing can be shrunk and slotted into the middle of the outer monument plan by placing the **inner** face of the Sarsen Circle, (Inner Monument circle of 10 sticks radius) exactly on the circumference of the circle drawn in step 19.

Having drawn the completed plan on the ground, the builders need to dig up all the pegs, and place the stones.

I suggest that you leave the chord lines in place for now, do not erase them entirely, they are useful for calculation.

For finishing touches the ‘Y’ and ‘Z’ features of the outer monument can be permanently preserved in the chalk by digging holes, possibly intending to place stones in these holes.

These are shown here but not exactly as they appear on the archaeological maps.

In an ideal world it should be possible to compare the drawing with the archaeological measurements, and this can be done up to a point. There are many archaeological details that I have ignored or overlooked as a matter of necessity because the available data is not precise.

For example, the archaeologists inform us that there is no unique central point from which all the circles are drawn, but it is not clear how many centres there are, or where they are.

It is also true that some of the features I have placed have been moved at some point after the monument was first built, and there are areas of confusion in the detail.

I cover all these criticism and objections by reminding you that we are not involved in writing an archaeological treatise, we are involved in a treasure hunt, and if this drawing helps us find the treasure, as it does, then we need not worry ourselves unduly about the finer points of detail.

Fig 7 - This is drawn by hand, following the directions in this book, just to show it can be done. (Blobs to simulate holes and stones)

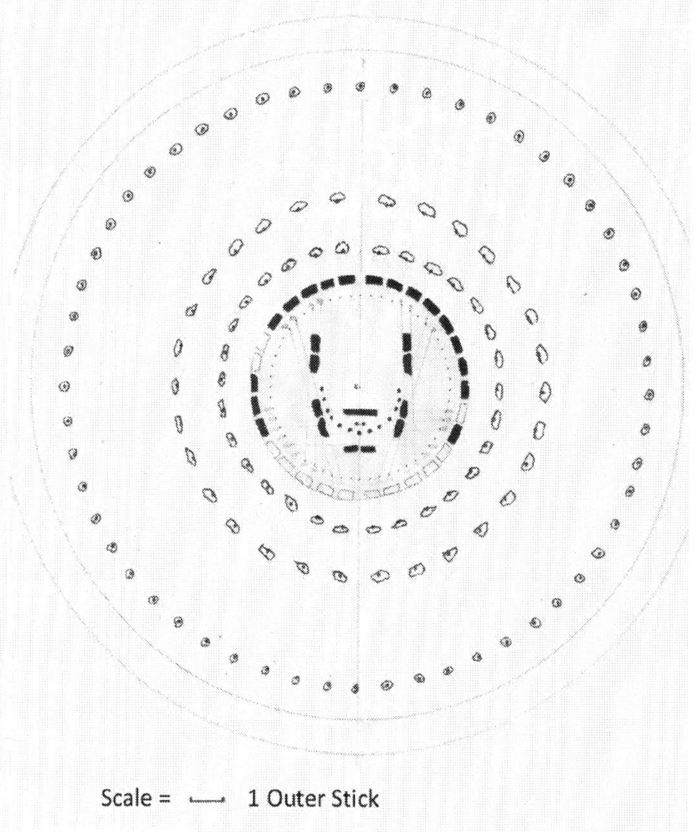

Details of Stonehenge

There are some details that confirm that the geometric construction outlined above was actually used.

- The method allows for 56 holes to be evenly spaced around a circle.
- The method delineates the guide lines for the outer bank and ditch.
- It allows for 30 radials to be generated from the 56 holes.
- These thirty radials are disposed symmetrically on either side of the axis in the same manner as the radials on the actual Sarsen Circle.
- If a slight error is made in the radius of the vernier, the result would be a larger gap between the first two radials either side of the axis. Such an effect was reported by Professor Atkinson.
- The process of producing 30 radials also produces the 'Y' feature, or something remarkably similar.
- The same construction template allows for the accurate placing of the Sarsen Circle, with its 30 radials, and provides a location for an early version of the Bluestone circle, (in 'Q' holes).
- The method results in an integrated design, relating the inner monument to the outer, and linking the two to form a homogenous whole.
- The method accurately reproduces much of the ground plan as described by archaeology.
- The method can reproduce 'mistakes' made by the builders during the layout of the 'Y' and 'Z' holes. (See figure 12).

The over-all consideration is that the method provides a rational geometric design for the Stonehenge monument that is an integrated whole.

The actual construction work in placing the stones most probably took place over a period of a few years; the amount of work involved dictates that it would have taken some time.

If the ground-plan is a unified whole, as it clearly is, then the stonework and the construction must also be an integrated whole. This is discussed in more detail in chapter twelve.

The C14 dating spreads construction over a period greater than a thousand years. I conclude and declare that the C14 dates are wrong.

In addition, and most importantly, the evidence is strong that this method described above was used, from which we must conclude that the designer was not a primitive Neolithic man. *The designer had a powerful brain, and an advanced knowledge of geometry and trigonometry.*

It is also evident that primitive tools were used. We can conclude from this that the builder was from an advanced society living under reduced circumstances, and strongly motivated to devote so much effort and time into the building of such a monument.

That such a thing can be constructed with just a few pegs and some rope is quite remarkable enough but to find that the major features also relate exponentially to the orbits of the planets is beyond the belief of some, but it is a verified mathematical fact, as we shall see in the next chapter.

*

I hope you have been able to follow all that, and made a determined effort to draw the plan with your own hands. Some people just read the words and look at the pictures, and I guess that is better than nothing, but to really get to know, and feel the truth of it, it is best to do it yourself.

There is no substitute for experience.

It gets a lot worse in the next chapter.

Chapter Nine

Sticks and Stones and Outer Space

I am glad you decided to stay with me, but I should warn you that from now on things tend to get a bit more complicated. There is no need to worry if you can't follow it, all that is needed for the moment is to accept that this is real, and not made up, you can get it checked later.

The point of this chapter is simply to demonstrate the correlation between the graphs in chapter 3 (Figs 8a & 8b) and the archaeological measurements in Professor Atkinson's book, with the geometry in my chapter 8, and the astronomical orbits of the Solar System. A four-way comparison demands a lot of calculations, which would be pretty boring. I have actually done all these calculations, but I have only given a few examples here.

This is not a book about astronomy, but if you are not familiar with the Solar System, I should explain that the planets beyond Jupiter are 'spread out' over huge distances, whilst the planets within the orbit of Jupiter are 'cramped up' which is one of the reasons for two different scales. The orbital figures are given in table one, page 299.

The point is, I can do the calculations, I have done them a great many times during my researches, but there is no reason why you should believe me. I might be cheating on the figures.

I am not cheating, but the only way I can prove that is for you to verify the results yourself.

So I propose to show how I do it, to prove that I can, and also work a few examples.

I have put the results on the monument plans, (fig. 8 – Note, I have turned this 'upside down' for clarity) to illustrate the calculated relationship between the monument features (Chord lines) and the orbits.

The Astronomical Features of Stonehenge.

Note. The important points are where the chord lines cross the axis.

At one point in the construction of the peg-and-string pattern, it occurred to me that the features of the monument were placed by the builders to draw attention to the chord lines in the ground plan. This is the complete reverse of the methodology I had employed to draw it.

It makes sense, if the designer wanted to pass on numbers or figures he could not rely on the actual stones, because they would become weathered and eroded and dilapidated over the years.

Chord lines drawn from a circle of 56 points can be calculated exactly.

Chord lines are useful for calculating distances. They subtend angles; which means that trigonometry can be used to calculate the distances from the centre in units of 'sticks'.

Each Aubrey segment subtends an angle at the centre of (360/56) degrees, which is 6.425754998...degrees.

The radius of both of the Aubrey circles is calculated at 8.907235428, for both inner and outer sticks.

Using the chord lines of the model, values can be calculated exactly.

Science would point out that there are a huge number of chord lines to choose from, and some of them are certain to be right.

I acknowledge this, and reply that we only concern ourselves with those chords that are indicated by the placement of monument features.

Thus, the features of the monument have been placed by reference to chord lines in order to draw attention to those chords, and identify the correct chord lines to use in calculation.

Since the chords we used span multiple Aubrey segments, the number of segments spanned multiplied by (360/56) gives the total subtended angle.

Trigonometry can be used to calculate the position of all or any of the chord lines with more accuracy than is actually needed, the result being presented in 'sticks'.

This is very useful for two purposes.

1) In a plan as big as the real monument, the outer stick would be 194 inches in length, and the inner stick would be 58.2 inches in length. The

chord calculations allow for the model to be checked against the archaeological measurements, if desired. (For metric system units, feel free to convert.)

2) The astronomical calculations I will demonstrate shortly also gives results in 'sticks', so the chord calculations will provide a useful and accurate comparison of astronomical features with Professor Atkinson's measurements of the Stonehenge features.

Astronomical Comparison.

List 1, Inner Monument and Inner Orbits.

The monument features relate to the following orbits, working from the inner to the outer.

Altar Stone inner edge - Mercury perihelion distance.

Altar stone outer edge - Mercury aphelion distance.

'Back-Sight' holes - placed to Venus mean.

Bluestone Horseshoe centre point - Earth.

Central Trilithon, inner edge – Mars perihelion.

Central Trilithon, outer edge – Mars aphelion.

Bluestone Circle; and Q&R holes (?) asteroids.

List 2, Outer monument and outer Orbits

Sarsen Circle– Jupiter

'Z' holes - Saturn

'Y' holes - Uranus

Vernier Circle - Pluto.

The Neptune circle was added by me just because I thought it should be there.

These allocations are not just guesswork; the features actually do have an exponential relationship to the orbits they are paired with.

It is real, as will be demonstrated in the next few pages.

*

The outermost bank and ditch might well be regarded as representing the Oort cloud of comets, and the Heel Stone might well represent something huge a long way off, but I have not considered these things.

*

The main objective of my investigation into Stonehenge was to test the notion that it might be connected to the 'heavens' in some way.

After a considerable amount of preliminary investigation there was no doubt in my mind that it was, but the data available from direct measurement of the monument features was not good enough to derive suitable exponents to demonstrate that relationship. It was because of this that I decided to investigate the geometry, which advanced my understanding of the monument somewhat.

With the geometry described in chapter eight as a tool, I could calculate the positions of the features, using simple trigonometry, relate them to the orbits of the relevant planets, and thus obtained two exponents, one for the outer monument relating to the outer system, and one for the inner monument that related to the inner system.

The exponents I derived from the geometry were long strings of decimals that worked, but not all that well.

At this stage I knew I was right, but I needed the exponents expressed in more meaningful terms.

*

I was walking my dog one morning when a thought popped into my head concerning the Great Sarsen Circle.

According to Prof. Atkinson's book, (page 38) the inner faces of the stones of this circle had been carefully dressed, and accurately placed, as if it were intended to be some kind of datum reference.

The inner face of the circle as constructed from my geometry had a radius of ten units of 'inner sticks', but it also had a circumference of thirty stones placed on thirty radials. School book learning tells me that the circumference of a circle is the diameter multiplied by π.

The circumference therefore should be 20π, but the designer of the monument had made it 30.

The designer seemed to be drawing attention to a silly equation.

$$\underline{\mathbf{30 = 20\pi}}$$

Or

$$\underline{\mathbf{1 = 30/20\pi}}$$

This was nonsense, but $(30/20\pi)$ is the same as **$(3/2\pi)$** which worked extremely well when I tried it out as an exponent for the orbits of the outer Solar System.

It seemed like magic, like the long dead designer was telling me things, and I thought I was going mad. It really gave me a weird sensation, but I had my exponent for the outer system.

Mad or not, I pressed on regardless.

This figure $(3/2\pi)$ is the radius of a circle of circumference 3.

So, I decided just to try other properties of such a circle, properties like the area, which is easy enough.

The area of a circle of circumference 3 is **(9/4π).**

This also worked extremely well as an exponent for the inner system.

These two expressions tallied well with the values I had previously determined, but were clearly easier to remember and use. They also gave better results.

Believe me or believe me not, like magic, I suddenly had both my exponents and could relate the orbits of the Solar System to the Stonehenge features, without using long strings of decimals for exponents.

Just for interest, these two relationships are.

Ki $(AU)^{(9/4\pi)}$ relates inner system planets to the inner monument features measured along the axis in 'sticks'.

Ko $(AU)^{(3/2\pi)}$ relates outer system planets to the outer monument features.

Lots of people get thrown by complex exponents, even when they are simple.

If I asked what is 3^2, most people would answer 9 because they know what it means. The '2' is the exponent.

(9/4π) is a constant; (9 ÷ 4 ÷ π) it has a numerical value of <u>0.716197243</u>...

(3/2π) is also a constant; (3 ÷ 2 ÷ π) it has a value of 0.477464829...

In general use, there are less buttons to press if we use the formulations, they are easier to remember, and more accurate.

(Compare these with my preliminary empirical figures of 0.72 and 0.48)

'AU' is the required orbital parameter expressed as Astronomical Units.

Ki and Ko are linear constants of proportionality, derived from Professor Atkinson's measurements, and are needed to account for the difference in linear scale between modern units of measure and 'sticks'.

Ki = 4.305 and gives results in short sticks, for the inner monument.

Ko = 1.386 and gives results in long sticks, for the outer.

These two functions give fairly accurate results, but are not perfect.

The results of the following calculations are shown on fig.8 in visual form. Please note that fig.8 is just for illustration only, do not scale; calculate.

Astronomical values are all from Norton's Star Atlas.

The actual calculations required are repetitive, rather a lot, and very tedious, and I do not propose to go into them all here. The following are for example only.

Calculation. (See Fig 8 page 296)

Example calculation

If 'n' is the number of Aubrey segments spanned, then the subtended angle is given by .... 360n/56 degrees

If we divide this by 2 ....360n/112 we get half the subtended angle.

We take the cosine of this angle, multiply by 8.907235428 to give the distance from the centre point to the centre of the Chord, in 'sticks'.

In general the distance from the centre to the Chord is given by-

Distance in sticks = 8.907 × Cosine (360n/112)

This is valid for both inner and outer monuments.

This is the simple case where the Chord crosses the axis line at right angles. Some of the points we may need are a little more involved because the chords cross the axis at a different angle. For simplicity I have ignored these in this demonstration.

Example 1

Let us take the 'Y' circle, the chord for this spans 16 Aubrey segments, so n=16.

Put this into the calculation described above, and the answer is 5.5534..sticks (outer)

Now take the perihelion distance of Uranus as 18.275 AU, and raise to the power ($3/2\pi$) you get 4.00398. Multiply this by Ko which is 1.386 gives 5.549 sticks.

Compare this with the chord line value. They are very close, in fact on the scale of the real monument the difference is about three quarters on an inch.

Example 2

The chord for the central Trilithon inner face also spans 16 Aubrey points, so the calculation is the same as the one we have just done, and the answer is the same, 5.5534 sticks, (inner)

Now take the perihelion distance of Mars as 1.381 AU and when raised to the power of ($9/4\pi$) you get 1.260. Multiply this by Ki which is 4.305 gives 5.424 sticks (inner). Compare with the chord line value. They are again very close, on the scale of the inner monument the difference is seven and a half inches.

Example 3

The cord for the outer edge of the central Trilithon spans 14 Aubrey segments so the calculation for the chord distance from the centre of the monument gives

6.298 sticks (inner)

The astronomical calculation from the aphelion of mars gives 1.441328 and this multiplied by K_1 results in 6.2049 sticks, a difference of about five inches on the scale of the actual monument.

Example 4

Mercury perihelion is .306 AU, and when this is raised to ($9/4\pi$) we get 0.42823;

Multiply this figure by Ki (4.305) gives a result of 1.8435 sticks.

The chord that crosses the axis on the inner edge of the altar stone spans 24 Aubrey segments, so the distance from the centre is 1.98 sticks.

The difference is eight inches on the actual monument scale.

Example 5

I have determined that the outer edge of the altar stone is marked by a chord that spans only 23 Aubrey segments, which calculates at 2.466 sticks.

The aphelion distance of mercury is 0.467AU which calculates as 2.495 sticks, which is a difference of 1.7 inches.

Distance of Altar stone from Main trilithon.

In example 2 above, the inner face of the main central trilithon as calculated by trigonometry is 5.5534 sticks.

The outer edge of the Altar stone as calculated by trigonometry is 2.466 sticks.

An inner monument 'stick' as previously mentioned is equal to 58.2 inches, so the distance is found by subtracting the two figures and multiplying by 58.2, then dividing by 12 to get feet.

5.5534 – 2.466 = 3.08 sticks, which at 58.2 inches per stick is **14.97 feet.**

The outer edge of the altar stone is hence calculated from both astronomy and chords as being approximately 15 feet from the inner face of the main trilithon, as measured by Professor Atkinson. (See page 56 of 'Stonehenge')

Width of Altar stone.

The width of the altar stone is found by subtracting the results obtained in example four from the results obtained in example five. This gives two different calculations, one from the astronomical data and one from the chords.

The astronomical data gives a width of 2.495 – 1.843 = 0.652 sticks or 38 inches.

The chord calculations give a width of 2.466 – 1.98 = 0.486 sticks or 28.2 inches.

The Professor gives a measured width of 42 inches, so we can see that the accuracy is not inch perfect. The astronomical calculation is out by 4 inches on the width, and the chord calculation is out by 13 inches on the width.

*

All the features that we have so far considered and drawn on the ground plan of the monument can be related to orbits in this way, and all of them suffer from the same discrepancies of a few inches on the scale of the actual monument.

The examples above are intended to give you an idea of how to calculate from trigonometry and astronomy to compare the results. They are not particularly accurate, because the chord method is rather crude and cannot show fractional quantities, however if we take the overall size of the monument into consideration, the results have to be considered as pretty good. The inner monument is 97 feet in diameter, and the whole monument out to the outer Aubrey circle is 288 feet in diameter, so the calculations should be seen in this perspective.

The whole point of the exercise is to demonstrate that there is a close correlation between the features, chords, and the orbital parameters of the planets, and I think it succeeded.

We should also consider that the scale factors Ki and Ko are derived from Professor Atkinson's measurements of the physical monument as quoted in his book. This means that Ki and Ko are subject to possible inaccuracy because of weathering and erosion.

It is accepted that the procedure does not lend itself to great accuracy, but accuracy is not required for the monument to fulfil its main function, which is to pass on the message that we will shortly discuss.

We do not even need to do a statistical analysis; we have enough information to continue with our treasure hunt. The next clue will not be long in coming.

*

Once I had managed to formulate the two relationships described above I believed that I had successfully demonstrated that the Stonehenge ground plan did indeed connect with the heavens and could therefore be identified as the fabled 'tower' of Babel.

There was no doubt that the ground plan of Stonehenge was a twofold model of the Solar System. It was a geometric representation, made with the peg-and-string method, which was related to the real Solar System by exponential equations. Under such circumstances one would not expect accuracies at the micron level.

I rested on my laurels, but only for a while.

*

I soon realised that this was not enough. It would not be acceptable to science, and it did not explain why the builders had gone to so much trouble.

Would anyone shift a thousand tons of stone by hand just to say "we were once advanced enough to measure the orbits."?

I wasn't sure, so I needed to have a little time thinking about things.

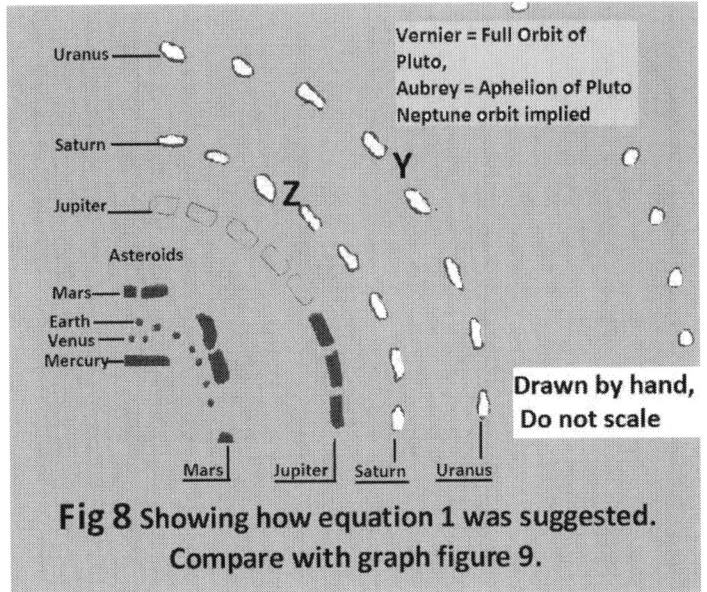

Fig 8 Showing how equation 1 was suggested. Compare with graph figure 9.

Interim Conclusions.

I had managed to convince myself that I had actually found Babel, mainly because I had looked for a connection with the 'heavens' and I found it.

A scientist would find lots to complain about, of course. I had put in a couple of planets myself, and this is not allowed. I did this mostly because of the lack of accurate archaeological data.

A critical scientist would also argue that the chords were selected on an ad hoc basis, with 'a priori' knowledge, and the scientist would be right, but that doesn't change the facts.

The monument really is an exponential model of the Solar System.

Science will not, cannot, accept this, for reasons explained in the main text, so you may feel confident that there will be no chance whatever of scientists considering this work.

Another criticism they could level, also somewhat justified, is the well-known effect of using exponents; the errors shrink.

I will not trouble to explain this, but a mathematician will understand.

*

None of this matters, because of what happened next.

*

The conclusions so far were quite easy to come to. Whoever designed the monument in the first place was a mathematical genius, who knew a huge amount of astronomy.

How can you portray the Solar System with a peg-and-string model?

The designer was most certainly not a Neolithic man.

Since the process of thought that led to this discovery was started by the book of Genesis, and the story of the flood, and Noah, and the Tower of Babel, I had to consider that all those things had some basis in fact.

This raised a major problem of conflicting truths.

The Monument tells one story about history, it tells the Biblical story.

This is in stark contradiction of the established and accepted story as told by modern scientists.

They cannot both be true.

In this war between truths, Stonehenge has the distinct advantage of being provable with mathematics.

The scientific version is theoretical, a hypothesis, and

cannot be proven with math.

We are forced to make a choice; we either accept the facts of Stonehenge, or the more attractive guesswork and hypothesis of Science.

I am biased, it was my discovery after all, and I cannot deny my own work.

I accept the monument. I accept the facts written in sticks and stones, and outer space, and reject the hypothesis of science.

The only defence science could offer is to claim that this is all a concoction of ad hoc, a priori, arbitrary chance and guesswork.

Unfortunately for science, what happened next puts the lie to that.

I noticed a few little oddities about the monument that set me thinking.

Table 1 **Orbital data in Astronomical Units** **Abstracted from Norton's Star Atlas (17th edition)**			
Planet	**Perihelion**	**Mean**	**Aphelion**
Mercury	0.306	0.3870987	0.467
Venus	0.718	0.7233322	0.728
Earth	0.983	1.000	1.016
Mars	1.381	1.5236915	1.666
Asteroid Belt	Nominal 2.0	-	Nominal 3.0
Jupiter	4.951	5.2028039	5.455
Saturn	9.008	9.5388437	10.069
Uranus	18.275	19.181871	20.088
Neptune	29.8	30.057924	30.316
Pluto	29.58	39.439	49.19

Chapter Ten

A New Heaven

If you have stayed with me this far then I must be doing quite well.

This section is about the worst, and if you find it difficult to read, then try to imagine how hard it was for me to write it.

I am trying very hard to make a convoluted and complex process look easy, but I think I am failing.

*

During my work on Stonehenge there was always one question uppermost in my mind, and the question was; 'why?'

Why did people who had just survived a major disaster that had destroyed their world spend so much of their precious time and energy constructing such a huge and complex model of the solar system?

What was so important about it that the Elohim would 'come down' to inspect it, and force the people to stop what they were doing?

The archaeological record bears tacit witness to the sudden cessation of work on the monument. Holes that were intended to hold stones were left empty, and the digging of the 'Y' and 'Z' holes appears to have been carried out in a hurry, notwithstanding the 'deliberate errors' that provided me with my clues.

The over-all impression is one of hasty finishing and

hurried departure.

The question of motive plagued me, and I spent hours just staring at the plan, trying to see into the designer's mind.

*

I noticed that the Trilithon Arms were deflected inwards. The stones of these arms were placed between chord lines that spanned 17 and 19 segments, quite different from the main central Trilithon.

I perceived this as another clue, designed to make me ask the question 'Why?'

According to the rules I was working to, this suggested that the arms were built to a different scale than the rest of the inner monument.

I already knew that the outer monument was a different scale, and wondered if Mars were being represented on both scales, for some reason. This turned out to be true, calculations showed that the side arm trilithons were in accord with the outer monument scale, but carried an offset of about 0.5 sticks. This turned out to be useful later.

I then remembered that the inner was drawn to the same template as the outer, and that several of the features and orbits used the same chord lines on both templates. They appeared to come in loose pairs, pairs like Earth and Saturn, Mars and Uranus, which made it look as though the inner monument would graph against the outer, but I didn't quite see the point of doing that.

One thought led to another, and the final thought was

that the designer of the monument was sending a message down the millennia.

The message was not; graph the inner monument against the outer, but rather it was "Graph the inner Solar System against the outer Solar System."

This was actually much the same thing, since the monument represented the Solar System.

It was telling me that in some way I could use the exponents to produce a relationship between the inner Solar System and the outer Solar System.

I could even figure out that Mars was to appear in both, it was represented to both scales, and Jupiter was to appear only in the outer.

I realised that to graph one set of astronomical figures against another I would only be using astronomical data, so the monument features with their ruined condition would no longer be involved.

All its dilapidation, weathering, and detailed archaeology would be left behind.

All the difficulties with placing chords and calculating errors and confused features would be a thing of the past – they wouldn't matter anymore.

Any scientific objections to the ad-hoc nature of the monument calculations would also be rendered ineffective.

Eagerly, I set to work to try to find a way to relate the inner system to the outer.

It would have been an impossible task if I had been working alone, but the designer of the monument, though long dead, had left little clues to help in the most difficult parts. Not least of these were the dispositions of the Trilithon 'arms'.

I have already described how I came upon the two exponents, in the most unscientific way possible, yet they appear to work very well in relating the Solar System orbits to the monument.

I decided to keep them, and try to use them to relate the inner orbits to the outer orbits.

I started by drawing up a list of the orbital mean of the planets, (From Norton's Star Atlas) and these figures raised to the powers of the exponents. The results were then written down as 'y' and 'x' values on a look-up table for a proposed graph. (Table 2 on next page)

These 'x' and 'y' values are the same values that when multiplied by Ki and Ko would provide monument distances in 'sticks'.

Please note that the 'y' is now used in a different context, and is not to be confused with the 'Y' feature of the monument.

These values graphed against each other fairly well, (fig 11) but I still needed to obtain a slope for the line, and the offset, so that I could formulate an equation.

It wasn't easy determining the slope or the offset, and the procedure I used for finding them is a little too ridiculous to believe. I wanted, if possible, to use clues from the monument.

The reason I wanted to use monument clues was simple. It wasn't because I believed in numerology, it was because I wanted to be able to say, with hand on heart and without blushing, that this was genuine, honest to goodness, antediluvian knowledge.

I was using modern astronomical data, you see, and

modern calculating instruments. I wanted to represent as much of the monument as I could, without distorting the whole scenario.

Does that make sense?

<u>Table 2</u> **<u>Look-up table</u>** **Ready-worked figures for graphs**			
<u>Planet</u>	**<u>Mean</u>** **AU**	**<u>X axis</u>** **$AU^{(3/2\pi)}$**	**<u>Y axis</u>** **$AU^{(9/4\pi)}$**
Mercury	0.3870987		0.506756171
Venus	0.7233322		0.792972486
Earth	1.000		1.0000
Mars	1.5236915	1.222719691	1.35204255
Jupiter	5.2028039	2.197749527	
Saturn	9.5388437	2.93545051	
Uranus	19.181871	4.097654299	
Neptune	30.057924	5.077774766	
Pluto	39.439	5.7809403	

Equation details

One of the numbers that cropped up in the monument was 20π, and of course the value π on its own is fairly ubiquitous in a stone monument consisting largely of circles.

So, I related π AU to 20π AU, raised to the appropriate exponents.

Believe it or not this led to me being able to formulate the equation which I still use today.

$$\mathbf{AU_i^{(9/4\pi)}.ln30 - F = AU_o^{(3/2\pi)}} \text{......equation 1}$$

You have seen this before in an earlier chapter, but it may be worth pausing a while to look at this equation again, especially if you don't understand it. (Represented by graphs, see figs 9 & 10 pages 333 & 335)

The expression on the left, $\mathbf{AU_i^{(9/4\pi)}}$ is the same expression that we used to relate the orbits to the inner monument. It does the same job here, except that because the monument isn't here, and we are not measuring in sticks, we do not need Ki.

The expression on the right, $\mathbf{AU_o^{(3/2\pi)}}$ is the same as the one we used to relate the orbits to the outer monument, except that we do not have the monument so we do not need Ko.

Or, the left hand side equates orbits to the monument

and the right hand side equates orbits to the monument, but we have taken the monument away, so the left hand side equates to the right hand side, without bothering with the monument.

So in that respect, we are equating the inner monument to the outer, without the monument.

The number 'ln30' is just a mnemonic for the constant 3.401197382, and uses less buttons to enter, and is easier to remember. It does a similar job as the scale multipliers Ki and Ko, only we don't use them because we don't have the monument any more. Yes?

1/ln30 also happens to be the slope of the graph line in figs 9 & 10.

The value of 'F' is calculated like so...

If we substitute π in the place of AUi and 20π in the place of AUo into equation 1, then 'F' becomes the only unknown and we can find the value, which is a constant.

$$\pi^{(9/4\pi)}.\ln 30 - F = (20\pi)^{(3/2\pi)}$$ ......equation 1b

Solving for 'F' ... **'F' = <u>0.500772097</u>**:

These values of $\pi^{(9/4\pi)}$ and $(20\pi)^{(3/2\pi)}$ are represented as a point on the graph line in figs 9 and 10.

The values of π Astronomical Units and (20π) Astronomical Units are applied as the upper limits for

the inner and outer Solar System respectively.

The main equation, equation 1, relates inner orbits to outer orbits and vice-versa. This should not be possible in a natural, random, Solar System. The function of the equation is shown graphically on **fig 9.**

*

I can imagine you looking rather bewildered, and that is to be expected.

Much may become clarified if you stay with me for a few more pages.

I think we should take a little break here, and let me rest my aching head. Let us have a little chat about just where we are, and what we are doing.

Tea break.

Let us have a nice hot cup of refreshing tea, and a couple of digestive biscuits, and while we are slurping and munching, we can chat.

It is clear to me, if not to you, that the design of the monument originated in antediluvian times. Unless we are to suppose that the survivors of the disaster brought telescopes with them, and all the paraphernalia of technology needed to measure orbits, we must assume that all the design details were finalised before the flood came. Noah carried the design on the Ark, in the form of a drawing or a set of written instructions.

This must mean that the orbital data from the Solar System planets used by the monument designers was data obtained or measured thousands of years BC.

I do not know how long ago the monument was built, but it was the only structure on Earth at the time. It must predate the pyramids of Egypt by a long, long way.

Modern astronomers say that the orbits of the planets are slowly changing, but the work done here seems to imply that the changes cannot be that great, because we still have good correlation with the data used by the builders of Stonehenge.

In fact, if we compare modern data with that ancient data, as expressed in the monument features, it seems that the orbits have not changed much, if at all. Saturn diverges a little from the required place, but not by much.

I mention this because the order we see in the current system, which I will discuss shortly, has not been the result of chance acting on changing orbits.

The mathematical relationships we see today are the same as were evident many thousands of years ago. It has not changed since antediluvian times.

This observation would answer the question of motive. The antediluvians knew that the system was ordered, and they knew it was an artificially contrived order.

They knew it revealed the presence of the Elohim, the only power with the ability to create artificial order in the planets.

I can almost hear you asking, how do we know it is artificial? Could it not be natural?

The answer is simple. The equation that encompasses

and describes the order is itself totally artificial. There is no possibility of it being derived from natural law. It doesn't even involve gravity, or Newton's laws.

This is why the antediluvians decided to build the monument. We are their descendants, and they wanted us to know.

They seemed to have a prescient knowledge that they would be scattered, their language confused, their origins forgotten, and they wanted to build a memorial that would carry their knowledge down the millennia.

Knowledge, I might add, that exposes the Elohim, and lets us know they exist.

There can be no other explanation for order in the Solar System; it is not possible for it to happen by natural law or by chance.

For scientists, order in the orbits is an odious suggestion, because it puts the lie to all that science has been telling us for one hundred and fifty years.

This also explains why the Elohim intervened to stop the building of the monument; they didn't want that information to become generally known before its time. They didn't want their cover blown or mankind would not develop naturally.

We may now say, with some confidence, that the so-called 'tower' of Babel is real, we call it Stonehenge.

The data encoded into the ground plan is as sophisticated as any modern scientist could produce, yet the monument was built using primitive tools.

This means that it is highly likely that the flood was real, or we must find some other way to explain advanced knowledge inside a primitive monument.

The orbits of the Solar System are neatly ordered, which is something modern astronomers know nothing about.

Someone intelligent created that order.

Someone powerful moved the planets, including Jupiter, and put them in precise and artificial order, such that they conform to the rather simple and utterly artificial equation derived from Stonehenge.

When I say that the equation is 'simple', I am not being patronising. It is very simple compared to the mathematics involved in human-designed objects in everyday use.

The math inside a computer is horrendous, as it is inside a TV set or a mobile phone. In fact, the math used to design a bike or an electric kettle element is far more complex than this Solar System Equation.

That doesn't make it easy to understand, I appreciate that, and the truth is that you do not actually need to understand the math. All you need to do is recognise the order, to follow what it does, not so much how it does it.

So, while we relax and enjoy our tea and biscuits, I will try to make you understand what the equation does, rather than try to confuse you with numbers.

(If by chance you are already equipped to understand the math, then you can skip this bit and go to the next section.)

As it stands (fig 9) the equation allows us to calculate

the orbital details of one planet from the details of another. This is a fairly straightforward normal function of a linear equation, and it doesn't sound like much, but it should be impossible according to modern astronomical theory.

But that isn't all it does.

It gets a lot worse, and here I am looking ahead to the math I discuss after this tea break.

I will explain what it does, but not fully. You will need to follow the math for a complete understanding.

Because a little sub-equation involving just Earth and Mercury allows us to find the values of spaces between the orbits, (marked 'a,b,c' and 'A,B,C') we can also calculate our way around the entire system, hopping from planet to planet. In other words, the equation provides a way to interrelate ALL the planets.

This can be done because the orbits are arranged in a certain Pythagorean order, an order which is illustrated by the ugly grid of lines on Fig 10 (p 335).

Using this grid, we can 'travel' along the lines, up or down and side to side, and calculate any orbit we wish.

In more fanciful terms, the equation turns an ordinary calculator into something like a 'Star-trek' teleport machine, (although we never actually move), enabling us to explore the pathways through the Pythagorean grid, or jump from planet to planet.

It works for mean orbital distance and/or for orbital period. To change from distance to period or back again we just change the exponents used, as described elsewhere in this book.

You do not even need to do any calculations, just trace a fingertip along vertical or horizontal lines, from Uranus to Mercury, or from Mercury to Saturn, and from Saturn back to Earth. This sounds a little silly, but if you do this, your fingertip will be tracing out the pathways of possible calculations. See how many different pathways there are? In a manner of speaking, your fingertip is doing the same task as a calculator.

The hard thing for people to understand, I have found, is that this is not a computer game, it is not a trick; it is very real.

Being real, it means that the Solar System is not natural. The order is not natural.

The main message of the Monument, and the main message of this book, is that the Solar System is arranged in a completely artificial pattern.

If you can understand that much, then I have succeeded, this book has done its job.

Have another biscuit!

It is odium for a scientist, a scientific odium of ordered orbits, because it completely throws all their theories into confusion; it is not possible for the Solar System to be ordered. For a scientist, it is worse than being confronted by a ghost, a UFO, and the Loch-Ness Monster, all at once.

The only way that science and religion can deal with this is to ignore it, and hope it goes away.

Now we must get back to work, tea break is over.

The Mathematics

Part 1 - Simplifying the Equation

Consult with figure 9. (Page 333)

My initial equation, as obtained from the monument is in the form as shown earlier, which is my own personal preferred way of presenting it, however I was advised by a mathematician that it would be better if I simplified it.

$$AU_i^{(9/4\pi)}.\ln 30 - F = AU_o^{(3/2\pi)} \text{.......Equation 1}$$

This equation can be simplified if the look-up table of pre-worked values is used (p 307). So instead of working the exponents every time, we just look them up in the table.

The equation then becomes $(y.\ln 30) - F = x$

Since ln30 and F are both known, the equation simplifies further to

$y = (x + 0.500772097) / \ln 30$

Or... $y = 0.294014103\,x + 0.147234059$

This equation is shown graphically in fig 11, and fig 9.

This is the standard schoolbook format of a straight line relationship. Apparently different countries have a different way of representing it, but in the UK we use

‘y = mx + c’.

This represents the modern ‘correct’ way of presenting the equation, but I don’t like it much.

It means that once the exponents have been applied, the orbits of the planets are revealed to be related by a simple linear function. This means that it is possible to calculate from inner orbits to outer orbits and back again.

The mathematician also found that the correlation coefficient was;-

r = 0.999900,

This apparently means that the equation is valid. Something I already knew.

The equation is actually very simple, it is just the circumstances of its origin and applications that make it seem complicated.

This simplified form ‘**y = mx + c**’ is no different than the original, and it is easier to follow. My objection to it is based on the fact that it tends to hide the factors that came from the monument, obscuring some important properties. (For example the relationship to Kepler’s third law is hidden.)

When presented in this standard configuration the resulting graph (fig 9) is easy to understand and to use, it relates inner orbits to outer orbits.

However, it does not reveal the whole story. In the original format, as derived from the monument, things are not as simple as they seem.

Things get a lot worse.

Part 2 - Pythagoras and An Equation for Venus

Consult with fig 10. (Page 335)

Let us imagine that we do not know the mean orbits of any of the planets, except Earth and Mercury. We may accept that we know that the planets exist, and we know their names, but not their mean orbital distances.

All we know are the mean orbits of Mercury and Earth.

We will accept that Earth has an orbital mean of unity, **1AU**, which when raised to the power of anything remains as unity.

Mercury mean of **0.3870987AU** is raised to the power of $(9/4\pi)$ to give the 'y' axis value of **0.506756171.**

From Earth at unity, and Mercury 'y' value of 0.506756171, ***we can calculate all the other orbits***, but first we need to find the orbit of Venus.

*

Let 'V' = the mean orbit of Venus in AU, assumed to be unknown.

Then: $$V = (1 - V^{(9/4\pi)}) \div (V^{(9/4\pi)} - 0.506756171)$$

I will refer to this as the 'Equation for Venus'

It is possible to solve this for V, by a process known as

iteration, or successive approximation.

When this is done, we get the answer:-

V = 0.723331002…,,

This is near enough exactly what science measures it at. (0.7233322.. AU)

Having completed the above calculation, in the final iteration we should also have obtained several by-products, one of which is $\mathbf{V^{(9/4\pi)}}$ which is the 'y' axis value for Venus.

This is **0.792971546**.

We must also have found a value for:-

$$\mathbf{(V^{(9/4\pi)} - 0.506756171)}$$

which we will call 'a'.

'a' = 0.286215375

And we must also have obtained a value for:-

$$\mathbf{(1 - V^{(9/4\pi)})}$$

which we will call 'b'.

'b' = 0.207028454

Thus, from the two planets Earth and Mercury we are able to calculate a figure for Venus, and the values of 'a' and 'b'.

We then calculate 'c' by assuming that 'a' and 'b' are

related to 'c' by Pythagoras.

Figures obtained from the Equation for Venus are:-

a = 0.286215375

b = 0.207028454

c = 0.353242157 by Pythagoras

Multiply by ln30 gives

A = 0.973474984

B = 0.704144635

C = 1.2014463 by Pythagoras.

With these values we can create the conceptual Pythagorean grid illustrated graphically on Fig 10.

(Note, bodies orbiting beyond 20π AU are outside the range of the equation and are not represented on the grid, - e.g. Comets, Eris etc.)

Locating the Grid (see fig. 10)

To locate a datum placement point for the grid (Circled on fig. 10), and hence the whole grid, we can use the 'y' value for Mercury and derive the 'x' value from this by putting it through the equation.

From Mercury, the 'y' value is **0.506756171**

Multiply this by ln30 and subtract F.

0.506756171 x ln30 = 1.723577762,

Subtract 0.500772097 = 'x' value is **1.222805665**

These two figures locate a datum point for the grid. (Corner marked with a double circle on fig. 10)

0.506756171 on the 'y' axis and **1.222805665** on the 'x' axis.

So we can produce and place the grid to any degree of accuracy we wish, and I have chosen to use as many decimal places as possible on my calculator.

The entire grid is placed by calculation from the mean orbit of Mercury, which is derived via the exponent from the measured value given in Norton's Star Atlas. Being a measured value it is not an absolute, so we will define it as an absolute.

Note; the grid is defined as being made up of sectors which are in a 'perfect' Pythagorean relationship, though calculation is only taken to nine decimal places.

No actual triangles are visible. Conceptual triangles are implied.

We now have a defined perfect Pythagorean reference grid with which to compare the orbits.

Since we know the 'y' and 'x' values for the datum corner of the grid, (circled) and we know the values of a,b,c and A,B,C we can now *use the grid* to calculate all of the 'y' and 'x' values for the places where the perfect grid projects onto the axes, as accurately as we can. (See fig 10)

This is a simple matter of adding up.

Once we have these 'y' and 'x' values, we can convert them into Astronomical Units by raising them to the relevant inverted exponents **(4π/9)** for the 'y' axis and **(2π/3)** for the 'x' axis.

When we compare the resulting AU values to the table of planets we find that with the sole exception of Saturn, the figures correlate to a very high degree. See **table 3** at end of this chapter, which lists the results I obtained.

Saturn is out by 2.5% (Compared to the measured figure in AU).

The comparison is shown graphically on fig 9, where the only discrepancy visible is that of Saturn, which shows as a double line. All the others are so small they are less than the thickness of the lines, so are not visible.

I cannot change the orbit of Saturn, and there must be a reason for it to be so far out (compared to the others).

However, it is worth noting that the discrepancy is well within Saturn's orbital deviation, the variation between perihelion and aphelion, so twice in its orbit, Saturn complies as accurately as all the rest.

(There are other annotations, P1, P2, P3, and Px marked on fig 10, these are discussed a little later)

*

If I could now just ask you consult table 3 with figs 9 and 10 and to take a minute or two to consider what we have just described, and done.

We have described how we can calculate all the planetary orbits of the Solar System from just a prior knowledge of two, Mercury and Earth.

And of course, I have done these calculations, and so could you, if you had a mind to.

[Note, we can also obtain orbital periods by using the

modified exponents ($2\pi/3$) for the 'y' axis, and (π) for the 'x' axis. Astronomers may observe the built-in functioning of Kepler's third law.]

It is also a fact worth commenting on that the Pythagorean relationship is ubiquitous throughout the Solar System.

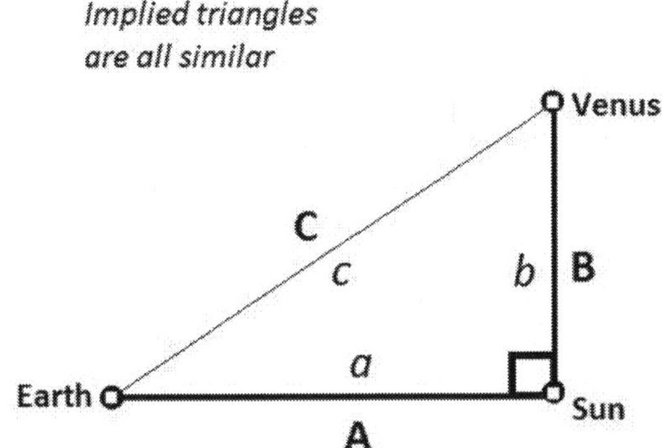

It is worthy of note that 'Pythagoras' implies conceptual triangles, and the triangles are all 'similar' in the geometric meaning of the word, and all are also similar to the triangle formed when 'real space' Venus and Earth form a ninety degree angle at the sun. (Here I refer to calculated figures).

The ratios b/a and B/A, as derived, both equal the measured orbit of Venus in AU to five decimal places, which means that the orbit of Venus in AU is somehow involved in placing all the other orbits.

It is very true that I had a fair amount of 'a priori' knowledge, but it still represents something that should be utterly impossible in a natural System.

It is also possible to relate any orbit to any other, using the grid, thus demonstrating that the planetary orbits of the entire known Solar System are interrelated and integrated into an artificial, Pythagorean, whole.

The real scientifically measured Solar System conforms very closely with this completely artificial Pythagorean construction.

Statistically, there is no chance at all that it could have come about by natural forces.

I rest my case. That is all I wish to say about the order in the system. There is more, but it is trivial in comparison.

If the artificial Stonehenge equation (fig 9) and the artificial Pythagorean grid (fig 10) are not enough to convince people, then nothing else will.

We live in an artificially ordered Solar System - Q.E.D.

There are a couple of other minor points I would like to make before I close this chapter, but the most important matters are completed.

Table 3

Results calculated from Venus Equation

Percentage difference from Norton's figure.

Planet	**Mean AU From Norton's**	**Calculated In Chapter 10**	**Percentage difference**
Mercury	0.3870987	**Datum**	**Not applicable**
Venus	0.7233322	0.723331002	-0.00017%
Earth	1.000	**Datum**	**Not applicable**
Mars	1.5236915	'Y' = 1.52554 'X' = 1.52391	+0.124% +0.0147%
Jupiter	5.2028039	5.195539524	-0.14%
Saturn	9.5388437	9.3020245	-2.5%
Uranus	19.181871	19.22324153	+0.217%
Neptune	30.057924	30.02787608	-0.1%
Pluto	39.439	39.41830763	-0.0525

A Little Exercise Relating to Px

I have marked some other points on the graph which apparently correspond to empty orbits. Points P1, P2 and P3, appear to relate to the asteroid belt, and are rather meaningless.

Point Px is useful to illustrate the functioning of the grid, as an example calculation.

We can find the x axis value of Px by a variety of means, but the simplest is just to add two lots of A + B + C to the 'x' value of the datum corner of the grid, (see above).

This totals to give Px an x axis value of **6.980937489**

We can now do two things with this figure.

1) We can raise it to the inverted exponent ($2\pi/3$) to give a mean orbit of **58.5448... AU.**

2) We can raise it to just (π) to give the orbital period in years as **447.95...years**

This describes the orbital parameters of a hypothetical missing planet, but it does not mean that the orbit is actually occupied by a planet. I have no idea if this planet exists or not, but if astronomers ever discover a planet in that orbit, I will not be surprised. I suspect that it will be at a high inclination to the ecliptic, higher than Pluto.

*

Well, that is it. I have nearly finished all I wanted to say.

There are just a few more chapters to go, which are back to chat, not many more technical details.

If you managed to get through this entire book so far, you can rest now.

If you will, have a look at the summary before reading the last few chapters, while I have another cup of tea.

Summary

1) The major orbits of the Solar System are interrelated by the main equation.

2) The orbits are related by the same equation that relates π to 20π.

3) The orbits can be calculated from Pythagoras.

4) The orbits can be calculated with the use of trigonometry.

5) The implied triangles (a,b,c & A,B,C) are all similar, and similar to a triangle constructed from Venus/Earth mean orbits.

6) Orbits can be calculated by adding and subtracting constants.

7) The exponents of the equation allow orbital distances to be interchanged with orbital periods. The function of Kepler's third law is integral part of the equation.

8) The ratio (b/a) and of course (B/A) is equal to the orbit of Venus in AU but is also *determined by* the orbit of Venus. This is not simply an approximation; it is accurate to five decimal places, and unique.

9) The orbits can be calculated by a number of different routes from any datum orbits. Divergence from

Norton's data will vary very slightly depending on the route taken.

10) The exponents are related one to another and to functions of a circle of circumference 3.

11) The equations are dimensionless, and do not involve gravity or mass, they are totally artificial.

*

Figs 9 & 10 follow.

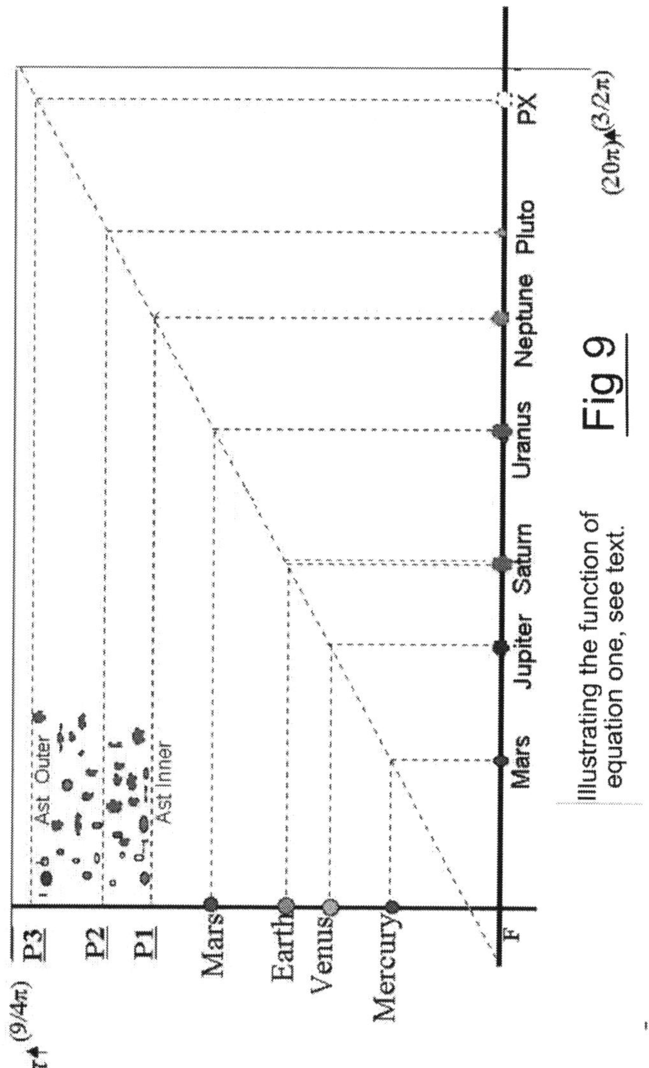

Fig 9

Illustrating the function of equation one, see text.

....

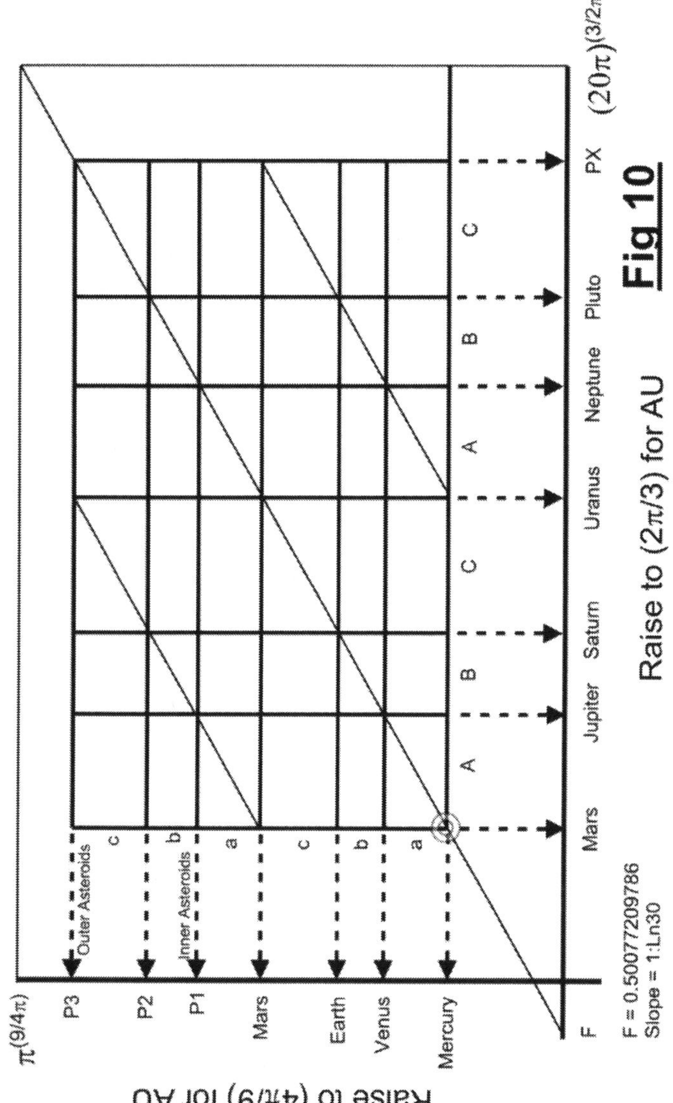
π^(9/4π)
P3
P2
P1
Mars
Earth
Venus
Mercury
F
Outer Asteroids
Inner Asteroids
c
b
a
c
b
a
Mars
A
Jupiter
B
Saturn
C
Uranus
A
Neptune
B
Pluto
C
PX
(20π)^(3/2π)
Raise to (4π/9) for AU
Raise to (2π/3) for AU
F = 0.50077209786
Slope = 1:Ln30

Fig 10

…

Ancient Knowledge

Part Three

Discussion of Implications

First is a reconsideration of the reasoning in part one, followed by a discussion of the implications for some of the sciences.

Chapter Eleven

The Hard Facts of the Matter

I know I have already mentioned it, but I would like to say a few more words about the existing scientific theory known as the 'Nebular Hypothesis' which purports to explain the origin of our Solar System.

The theory was apparently first proposed by a man named Swedenborg in 1734, and supported by Kant in 1755, but its most well-known proponent was an astronomer named Laplace (1749 – 1827).

The theory holds that a cloud of rotating dust and interstellar gas collapsed under gravity to form a disc rotating about the sun.

It is proposed by the hypothesis that as this disc rotated various parts of it coalesced into larger lumps, and gravity caused these larger lumps to collect other material from the dust cloud. This accretion of material by gravity continued until planets formed. The full theory is somewhat more complex, because there are problems with it that need not concern us here. Even for scientists it is not a perfectly understood theory.

This nebular hypothesis is foundational to many other theories, and has been extended out into the cosmos to explain the birth of stars. It has been used to calculate the age of the Earth and the other planets.

The age of the Earth is fundamental to the functioning of Hutton's and Lyell's geological principle known as uniformitarianism, and essential to Darwin's theory of evolution.

It becomes apparent that a great deal of science hangs on the validity of the nebular hypothesis, and it is important that we do not take these matters lightly.

It is obvious that this hypothetical process of planetary formation would not result in the neat Pythagorean arrangement of orbits that we have just seen in the previous chapter and in fig 10 in this book.

It is very clear, very evident, that the Nebular Hypothesis has no explanatory value with respect to this Solar System, and should not be applied to our System, or used to explain our origins.

Astronomers should not continue to promote the hypothesis as if it was a known fact, and any self-respecting professional astronomer with even a small degree of intellectual integrity should acknowledge this.

If it is accepted that the nebular hypothesis fails, then it follows that the calculated age of the Earth (5.5 billion years) is also without foundation, as is the theory of evolution.

By the middle of the 19th century the nebular hypothesis, uniformitarianism, and Darwinian evolution, had all been accepted as satisfactory by the scientific community, taught in our universities and colleges and presented as fact to the general public.

None of these theories have any validity; they all fail in the face of the ordered orbits of chapter ten.

It is for this reason that I maintain that science has been misleading humanity for 150 years.

*

However, it is not enough just to show that science is mistaken, it is also necessary to show that the observed order is explained by intelligent intervention.

I assume that you have been able to follow the mathematics, and are now fully aware of the situation? I used maximum decimal accuracy on the Pythagorean grid calculations because I wanted to show that the relationships are not a product of 'pyramid-ology' or 'numerology', both of which terms will no doubt be used by critics as arguments against the reality of these matters.

I wanted to show that there is no cheating going on, no 'arbitrary approximations' or any other kind of deception.

I have said in a previous chapter that the Elohim are real, and that they are physical. I used anecdotal comments from the Bible as a basis for this assertion, and in that regard I can see a slight problem with the reasoning. The problem is that the scribes who wrote the Bible might have been inventing their stories. Just because the ancient scribes believed in the reality of the Mighty Ones, doesn't mean that we should also believe.

In this chapter I would like to attempt to demonstrate that this reasoning is wrong, or mistaken.

What I would like to do, if you do not object, is to run through the whole thing again, only this time I propose to work the logic backwards.

Instead of starting with the Bible, I propose to start with the astronomical calculations of figs 9 & 10, and work in reverse.

I need to apply a little logic to the situation, and start with the known facts. I propose to engage in reasoning from the facts, and the known laws of physics, to arrive at a rational explanation.

*

The first thing I would like to do is to look at the 'order' a little more closely, to see if there is any possibility that it might be natural after all.

Mathematics is just numbers, and numbers do not make much impression on people. The meaning of the numbers is a matter that only becomes evident if the relationships between them are understood.

Some people tend to inject their own personal prejudices into their evaluation of these things.

If the numbers reflected a natural law, they would be acceptable to science, but if they do not obey natural law, then they would not be acceptable to science. If the numbers we are using describe an artificial structure, science will not be interested.

The situation is akin to the difference between a crystal, the form of which reflects natural law, and a domestic building, which may look similar to a crystal, but does not reflect natural law except in regard to the structural load calculations, etc.

In both cases it is possible to generate a system of related numbers. The one case is 'natural' and acceptable as reflecting natural law; the other is man-made, artificial, and not acceptable.

A building may be any shape or size, determined by the designer, there is nothing in natural law that will predict the shape of the designers finished product. A crystal, on the other hand, can only take on one of the few forms permitted by its molecular structure.

So one possible way to determine if a regular structure is the result of intelligent design or natural law; is to see what degree of freedom is exhibited by the structure.

I am claiming that the mathematics we are dealing with in these pages falls into the second category. I am stating that it is not in accord with natural law, as defined by scientists.

What this means is that scientists will never be able to explain it. It is something that comes more under the jurisdiction of an architect than a physicist.

*

It is an important matter, and worth taking some time over. We need to be certain that these things are correct, not just the calculations but the reasoning that derives from those calculations. If I can show a significant error in the calculations or false reasoning in the logic, then it is as well to make such a mistake known.

As far as the calculations are concerned, all I can say is that they have been checked and rechecked so many times that it is highly unlikely that any error could have survived undetected. The lower order decimal digits can vary depending on the route the calculation follows, and this is to be expected and means very little. The last decimal place represents a couple of hundred yards/metres on the scale of the Solar System.

That leaves only the logic and the reasoning, and it is up to you to determine if my logic is rational or defective, you are the judge in these matters.

*

One thing that many people do not notice is that the equation and the graphs are ‘dimensionless’. This means that they do not need measures like centimetres or miles or kilometres. They operate with just numbers, which can be described as ‘dimensionless’ quantities. Nor do they involve any natural forces like ‘gravity’ or ‘mass’.

I have used Astronomical Units for measurement, and referred the equation to astronomical orbits, but the equation is not ‘tied’ to the Solar System, or AU, or any other form of measuring units.

It will work just as well on other objects on other scales, if they are placed in the right order. Just like the Stonehenge peg-and-string model, the math is ratiometric. It works on any scale.

Since I mention Stonehenge, might I remind you at this stage that the ‘y’ scale of the graphs is a direct one-to-one comparison with the inner monument features, and the ‘x’ scale is the same for the outer features. These graphs that we now have floating in space are mathematically identical with that old monument.

*

To continue with what I was saying. We could place objects on a table in the same order as the planets, and the equation would relate them just the same. All it needs is for one point to be set at ‘unity’ in whatever measuring system is used. It follows that the equation is not dependent on any particular scale. It would work with feet, miles, anything.

The whole equation is relative to the point that has been set at 'unity'; the calculation then works from that point, and in terms of the Solar System that point and that 'unity' is the notional mean orbit of planet Earth.

For the equation to work in AU is rather odd really, since it was human astronomers who decided to use the Earth's mean orbit as a measure of distances within the Solar System. One Astronomical Unit is a human invention, devised because we just happened to live on Planet Earth. It seems that the antediluvians used the same measure, as did the designers of the Solar System. That is why I say that they ordered the orbits *relative to the Earth.*

*

Although we can use AU to measure the orbits, the equation itself works with just numbers, empty spaces, and empty orbits. There is nothing in the equation to suggest that a planet must occupy the predicted orbit. Take Px for example. I calculated the orbit in the last chapter, but there is nothing to say that there has to be a planet there.

The same could be said for all the other planets. The orbits calculated could all have been empty. There is no reason to suppose that Mars should exist, just because we calculated its orbit.

If we wished, if we were able, we could draw out the whole calculated result on a totally empty volume of space. There would be no argument then, the drawing is clearly artificial.

It is easier to follow if we draw it on paper, and I have done this in figs 9 & 10. Note that the equation and the graphs work on a small scale on paper just as effectively as they do in AU.

Let us make no mistake, in the cold hard light of day, the equation and the graphs are dimensionless artificial constructs that describe the relationships between empty 'number slots', with lower limits determined by the offset and zero, while the upper limits are $\pi^{(9/4\pi)}$ and $(20\pi)^{(3/2\pi)}$, and we should note that both of these limits are themselves dimensionless.

We put dimensionless numbers in, and we draw it on paper, or we could mark it out to a larger scale on a table top, or set it out on an even larger scale with marks on the turf in a grassy field, or we can draw it really huge and (conceptually) put it in space.

We see our graph as just numbers; there are no objects or planets in it.

We are talking about an abstract mathematical pattern, not solid objects that interact.

There is no argument possible regarding the equation and the number range used by it, it is an abstract mathematical pattern and unambiguously artificial.

Design your own Solar System.

If we imagine fig 9 or 10 without any planets marked on it, without the vertical and horizontal dotted lines, just as a blank graph with nothing on it but the sloping graph line, then that will suffice to represent the 'empty' equation, and you can use that empty equation graph as a starting point for designing your very own Solar System.

You can mark as many points as you wish on one of the axes, and they will be reflected on the other, according to the working of the equation.

If you wish to design a random Solar System, you will find it is not possible. Random systems, and a System with only one planet, are the only Systems you cannot design using the equation.

The reason is simple; if you want to have a random solar system you can place a random set of points on the 'x' axis. You can put them there, but they will be reflected on the 'y' axis, and vice versa, so the total will not be random.

If you only put one point on one axis, it will be reflected on the other axis, so you will have two.

You cannot make a totally random system; if you use the equation you automatically produce a simple kind of order. The only way to produce a random Solar System is by not using the equation.

If you should wish to try to design your own Solar System I have included a 'blank' (Fig 10b) for that purpose. You should avoid going near the offset area, that is negative space-time and nobody knows what happens in there.

You can put a point on either axis, and draw the lines to project it onto the other axis. Or you can use the equation to calculate where the second point should go.

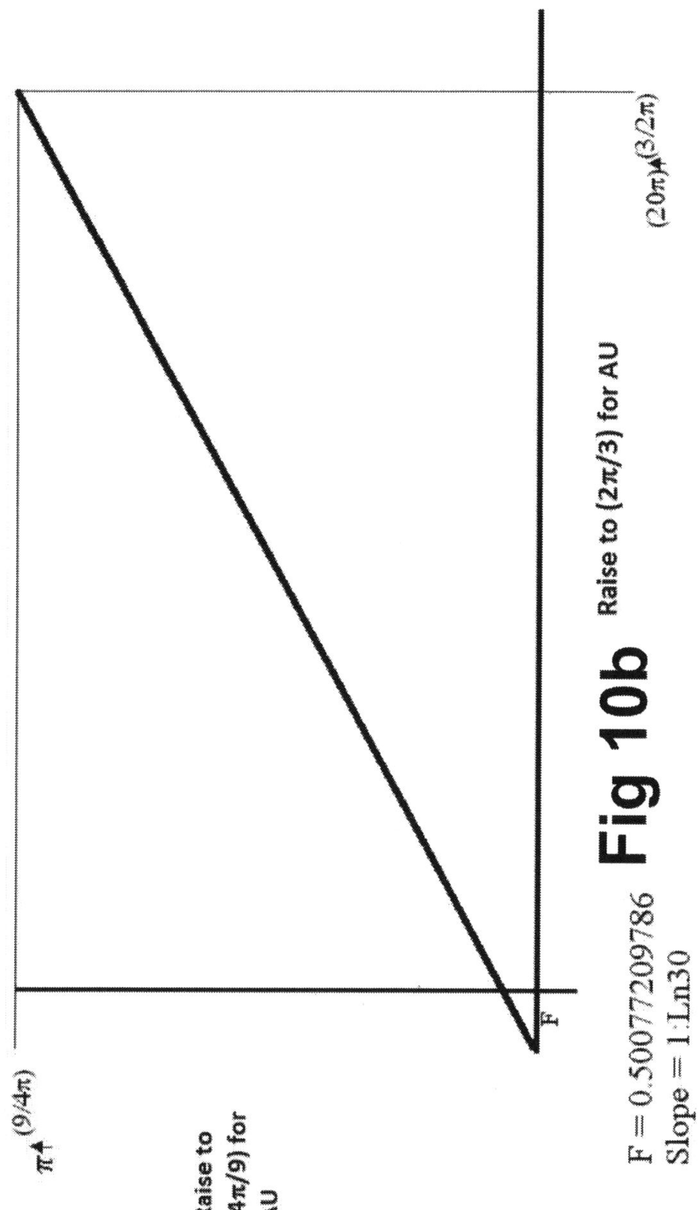
π↑(9/4π)
Raise to (4π/9) for AU
F
(20π)↑(3/2π)
Raise to (2π/3) for AU
F = 0.50077209786
Slope = 1:Ln30

Fig 10b

Perhaps you might like to put your selected points in a more complex specific order, for example you might decide to place them such that they are all equally spaced. The order will be reflected on the other axis.

You could go further and start to show off a bit of mathematical skill. You could devise a complex repeating Pythagorean pattern, and introduce quite a few interesting mathematical curiosities, and put the whole artificially contrived pattern of points and lines onto the original blank.

You could design a layout of points as complex or as simple as you like. It would still be a design, it would be abstract, and it would not be real.

You would still be working on paper.

So let us assume you have drawn out a totally artificial abstract design on paper, one of your own designs, but without the names of planets marked on it.

The next stage is to provide some way of projecting this artificially contrived pattern onto the empty space around our sun, and if you could do that little thing, marking your design in space, perhaps with fictional lasers, it would still be an artificial abstract design.

Now it gets a little more complicated because the graph axes scales on figs. 9 & 10 are linear scales produced after the exponents have been applied, and the same must apply to your design.

So now that you have your abstract design, and you know the numbers, you need to back-calculate with the inverted, artificial, exponents to expand the design into real space, and find where to put the 'real' orbits.

But even after you have calculated all the 'real' orbits from the design, you are still dealing with an abstract, because so far the 'real' orbits are all just empty 'number slots', empty regions of space.

You could do all that yourself, in concept, on paper. You could design your own Solar System using a blank graph like fig 10b if you wished. You could even do the calculations to expand it into real space, or at least obtain the numbers, the orbital values in AU.

What you could not do, because you do not have the power, is to put real planets into the calculated orbits.

To finalise the design you need to put real planets into the number slots, and this is where it would be possible to make a mistake. If you miss the number slot, the planet would still be in orbit, but it would not exactly match your designed point. Saturn is an example of such a miss.

Having established the planets, you could perhaps decorate the finished product with an asteroid belt. You could even leave an original pre-existing cloud of comets in the outer reaches, beyond the limits of the equation. (Bank and ditch on the monument) Garnish the whole thing with a light sprinkling of wayward meteors, and the job is done.

As mentioned above, there is no physical law that states that planets must exist at all; far less is there any law that says they must conform to an artificially contrived order. Yet they do.

All the above, 'design you own Solar System', is not just for fun, it is a test to see if there is freedom of design, or if there are constraints placed by natural law. I suspect that you came up with a different design than anyone else. Your design would be unique.

One thing you may have noticed is that I left the existing exponents and offset, and the same slope. I did not change the equation. There appears to be a large degree of design freedom within the existing equation, but you could produce a different pair of exponents, and a different slope and offset, to really design your own Solar System.

If you have enough understanding of mathematics it is possible that you could produce a wide variety of artificial designs, and the only natural constraints are those of mutual gravitational attraction and the possibility of collisions. Perhaps it would be best to keep your orbits fairly widely spaced apart.

The conclusion has to be that the real Solar System is just as much the product of design as yours is.

The Solar System order does not conform to any natural law, and does not need to. The equation graph reveals an artificial abstract design, and the planets have been moved to comply with the requirements of that design.

*

Just to reinforce that conclusion, there are one or two quirky little mathematical curiosities in the array, the 'Equation for Venus' is one of them.

I am not proposing to go into any more mathematics here, enough is enough, but mathematicians might find it interesting to note that a point corresponding to Mars appears on both axes, and also that the Mars point on the 'x' axes relates to a point corresponding to Mercury, and the Mars point on the 'y' axis relates to a point corresponding to Uranus. Both these Mars points when processed through the relevant inverted exponents yield approximately the same numerical value for the mean orbit of the planet Mars in AU.

We can see from this that the mean orbit of Mars in AU closely relates to both Mercury and Uranus, so it follows that there must be an expression that relates Mercury directly to Uranus.

Couple that with the results of the Equation for Venus, which involves the Mercury point, and produces, via Pythagoras, the Mars 'y' point. (Note I use the term 'point' rather than 'orbit' as I refer to abstract mathematical arrangements.) It can get very intricate, and very interesting, and for every little quirky calculation there is another reason for saying it is artificial.

Here is a challenge for you; if you attempt your own design you might try to produce one that is more intricate and ingenious than the real one? That will give you a feel for just how artificial our System really is.

I would love to go into these things in more detail, but this is not a math book, so we will leave the mathematics for now.

*

If scientists wanted to construct a natural law that would produce such a varied range of relationships it would have to be such a convoluted and contrived 'natural' law, that should it ever be proposed, we would be fully justified in accusing such a law of being itself 'artificial'.

*

Let me just repeat, that there can be no doubt that the Solar System is closely in accord with an intricate and very clever abstract mathematical design. There can be no doubt that it is artificially ordered.

The conclusion has to be that we live in an artificially ordered Solar System.

Now we need to answer the question ‘who or what ordered it?’

*

It is conventional wisdom to suggest that the One True Creator God; or the ‘Big Bang’, created the Solar System, along with the Universe.

Perhaps we should examine that possibility before we jump to conclusions.

It could be argued that if the Infinite and Omnipotent One True God had put the planets in order, He would not have left the small error in the placement of Saturn. In other areas where the One True God is credited with creation, for example in subatomic physics, atoms and molecules, He is very precise in His work.

It is the same in the Solar System, the One True God makes the laws of gravity that all the planets are subject to, and these laws are accurate and applicable across the whole Universe and for all of time.

We have to rule out the possibility that the One True God put the planets into the order that we see, because although the abstract designed order is precise, we see that the actual placing of the planets is not precise enough.

If this argument is acceptable, we could extend it to any possible claims that the ‘Spiritual Angels’ did the work. The same argument would apply, from the viewpoint of the Perfect Infallible One True God, the work must surely appear to be defective and faulty, and the One True God would not accept such slapdash and shoddy workmanship.

To say this in a more prosaic way, natural law allows for no exceptions. If there is an exception, such as Saturn, then we cannot appeal to natural law.

We may consider that this is true, but the discrepancies are so small in all cases that they cannot affect our determination that the system is artificially ordered. Even Saturn is a 'direct hit'; it just misses the bull's-eye by a small amount, which it would not do if it was placed by natural law, or placed by a One True Creator God.

There is also the previously noted comment that the One True God would lack a motive for installing such order in the Solar System.

I have tried to conceive of a motive, but have been unable to do so. Perhaps someone holier than I am might find a suitable motive.

*

There is a difference between the notions of 'Creating' and 'creating order'.

It is probable that we can assign the job of 'Creating' to the One True God, or to the 'Big Bang', such that the original primal Solar System was in accord with scientific natural law. (See below)

But that was long, long ago, millions of years in the Solar System's past.

In these modern days the same planets are no longer orbiting in accord with the primal natural law, but match very closely with a very un-natural mathematical scheme.

If the current order is not due to a One True God, or natural law, or the Big Bang, and if the odds against it happening by chance are impossibly huge, then by a simple process of elimination, we are left with intelligent intervention.

We have nothing else left; we must assign the task of 'creating order' to intelligent intervention.

By intelligent intervention I mean someone physical and therefore fallible. Entities that are 'spiritual' or non-physical, are assumed to be infallible, and do not make mistakes like the discrepancy on Saturn.

This means we are left with only one possible answer, the work on the Solar System was carried out by very powerful, but fallible, 'almost gods'.

In other words; the work was done by physical entities of some kind, perhaps super-powerful 'aliens'.

It sounds incredible, unbelievable, insane, but it is the only alternative to shrugging the shoulders and walking away, muttering obscenities about mysteries.

*

So if you have not discarded this book and wandered off in disgust, we need to continue with our analysis.

We have deduced that the orbits were ordered by powerful but fallible, and therefore physical, 'entities'. For want of a better description we call them 'gods' with a small 'g'.

These 'gods' must have come from somewhere, since the Solar System could only have been ordered by an outside agency.

It would be easier to accept that possibility if we could also accept that the Universe, and in particular, this Galaxy, contains life that is far older and wiser than our own human life.

We humans have been developing science and technology in a modern sense for, at most, just two-hundred years. It is within the realms of possibility to suspect that far away in the heart of the Galaxy there are beings that have been practicing science for millions of years, or even billions of years.

It takes time to develop technology, and aliens who have been doing research for millions of years would be so far advanced that we could well regard them as 'gods'.

In that kind of time span they could have solved all the problems that we deem to be impossible. They could well have solved problems like immortality, health, faster than light travel, faster than light communications, how to move planets, and lots more. We humans do not have the ability to move planets, so it is clear that the power that did it to our Solar System was from somewhere else, and we can only assume they were from a very ancient civilization.

It also follows that in order to move all the planets, the gods would need somewhere to stand and watch. They would not likely wish to be on a planet while it is being moved, I would not have thought. The essential need that springs to mind is that they would have a spacecraft of some kind. This would be needed in order to get here, and would also serve as a base while the changes are being made to our System.

*

The next question to consider is whether or not our system is the only one that ever got changed?

It doesn't seem to be very efficient for the gods to come all the way to here, and pick on this system as the only one. It would make more sense to suggest that we were just one of many. If we accept that we are just one of many, then it would follow that the gods must be engaged in touring the Galaxy looking for suitable Solar Systems to change.

And why would they do that?

They must have had a reason. They expended an awful lot of energy and time to do such work on our system, so we must assume that they were highly motivated.

I would like to suggest that they would do that for the same reasons that our early explorers set out in sailing ships to start new colonies in new lands. When our explorers found a new land; they raised the flag to show who owned the territory. Shortly thereafter, they would establish a colony.

All life-forms reproduce and multiply, and over time any population will run out of living space, or food, or both. If the 'gods' are from a very ancient star-system, from a very ancient race, they must have long ago spread out from their home planet to explore and colonise other stellar systems.

If these mighty gods are expanding an empire, looking for new 'lands' to start a new colony, and establish ownership, as it were 'plant their flag' with the equation coded into the orbits, then they would only be doing on a grand scale what we humans have often done on a merely global scale.

The notion that a very ancient and highly developed intelligent civilization might wish to expand an empire would satisfy the need for a motive.

*

The next obvious question to spring to mind is 'where are the colonists'?

If they are setting up a colony, there should be colonists in the system somewhere, surely?

This question ties in with the further question about when these changes were made. We could assume that the system has always been ordered; right from the start, but that would run us into problems.

We have to accept the scientific assertion that many of the rocks that make-up the Earth's crusts are millions of years old. We might not necessarily appreciate what scientists say, but they are not always wrong. If we maintain that the order was placed at the very beginning, before life and the dinosaurs evolved, we would then have to accept that these 'gods' waited for billions of years before establishing their colony, because there is no sign of non-human highly intelligent life in the fossil record. (That is, according to paleoanthropologists).

It is far more likely that the Solar System pre-existed the ordering of the orbits as a naturally occurring random system. We may accept that previously it was as science would wish it.

We could postulate that to start with there was a Solar System created by the Nebular Hypothesis, or the One True God, or natural law. This System had the same planets but in naturally random orbits, perhaps with the Earth nearer the sun. The early Earth might have been a hot tropical paradise full of fierce carnivorous dinosaurs and such.

Millions of years would have passed with the Solar System in this original natural state. The Earth would have remained in that state, in that orbit, whatever it was, accumulating all the evidences of ancient life, and evolution, for as long as is required.

*

Then one day not so very long ago in cosmic terms, the gods came and set to work, they moved the planets, putting them into the order we see today.

The ordering of the orbits took place before we humans came into existence, because it is fairly self-evident that the energies used to move planets would have wiped out most, if not all, of the life on the surface, including us, had we been here at the time.

Planets are best moved by speeding them up or slowing them down, so as to persuade them to change orbits, and this is likely to take rather a long time and involve the expenditure of a lot of energy. It also runs the risk of unintended collisions, so needs to be done with a lot of advance planning and great care.

Once that work was completed the gods could start their colony almost straight away, after a relatively short settling time.

For maximum efficiency, it would be most likely that the colony would be established as soon as possible after the re-establishment of a viable ecosystem.

So we might ask again; where is the colony?

If we are looking for colonial settlers, we need to look for intelligent beings who are relative newcomers, living on one of the planets of the solar system.

Humanity has explored the Solar System, and we are the only intelligent life anywhere in it, as far as we know (apart from the elusive gods).

If there are any colonial settlers here, where are they?

The only reasonable answer is - we humans are the colonial settlers.

*

We do not live long enough to travel between the stars, and it is clear that the 'gods' do. So there is a distinct difference between us and the supposed colonial force. We would be hard pressed to say that we are the biological children of these 'gods', we do not share their evident and necessary longevity.

It is possible that fecundity amongst the gods is low, by deliberate choice. Alternatively, if they in fact have children, would they maroon their own kids on a frontier planet? It is possible but it seems unlikely, highly intelligent life would be expected to be lovingly protective of its young.

However, there are no such emotional attachments to clones.

They could clone themselves, and use the clones to establish a presence on the frontier planet.

Clones would do the job of colonisation just as well. The clones would carry the god's genetic makeup in their own body cells, copies of the DNA slightly altered to shorten life expectation.

The gods could place cloned versions of the entire crew, or perhaps from frozen samples taken from back home, from many members of their race, onto the surface of the new Earth.

They would need to nurture and protect the clones for a while, instruct them in rudimentary survival techniques, teach them about the wild animals, and show them how to make clothing.

When the clones are deemed to be ready, they would be told to go forth and multiply, not that they would need much instruction in that regard.

After that, the 'gods' would just have to leave a skeleton crew here to keep an eye on progress, while the main party moves on to pastures new.

Those left behind would keep a very low profile, waiting until the clones are mature enough to read the message in their Solar System, and desire to make contact with their colonial 'grandparents'.

Mind, the Gap

There is another rather obscure argument that I would like to explore concerning relative intelligence levels. I am not going to argue about what constitutes intelligence, it is easy to define, it means being intelligent enough to know what the word 'intelligent' means.

I would include all modern humans in this definition, of whatever intellect, even if they are not smarter than the average, even if as individuals they are not able to understand the math. I am not being elitist here, all humans fall into the category of 'high intelligence' as far as this book is concerned, and that includes you.

If pushed, I would even include politicians in the definition of 'intelligent', because some of them can actually read.

*

In the category of intelligence I would list the following:-

1) We have observed that Stonehenge was not built by Neolithic man, or modern man. It follows that another intellect designed it, an intellect that is not recognised by historians or scientists. We will call this intellect **'antediluvian'**.

2) We have also determined that the Solar System is intelligently ordered, and since that could not have been done by modern human or by any previously existing or antediluvian human, we must assume it was done by another intellect, which we call '**Elohim**'.

3) We can also perceive that the Monument and the Solar System designs were both elucidated and understood by yet a third intellect. That means you, and you are what we may call '**Human**'.

In the above short list we can see that there are three different intellects at work, antediluvian, Elohim, and Human.

Antediluvian mankind preceded modern man, and as far as I know there are no true antediluvians left, but for the purposes of this discussion I will refer to them as if they were still around, as if they are still capable of thought.

I would point to the fact that the level of intelligence of antediluvian man can be roughly gauged by the degree of ingenuity and knowledge of astronomy incorporated into the ground-plan of Stonehenge.

The knowledge incorporated into it is, in some respects, greater than that of modern science, in that it directs us to the order in the Solar System, which modern astronomy knows nothing about, prior to this book.

We may estimate that the intelligence exhibited by antediluvian man was evidently on a par with our own, or greater. They understood exponential math, and geometry, and the level of astronomical knowledge about the Solar System was certainly in advance of ours.

The level of intelligence of the Elohim can be similarly gauged by the degree of ingenuity incorporated into the math of the Solar System. This is evidently very high, but must be magnified by the assessment of the power and technology evidenced in the bringing of the design into practical reality. We might also assume the math has been 'dumbed-down' for our benefit; Pythagoras is pretty basic, and was probably deliberately included to make it easier for us to recognise the artificial nature of the system.

Of these three intellects listed above, it is obvious that the highest level is without doubt that of the Elohim, with the antediluvians and modern humanity running for second place.

I do not suggest for one minute that antediluvians and modern humans are anywhere near to the Elohim in levels of intellect, but that *all three are of the same 'kind' of intelligence.*

For example, it is evident that both modern humanity and the antediluvians are capable of understanding the Elohim mathematics. When I first encountered Stonehenge, it seemed to be alien in nature, but that was just me being dim, and the feeling didn't last long. I needed to learn, and after a while the mathematics began to make sense. I could understand it, and I could also understand the Elohim design of the Solar System, which is the point I am trying to make here.

In this respect all three minds share the same *kind* of intellect. We all have something in common.

We all three speak the same mathematical language, we share the same sense of logic, and that must mean that we share similar thought processes, which in turn means we all have the same kind of mind and a similar kind of brain.

This leads us to make a very important and meaningful observation.

All three intellects listed above are separated from the evolved life on Earth by a very wide margin, a gap so huge that it is not really possible to bridge with evolutionary arguments.

This observation firmly places humanity into the same category as antediluvians and Elohim, and clearly demonstrates that we are not of Earth. It means that we three are all related, all kinfolk; we are of the same kind; we are of the same family. The antediluvians are our long-lost elder brothers, the Elohim our ancestral parents, and we are on the way home.

*

There is a belief, prevalent amongst people who think that we evolved, that intelligence must have evolved fairly often in the Galaxy. Evolutionists assume this to be true, as do supporters of SETI and the 'Drake equation'.

I believe the assumption they make to be over-optimistic and totally unjustified. It is not supported by reason, and certainly not by observation.

Evolutionists seem to assume that the development of intelligent life is inevitable, the unavoidable culmination of millions of years of evolution.

According to science life began in the pre-Cambrian period of geological history, about 540 million years ago. Since that time there must have been uncounted billions of different species on Earth. Current estimates for species alive today range from 8 million to 100 million, nobody really knows. Ancient life is not available to be counted, so we can only guess at the total numbers of species that have ever lived on this planet, and either evolved or gone extinct.

We may observe that of all those uncounted billions of species none of them were known for their intelligence. For half a billion years this planet full of life managed to get along without any intelligence on it at all, beyond that of dinosaurs and small squirrels. (According to evolutionists)

The standard normal product of half a billion years of evolution is therefore observed to be one hundred per cent *non-intelligent* life.

*

Evolutionists would argue that one evolutionary line did succeed in producing intelligence, meaning humanity, (I would deny this, we did not evolve) thus proving it can happen, and can therefore happen again.

It is a well-known mathematical fact that we cannot legitimately derive 'odds' from a single occurrence of a phenomenon. To establish any viable estimate of probability we would need to wait until highly intelligent life evolves a second or third time, perhaps from hedgehogs or bats.

It is not practical to wait that long, but we can say with some confidence that if we did, the resulting probability figure is not likely to be encouraging for those optimists who would like intelligence to evolve more frequently than is actually observed (sic).

*

In counter-argument, scientists could draw up a table of escalating levels of 'intelligence' that operates by a different definition than mine. The list would have dolphins at the top, second in intelligence to humanity.

Can we imagine the nature of an intellectual conversation between a dolphin and its human trainer?

Trainer, "Would you jump through this hoop please."

Dolphin, "Give me a fish."

Trainer, "I don't have any fish."

Dolphin, “Sod off then.”

We conclude that there is no actual evolutionary need for high intelligence. The survival of millions of unintelligent species adequately demonstrates that conclusion. The slugs in my garden are not intelligent, but they survive and flourish despite the huge amount of money I spend on slug-poison pellets, and they always appear be fat and healthy, and to live very happy and fulfilling lives.

This observation also highlights the profound difference between the ‘normal’ evolved low intelligence range, and the capabilities of ‘high intelligence.’

All species on Earth possess a rudimentary intelligence that is just sufficient to enable the species to survive. Clearly they would not survive if they did not.

High intelligence is the sole exception to that rule. High intelligence has far more capabilities than is required for survival on Earth.

Humanity could survive with the same intelligence level as an orang-utan or a gorilla. This observation has been made by many others, but it is worth repeating. We did not evolve the high level mental abilities that we possess by any evolutionary need.

High intelligence is fundamentally different from evolved intelligence, and there appears to be a large hiatus between evolved animals and high intelligence, a gap that is not filled or explained by any evolutionary mechanism that makes any sense.

If we consider that list with the dolphin at the top, the list of escalating mental capabilities, say from mice upwards, we would find fairly regular low level differences and similarities between species that gradually increase as we get up to cats and dogs and elephants and dolphins.

Then there is a huge, truly vast, enormous gap between the dolphin and the three intelligent entities at the very top, human, antediluvian, and Elohim.

Human intelligence does not fit the pattern of the evolution of life on Earth, which has been one hundred per cent non-intelligent for half a billion years.

Judged solely by the nature of our intellectual capabilities, we humans are much closer to the Elohim than we are to apes or dolphins.

*

Until high-intelligence happens again, we cannot allocate a meaningful probability figure, other than to say it is immeasurably or incalculably minute. In that perspective, highly intelligent life may only have evolved once in the history of this Galaxy; there are probably not enough suitable planets for such a rare chance event as high-intelligence to be more frequent.

This would appear to mean that there is only one intelligent species in the Galaxy. Such is the conclusion we must arrive at if we accept the reasoning of science.

*

The only sensible and intelligent conclusion I can come to is one that says we did not evolve, not here on this planet, anyway. If we did not evolve in this uniquely ordered system, then we must have originated in some other way – we were put here, we are clones of the Elohim.

That claim would raise yet another problem with science. If we are cloned, then what about the primitive ape ancestors that scientists keep finding? What about Cro-Magnon and Homo erectus and other primitive predecessors to humankind?

We will discuss these in the next chapter.

*

The Elohim must exist, because someone put our planets in order, and it wasn't us humans.

The Elohim may have evolved long, long ago on a planet circling a very old star, in a solar system that was not ordered, and they may have done so in the same manner that science believes humans evolved.

If they did, they were highly likely to be the only intelligent creatures ever to evolve by pure chance in this Galaxy.

If we accept that the Galaxy was once empty of evolved intelligent life, apart from the Elohim, then we have a good motive for what they are doing.

They are filling the otherwise empty Galaxy with intelligent life, and we are a part of that grand project. This conclusion is no different from the equally valid suggestion that they are expanding an empire by colonisation; it is saying the same thing in different words.

Since they are the only highly intelligent life to have evolved, we could not have come from anywhere else; we must be derived from them. Again, the conclusion is that we humans are clones of the 'gods' which we have been calling 'Elohim'.

We can go further and instead of using the term 'clone', we can use the word 'human' and say that the Elohim are spreading humankind throughout the Galaxy.

*

If the Galaxy is full of humans and Elohim, surely they must be detectable? Why do we not detect their radio? SETI spend millions listening for radio messages, and have heard nothing.

Radio is not much use for communicating between the far flung reaches of a Galactic Empire, it is far too slow. We may suppose that only newly established 'frontier' planets like ours would use radio.

In order to communicate between stellar systems across many light-years of space they would need to have some other form of transmitting information, a means that we cannot detect.

Einstein maintains that there is no way of communicating information faster than the speed of light, but perhaps the Elohim don't know that.

Colonies established before ours would probably be using a faster and better way of communicating.

A picture that emerges from all this deduction is one in which there is a Galaxy buzzing with intelligent life, but we are not aware of it, it is invisible to us because it is undetectable by our level of technology.

It is invisible until we apply the exponents to the orbits, and open our eyes and our minds and look at the neat order in the Solar System, and then we can see that all these things could well be true.

*

Let us return to the question of why they would go to all the trouble of ordering the orbits. Why, apart from the flag-planting possibility, do they not leave the orbits in their original natural places? I have discussed this elsewhere, and see no need to repeat all the argument here, beyond reminding you that it serves as a first-contact message.

If intelligence is really so rare, as discussed above, then that would obviously remove the need for any suggested 'no trespassing' sign, there would be no 'others', no trespassers, to worry about.

All that is left is the 'first-contact' message.

The 'first-contact message' is actually quite a reasonable suggestion, given that sooner or later the contact has to happen.

Once we clones, we humans, discover the hard facts about the orbits of the Solar System, we would not rest until contact had been made. It is built into our human nature.

At some stage, the clones would have to become like their progenitors, they would have to become 'Elohim' themselves, or at least quite a few would, in order to complete the colonial program.

There are two possibilities here.

The colonists could be left to develop on their own until they had advanced to the point where they would be indistinguishable from the original Elohim. This could take a few million more years, if we do not exterminate ourselves first.

If this scenario is applied then there would be no point in leaving a first-contact message, no point in ordering the orbits.

Or, since we, the colonizers, all carry a slightly altered version of the Elohim DNA, it would possibly be just a simple matter for the Mighty Ones to convert that DNA back to the original code, and thus change us from clones into actual immortal Elohim.

I prefer this latter suggestion, because it explains the motive for a first-contact message, a motive for an ordered system, much better than any other hypothesis.

They are telling us about themselves by means of the order in the system, not just because it is interesting or nice to know, but because we have a ***need*** to know.

The Earth ends up as a full member of the Galactic Empire, with its own breed of Mighty Ones going off into space to establish yet more colonies elsewhere, and again create man in their own image.

The Galaxy is a big place, and to fill it with intelligent life is a major undertaking, a worthy undertaking for physical 'gods' who live for ever.

*

We must also address the question of how long ago this 'ordering of the orbits' took place.

If we accept that as clones we did not evolve, we came 'ready-made' as it were, then we would have by-passed the millions of years scientists would say it took for us to develop. It is therefore possible that the ordering could have occurred a relatively short time ago, in geological terms. It is probably a period counted in thousands rather than millions of years.

It most probably happened not long before the early parts of the book of Genesis, because the people from those times plainly had some dim memory of stories of the Elohim and these events, or they could not have been written down.

One of the problems with trying to establish a date arises from the fact that accepted history is a little out of step with the events that I have been dealing with. Stonehenge really does contain sophisticated scientific knowledge, and that could only have come about if there was an advanced civilization, now destroyed. I cannot reconstruct dates when accepted history simply denies the facts.

I am not going to speculate further about dates for the ordering of the system beyond saying that it would predate the appearance of antediluvian man, by a short time period. Mankind did not exist when it happened, but we came into being very shortly afterwards. Allow time for a few trees to grow.

*

I must apologise again, I am sorry but I cannot think of any other scenario that will fit the facts of an artificially ordered Solar System and a real Babel. It would seem that my earlier conclusions still stand.

The strange thing about this is that I really haven't based my deductions in this chapter on anything said in the Bible. It is a logical progression starting from the fact of order in the orbits, yet I end up with a very similar account to the Biblical one.

*

The Earth had been put through a traumatic experience during the process of ordering the System, and when the young inexperienced clones were first released onto the surface of the new Earth, they needed the help of the 'gods'.

The clones, which I have come to refer to as 'antediluvians', remembered the 'gods' and called them Elohim, or Mighty Ones.

The first men made notes, those notes have survived for thousands of years and come down to us as the Genesis story, much garbled and confused, and redacted by later pious editors, but the pith of the story remains.

During the antediluvian period the people developed astronomy, they investigated the Elohim, found evidence of an ordered Solar System, drew up designs, and after the flood that destroyed their world, the survivors decided to build a huge monument to preserve and pass on the knowledge they had gained about the Elohim gods, so that future generations should be both warned and informed.

And this is where you and I come into the story.

*

I am forced by my own logic to concede that the Genesis story is correct. My elderly lady visitors were right. We should all read the Bible; it tells us the literal truth about our origins.

Strangely, the truth that emerges is not one to inspire religion.

*

At the end of the day, after due consideration of the hard facts of the matter, the Solar System remains artificially ordered, and the logical train of thought that follows from that fact appears to confirm the tattered remnants of the Genesis story.

The story of the Tower of Babel, and Stonehenge, are fully vindicated.

Does that take the biscuit? Have some more tea.

Chapter Twelve

Such a little change.

I would like to be very lucid, crystal clear, about something that is extremely important. The mathematical fact of order in the orbits is not simply a minor difficulty for science; it undermines the very foundation of science.

Science, in all its varied disciplines, relies entirely on everything in the universe being subject to natural laws. It is one of the main tasks of science, perhaps the only task, to elucidate these laws, and describe the functioning of nature in terms of those laws.

If it is ever shown that some aspect of the universe is ordered without regard to any natural law, if things can happen without law, without natural cause, then the whole fabric of science is shredded.

To an astronomer looking at the Solar System, it all looks natural. Once the exponents are applied, it suddenly becomes very artificial. The problem is; what else in the universe might exhibit the same kind of transformation if looked at more closely?

We do not know, and neither does science. Nothing can be relied on to be entirely natural.

Thus it is with the Solar System and the mathematics in chapter ten, it may be just the artificial tip of an artificial iceberg. It is not simply a trivial nuisance or an interesting diversion for science; it is a death sentence for science.

Unless science can explain the order in the orbits in terms of natural law, and only in terms of natural law, then science has no future, but it will not be the ordered orbits or the Elohim or anything else in this book that will bring an end to science, it will be the scientific method itself that will destroy science.

However, at this time, science does not know that it has no future, so it will continue with its work of unintentional deception.

It is not something to gloat about; and there is no individual to blame. The fault, if there is one, lies with the system of isolating the different disciplines. There appears to be no overall 'consolidation' of all the different sciences, so that evolutionists will not be familiar with astronomy, or archaeology, and vice versa. Not only this, but there is a deep seated conviction that there is no value in any truth other than that presented by the scientific establishment.

The self-appointed purpose of science is to understand and explain the world around us in terms that do not involve the supernatural. We might like to observe that the Elohim are not supernatural, they are physical entities that are far in advance of modern science.

If scientists had the audacity they could make the Elohim the subject of study. Science could study the Mighty Ones and their works in the same way that they study other things, but they would first have to recognise the reality of these superior beings.

This planet was specifically refurbished to provide a home for interstellar colonists, for us. We are supposed to live on it and develop in a natural manner, without constantly looking over our shoulders for the watching masters. Obviously, the world must appear to be natural, but that doesn’t mean that it is. If science could accept the possibility of an invisible but physical intelligence furtively acting for the development of mankind, then they might realise that many of the wonders of the world are the product of deliberate intervention, and study them accordingly.

Science (personified) will quite rightly ask for some physical evidence of these intelligent beings, and I would be happy to offer them the ordered orbits of the Solar System.

In the final analysis, we cannot have an artificially ordered Solar System and still keep a natural Earth. If there is anything artificial about the Solar System at all then there must be a superior power, and if a superior power exists then we might as well assume that nothing on the Earth is truly natural either. If the orbits are artificially ordered then the Earth is also artificially provisioned; everything has been arranged for us, so that we may live and thrive and develop naturally on this world that has been given over to our use.

The scientists would not accept my offer because they are not stupid and will recognise the truth of the above reasoning. We cannot sub-divide the world into ‘natural’ and ‘artificial’; it must be all one or all the other. Scientists will reject my offer, and they will continue to stand in the way of ‘first contact’, until such time as they recognise the reality of the situation. Once they accept that there is an intelligent power greater than mankind, only then may we hope that the scientific establishment will be sensible enough to concede the fact in public.

Until that happens, there will always be arguments and questions, all of which can be answered by reference to one or more of the three facts listed at the end of this chapter.

The mind-set of scientists is so deeply entrenched in their belief in evolution and other theories that they will laugh at the suggestion that we humans are clones. If we point out the mathematical order in the solar system, the evolutionists will dismiss it, because it is not their subject. If we point to the geometry and the astronomy in Stonehenge they will dismiss it, because it is not their subject.

One of the ways in which science succeeds in its unintentional deception is this division of responsibility. Astronomers stick to astronomy, and do not dabble in archaeology. Archaeologists know nothing of evolution, and will not countenance the possibility of advanced knowledge being in their Neolithic monument, and so it goes on, each scientific discipline specialises in its own subject, and passes responsibility for strange inexplicable occurrences on to other disciplines. It is a refined system of passing the buck, giving people the run-around.

This is a survival technique, arising by chance during the evolution of the scientific establishment, which allows it to mutate whenever needed, to baffle any opposition.

Science is dead, but it isn't about to lie down any time soon.

*

Radiogenic dating methods.

Perhaps now would be a good time to discuss the radiocarbon dating of Stonehenge, and radiogenic dating in general.

The figures in the following brief discussion are from Professor Atkinson's book, page 215, which presents a dating sequence derived from revised and calibrated C14 tests carried out on samples found at various places throughout the monument.

I would like to point out that nothing I say here should be taken as a reflection on Professor Atkinson or the quality of his work. All he did was send samples off for testing, in good faith, and he was not in a position to question the results.

In chapter eight of this book, I described in detail a rather simple way of producing the ground plan of Stonehenge. The method described was one that was able, very closely, if not exactly, to replicate all the main features of the monument, including the mistakes made by the builders.

I think I am safe in saying that the design I proposed was actually used to lay out the ground-plan of the monument.

It is a completely unified design, and I mentioned at the time that this implied that the monument was built as one integrated whole, because the design and method of drawing the ground-plan was an integrated whole. The reasonable assumption was that the entire monument would have been finished within a few years.

If we accept that the builders were intelligent and resourceful, they would have gathered the rocks together so that they would be close at hand before starting to build.

They would have planned the build sequence, and used their intelligence combined with animal power to erect the stones as efficiently as was possible under the circumstances. If there is enough animal and/or manpower, erecting a stone is a rather quick process, it has to be quick or it would never be erected at all.

It is the gathering, preparation and shaping that takes the time. There are only forty major upright stones, and even if we assume that all forty of them were actually erected, with division of labour, shaping and erecting one stone per month, it could have been done in as little as four years. This is a reasonable estimate, so it is possible to suggest that, including tea breaks, ten to twelve years would have been more than enough time to finish the entire structure.

We can accuse the workforce of being lazy, demanding holidays, time off for paternity leave, and other excuses for not working, and accept that it may have taken the indolent crew a full twenty five years to complete the monument, or even longer, but we cannot accept the time scale proposed by science.

*

In the Professor's book, the radiocarbon dates, which are described as 'calibrated' are so far spread out, that they make no sense to me at all.

The start of the sequence, the 56 Aubrey holes, together with the bank and ditch are radiocarbon dated to **2810 BC** (+/- 120 yrs.)

The 'Y' and 'Z' features are part of the same geometry and would have been marked out at the same time as the Aubrey circle, yet according to the C14 dating, it seems these holes were not actually dug until **1,270 years later.** (C14 dates at 1540 BC)

What this means is that, if the radiocarbon dating is right, the builders marked out the ground plan on the grass, and then waited for 1,270 years before digging the holes. That is rather a long tea break.

Most of the other construction dates fall in between these two figures, for example, the main Sarsen Circle is dated to 2120 BC or 690 years after the ground-plan was drawn which of course included the 30 radials needed to place the Sarsen Circle stones.

In short, the radiocarbon dates provided to the Professor by the laboratory give a total period for building the monument after laying out an integrated ground plan of somewhere in the region of 1,270 years or more.

Let me put that in perspective.

I suggest it would take perhaps three or four days for three men to lay out the entire ground plan as described in my Chapter Eight.

Let us give them extra time for tea and biscuits, let them have a few toilet breaks, and say it would take them a whole week.

Seven days to lay out the ground plan, and one thousand two hundred and seventy years to build it. It just doesn't make any kind of sense to me.

In 1,270 years the original ground plan would have been totally forgotten.

It is on a par with an Anglo-Saxon King of 730 AD drawing up plans for a new church, marking out the foundations, and taking until the year 2000 to put the doors on and complete the finishing touches, just about the same time as the Millennium Dome was finished.

Another example would be if William the Conqueror, in 1066 AD, designed a new Norman castle, marked out the foundations, gathered the materials, and started building, but it isn't finished yet, it won't be finished until the year 2336 AD.

To be frank, it is completely ridiculous and unacceptable time-scale for building such an integrated geometric structure as Stonehenge.

I do not anticipate anyone in the scholarly world will agree with me, certainly not the archaeologists and the laboratory workers who did the testing, but the only honest way I can describe these dates it to say they are completely preposterous. They are just plain *silly*.

And it gets worse, the dates are claimed to be ***calibrated*** dates, supposedly checked against dendrochronology, and therefore reliable and accurate.

I do not accept them; the design is integrated with the structure, it is not possible to extend the building of it over such a long period.

But it is not so much the duration of the build that concerns me, it is the ***start*** of the build. If the duration dates are so ridiculous then we cannot rely on the supposed start date either.

This means I do not have a date for the building of the monument.

I was going to say that I am not qualified to make such comments, but I believe I am, since it is not difficult to demonstrate that it was my geometry that was used to lay out the ground plan.

*

With the benefit of hindsight, the geometry I employed to draw the ground-plan of Stonehenge is just the sort of thing that Archaeologists should be good at. Unfortunately they were prevented from even considering such geometry by the C14 dates, which made it look like any coherent design was impossible.

Archaeologists should also have been able to recognise the connection with the Solar System by virtue of the distribution of the various features, but they were prevented from doing so by the powerful mental conditioning they underwent in university.

Before anyone ever looked at Stonehenge, it was 'known' in advance that it could not be anything other than a Neolithic temple. It could not possibly be antediluvian, because it was known in advance that there was no such thing as antediluvian. It was known in advance by everyone who examined it that it could not contain important knowledge, because it was built by ignorant primitives.

*

I have mentioned previously that science has been deceiving us for 150 years, and the circumstances outlined above are a good example of that deception, and how it comes about. Professor Atkinson's work was impeccable, I am sure there was no intention on his part to deceive but the deception happened all the same.

It starts with an educational system which teaches the particular mind-set that originated with Darwin and Lyell. When these theories were first put forward they were accepted by the educational system and have since taken firm root.

Imposed on top of that is the 'scientific' method, one rule of which states that any new research must 'further our knowledge', which means adding to and progressing the established opinion.

The system has been going for so long that it has built up a momentum, and is now like a huge and ponderous flywheel that flattens all opposing views. This in turn leads to a kind of academic arrogance where the beliefs and ideas of experts are not questioned.

This is how the deception comes about, it is not deliberate, it has just grown up, and one could say 'evolved', all by itself.

Professor Atkinson could not have refused to accept the faulty radiocarbon dates, even if he suspected they were wrong, because of this long established institutionalised academic arrogance.

*

It is the same kind of unintended deception that clouds the issue of human origins. It is declared in a loud booming voice, heard all around the world, that 'WE EVOLVED!' and then the whole machinery of education and science has become geared up and sets out to prove this unjustified statement. Everything has to be understood and interpreted in the light of that statement of faith, the evolutionist's creed. The scientists build careers on it, and academic acclaim, so the deception progresses and gathers strength and momentum with every new turn of the spiral of speculation.

*

The problems with the dating of Stonehenge and the unintended deception made me look at all radiogenic dating methods in a new and different light.

Radiogenic methods produce dates that are presented with a thoroughly undeserved air of confidence, and the misplaced confidence is extended to the entire structural sequence of the proposed history of the Earth.

In the case of Stonehenge, the start date and duration of building has now been permanently lost, exaggerated and randomised by any arbitrary amount, and nobody can question it, not even the Professor who was doing the archaeology. The Professor is sadly no longer with us, but I bet he would be extremely angry if he knew what these laboratory people had done to his meticulous and painstaking work.

Similar unwarranted confidence is put into the dating of human remains, and the structural integrity of the theory of human evolution depends on these dubious radiogenic dating methods.

Let me put it like this, the laboratory people who provided the dates for Stonehenge were the acknowledged experts, they reigned supreme; they issued the dates with an arrogant air *of utter confidence that they were checked, calibrated and correct.*

Their pronouncements cannot be challenged by such an esteemed and influential personage as a Professor of Archaeology, much less can they be challenged by the likes of this writer, but I do so challenge.

The radiocarbon dates for Stonehenge are wrong, totally wrong, utterly wrong, completely wrong, worse than useless, and meaningless.

I hope I make myself clear.

*

Radiogenic dating is widely used in a number of areas, but if the results presented for Stonehenge are anything to go by, they are of no scientific value.

If a similar overconfident attitude prevails in the dating for the theory of evolution or the story of humanity, who would know what falsehoods are being promulgated in the name of science?

It is no good the laboratory repeating the tests, and coming out with new figures. The old ones have already been declared to be calibrated, and subsequently shown to be ludicrously inaccurate, all future tests would be equally suspect.

The radiocarbon dating procedure is just one example of a class of dating methods that rely on the radioactive decay of isotopes. These isotopes must be either part of the structure of the item to be dated, or in close association with it. Carbon fourteen dating is supposed to be one of the most reliable, because it is used for relatively 'recent' dates, and can be checked against items of known age.

Unfortunately it is now clear to me that the method cannot be relied on at all. It is a matter of trust, more than anything else.

Carbon fourteen dates are the easiest to check, and if they have turned out to be so ridiculously unreliable, what can we say about radiogenic methods that relate to more ancient times, that are more difficult to implement, and more difficult to corroborate?

What are we to say about a radiogenic date of two million years if dates of a few thousand are so unreasonable?

It has to be said, though I do not like to say it, but all radiogenic dating methods must be regarded as highly suspect, virtually worthless, until proven otherwise.

A guest for tea.

We have a guest for tea. Let me introduce you to my friend Jack, who wrote the foreword for this book and did most of the drawings. He is joining us for a short chat. It was only because of Jack's importunity that this book was written in the first place, so I think he is worthy of our hospitality and a few cucumber sandwiches.

Jack knows that I will not argue about Creationism, I am not taking sides in what I consider to be a fatuous argument, so Jack and I are not going to discuss Creationism in this book.

Creationism is an aspect of religion, and this is not a religious forum. Creationists hypothesise about the origin of the entire universe, which is a topic that is far outside the scope of this book, and in my opinion well beyond the understanding of any mortal man, it is a matter for faith not science.

There are innumerable arguments for and against religious Creationism, but we will discuss none of them here. This book is supposed to be about ancient knowledge, not modern conjecture.

So Jack and I will not argue about Creationism today, and that is just as well, because if we did we would end up hurling crockery at each other, and you might get injured by the shrapnel.

Instead, we will politely sip our tea and engage in a more civilised discussion.

Jack would like to talk over the reports that the C14 carbon isotope has been found in diamonds, because it seems to him that this supports his belief in a young earth, as opposed to an old one.

In my own opinion all it does is to throw another spanner into the works of radiogenic dating methods.

Carbon fourteen dating is usually only applied to the remains of things that were once living. It works on the assumption that the C14 from the environment entered the body cells of a living thing, and it also assumes that the ratio of C14 to normal, stable, C12 has been constant throughout all of time. Consequently when the animal or plant dies, it stops absorbing carbon and the C14 in its tissue starts to decay at a known rate. The isotopic ratio changes with time, thus enabling scientists to calculate the time that has elapsed since the death of the organism.

This procedure doesn't work for diamonds, of course, because diamonds were never alive, they are simply crystallised carbon, usually formed deep inside the Earth and associated with volcanoes.

Scientists appear to be at a loss to understand how C14 could have got into the diamonds in the first place, since diamonds do not breathe air, or eat and drink. Without any acceptable explanation for how the isotope got into the diamond, the dating method cannot really be applied. It is also difficult to determine how much C14 was present originally. Did it arrived all at once or is it constantly feeding into the crystal? Diamonds do not 'die' so there was no point in time when the isotope decay dating 'clock' can be said to have started.

The main problem for scientists, as I see it, is that if C14 can get into inert material like a diamond, then it can also intrude into the remains of once living things. If C14 can get into diamonds, it can also get into the remains of a mammoth, for example, or a piece of burned wood, or a deer antler at Stonehenge.

This would obviously throw the carbon dating method into more confusion than it is in already. As a radio isotope C14 is no different from any other radio isotope, so what is true of C14 must also be true of other dating methods.

What it boils down to is that we cannot rely on any radiogenic dating techniques.

Jack and I get into a friendly argument over our tea and sandwiches about what exactly is proven by the discovery of C14 in diamond. I would say it proves nothing about the age of the Earth, because we do not know how or when the isotope got into the diamond.

If we go ahead and use the dating method anyway, then all it shows is that some diamonds are very young, but we already knew that, they can be formed at any time when the conditions are right, and synthetic diamonds are made in huge numbers commercially.

Unfortunately we cannot eat-up all our sandwiches and still have them on our plates. Jack and I would agree that radiogenic dating methods cannot be relied on, but that claim also works against us, for we cannot criticise such methods and then use them ourselves.

Jack and I finish our little sociable interlude by sharing a plate of biscuits while I explain to him my argument about the geometry of Stonehenge and how the integral nature of that geometry proves that the C14 dates for the monument are completely and unambiguously wrong.

Of course he agrees with me, because he it was who did the drawings in this book, by following my written instructions.

After a little bit of personal chatter, he has to leave, so now, if we have finished our tea, we will wish Jack a safe journey home, and get back to work.

I feel guilty. I may have given you the impression that I am in some way anti-science. If you think that to be the case then you would be slightly wrong. I am not against reason and rational thought.

As previously mentioned, scientific endeavour has been a great boon to humanity, so I am not against it. I am, however, against some of the methodology, especially the methodology of unquestioning acceptance of radiogenic dates.

I am also not in favour of methodology like that employed by Lyell, who we met earlier.

Lyell maintained that the 'present is the key to the past', which is a little slogan he seems to have popularized.

What this means is that instead of looking at Earth's features and trying to deduce events from the evidence, he states, prior to even looking, that geological processes in the past will be no different from those that are seen today. In this way he dictates, in advance of any investigation, how researchers are to interpret their discoveries.

This is the principle of 'Uniformitarianism'. It sounds reasonable, but it is contrary to the basic principle that we don't know until we look. I am opposed to such reasoning. I would say, 'let us look first, and reason on what we find.'

In fact there should be no 'isms' in science. A catastrophe either happened or it didn't, there should be no 'ism' to decide the case in advance of investigation and intelligent enquiry.

There should be no uniformitarianism or catastrophism, there should be just science, but since these words and notions have become embedded in language we will continue to use them.

Before those famous three, Laplace, Lyell, and Darwin, catastrophism was the generally accepted way of looking at geological history. Plenty of evidence was found for catastrophic changes in the earth, and these were associated with the flood of Biblical mythology.

The evidence for catastrophe is still around us, but is being interpreted differently; it is being interpreted by the a-priori, assumed knowledge of uniformitarianism.

These days just about everything is interpreted in accordance with uniformitarianism.

Evolution is the one exception, it is not a product of uniformitarian interpretation, but this is never made clear in publications on the subject. Uniformitarianism insists that ancient processes are to be regarded as no different from those that occur today, so, for example, large deposits of sediment are assumed to have been built up very slowly, just like sediments do today.

Evolution does not happen today, of course, at least, nobody has seen it happen, so there is no real method available for assessing how evolution behaved in the past. For this reason the principle of uniformitarianism cannot be applied to evolution, especially not human evolution.

If we were to apply the principle of uniformitarianism to evolution, we would have to conclude that evolution did not happen, because it is not happening today. Evolution is something that is assumed, not observed.

Scientists are quite happy to abandon Lyell's principle when it suits them, so they conveniently forget to apply it to evolution.

Uniformitarianism often leads to a situation that is a little like some of the popular archaeological programs we watch on TV (although it has to be recognised that it is just a TV show), where the archaeologists state in advance what they are proposing to dig up.

"Today, we will be excavating an Iron Age house." They then proceed to dig a hole and lo-and-behold, they find an Iron Age house. What a surprise!

Wouldn't it be nice if one day they dug up something they did not expect to find, and then spent the rest of the programme trying to figure out what it is?

*

More recently some elements of catastrophism have been allowed to creep back into mainstream geology, especially with regard to the extinction of the Dinosaurs, but these excursions into catastrophe are few and far between.

The worst thing about the theories of science is that they have been promoted by television shows and popular magazines as if they are absolutely established factual conclusions. We cannot question the reality of a fossil, but when we read or hear claims that it is a hundred million years old, and evolved into a giant squid, or some other creature, I begin to have doubts.

On the south coast of England, in Dorset by the sea, at Charmouth on the Jurassic coast, we find a great many ammonite fossils on the beach or in the rocks. We are informed that these are in the region of a hundred million years old.

My problem with that statement is this. The 'rock' that many of the fossils are found in is a soft black material that when exposed to water turns instantly to glutinous mud. In fact at Charmouth much of the beach is covered in a ten foot thick layer of soft and sticky fossil-bearing smelly black mud.

In some places the black 'rock' is a little bit harder than mud, it can be handled, and so I brought some home and experimented. I poured some water on it, and within a few minutes there was no rock left, just muddy black sludge, and a few small fossils that had previously been hidden inside the 'rock'.

I have to ask myself how the 'rock' can still be mud after a hundred million years.

Another difficult example is to be found on the East coast of England, on shingle beaches. On these beaches it is possible to find the modern and fossilised shells of a species of a bivalve *Gryphaea* commonly called a 'Devil's Toe Nail'. Both fossil and non-fossil shells mingle together in the shingle, distinguishable by the fact that one is made of shell, and the other of stone. If one explores at low tide, as I have done, it is sometimes possible to find outcrops of rock that are made out of the fossil form, with the living ones on the surface. Such an outcrop was found by this author exposed at low tide, far out across sand flats, off the coast of Yorkshire, near Redcar.

Scientists would call this a 'living fossil', but they would also claim that these little creatures cannot crawl around; they are a form of oyster. Somehow the ones I found in Yorkshire apparently survived for 100 million years in the same place, which was underground before the coast was eroded. They also survived when the North Sea was once dry land, and later they survived being crushed under a two-mile thick layer of ice during the ice age. And now the living creatures co-exist with the fossil form. This is a fact, according to science, so I do not need to prove it.

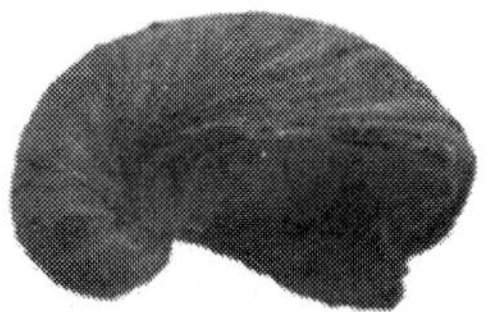

Catastrophes

Despite the problems understanding the great ages of fossils, we need to acknowledge an old Earth, if only for the sake of the dinosaurs. If we concede an old Earth, such that most of the claims of science can be left unchallenged, we are still maintaining that there have been two major catastrophes visited upon the planet in relatively recent times.

There was one when the Solar System was re-arranged, and another we call Noah's flood.

We need to ask where the geological evidence is for these disasters.

*

We should recognise that the changes to Earth's history that are implicit in the design of Stonehenge and the Solar System must somehow be reconciled to the observations of science, by which I mean their factual observations, not necessarily the theories generated to explain them.

Previously, I stated that there is a compromise, wherein science can keep its old Solar System, with its old Earth, and its dinosaurs and fossils, because all these things can be allocated to a time before the order was put into the System. We cannot be irrational, like some Creationists, and claim that all these old fossils were put there deliberately to deceive scientists. The fossils are real.

We might even concede that Laplace and Lyell and Darwin were all correct in their assertions, but only when applied to the time before the Elohim came to change our Solar System. By making this concession, it should not be inferred that I agree with the claims they make.

It can be inferred that the claims they make, true or false, do not impinge on the content of this book.

*

Science has something called 'scientific method', which works by the observance of 'scientific rules'.

One of these rules states that a theory has to be 'testable' or 'capable of falsification'. This means that any theory should be accompanied by a method that would be capable of showing that the theory is either true or false.

When it comes to scientific theories about the origin of the Earth, and the Solar System*, and evolution*, it is no longer possible to validate them.

It is no longer possible for scientists to claim that the Solar System originated by the nebular hypothesis, even if it actually did. The reason is because the nebular hypothesis cannot produce an ordered Solar System, and it is a fact that the Solar System is currently ordered, and there is no way of showing that it was ever in any other condition, even if it was.

It is such a little change, just move a few planets around, but it completely throws science into confusion.

*

Science cannot make assumptions about such matters, science needs facts that it can rely on.

It is always possible that everything science has established is actually true, but because of the rules of science, they can no longer demonstrate that truth, they can no longer test their theories, or depend on their dating methods.

To show that the Solar System is ordered, with just a little graph and a few numbers, throws a huge spanner into the workings of the Earth sciences.

It is not an exaggeration to say that if the scientific method were to be rigidly applied, then all the scientists involved with the Earth's history, evolution, and geology would have to start all over again, taking into account the fact that the Solar System has been changed. They would need to know when, and by how much, and by what means, before they could factor all those parameters into their methodology for describing the origins and history of Earth.

Astronomers are going to have a really difficult time trying to explain how the System could have become ordered, and an even harder time trying to explain how they missed it. Especially since the supposedly 'Neolithic' designer of Stonehenge knew about it.

The dating laboratories must explain how they could have got the dates for Stonehenge so wrong whilst claiming they were correct and calibrated. How do these laboratories propose to restore confidence in their methodology, and reclaim their lost credibility?

For scientists such little changes mean there would be so much at stake; it is far easier just to ignore the findings in this book, or hold a little ceremony and burn it.

However, we are not so cavalier, we need to know the truth, and so we will continue and try to find a way to fit the two catastrophes into relatively recent history.

*

The biggest catastrophe of all time would have been caused by the moving of this planet from its previous orbit to its current one.

How do we know if it has in fact been moved?

The mathematics of the system describes orbits that are arranged relative to unity, and unity is defined by the mean orbit of Earth. It follows that no matter where the Earth goes it remains as unity and remains as the reference.

Since the whole pattern is ratiometric the Earth could possibly have been left where it was, and all the others moved to conform.

But we should remember that Newton's laws of gravity still apply, even if gravity is not involved in the equation.

Mercury, Venus, and Earth must be in a precise relationship in order for the 'Equation for Venus' to work, but all three must also be in stable orbits relative to the sun. The sun is not part of the ratiometric scheme; it is fixed, very big and very hot, and it has a very powerful gravitational effect.

The overriding source of gravity is the sun, of course, but all the planets also have a gravitational influence on each other, in particular Jupiter has a significant influence. The design equation does not involve gravity but the problem is not just one of mathematical order, which is intricate enough. The design also has to take account of all the interacting gravitational forces and ensure that the final arrangement is stable.

Changing any of the orbits would change the gravitational stability of the entire system, so it would probably have been necessary to move the Earth a little bit, just a little change, to make sure that the finished newly ordered system also has long-term gravitational stability. This is something that does not show up in the mathematics and tends to be overlooked, but it certainly had to be considered by the Solar System designer, and is a factor that must be added to our appreciation of his mathematical skill and ingenuity.

So the guidelines for placing Earth in its orbit are not at all straightforward.

Earth must be in the so-called 'Goldilocks Zone', and preferably at a distance from the sun that would be most comfortable for humanity, but it must also be in a position where all the other orbits would combine in accord with the mathematical order to produce a whole structure that would be in a stable gravitational configuration.

It is unlikely that Earth would be found exactly in the right place by the chance positioning implied by the chaotic workings of the nebular hypothesis, although it was possibly fairly close. I say possibly close, because the fossil record declares that Earth has been in the habitable life-supporting 'Goldilocks Zone' for a very long time.

*

If the Earth ever did have a different orbit than it has today then the length of the year would also be different, compared with the present length. If the Earth was ever closer to the sun, then its year would have been shorter than it is now, and of course if it had ever been further away, the year would have been longer.

Such differences might be detectable in the fossil record. Assuming that other parameters had not also changed, there could be evidence in the relative duration of the seasons, or perhaps the ancient year could be measured in days or months. An Earth nearer to the sun would have had shorter years made up of hotter and relatively longer summers and shorter winters; an Earth further away would be the reverse.

Planets could possibly carry these records of their previous orbits along with them, in the form of a 'fossilised' temperature change.

We know that Earth was never too close or too far away from the sun for life to exist, because there are ample fossils to show that life flourished.

If the Earth had at one time been slightly closer to the sun, we would expect to find evidence of a hotter sun and a warmer climate in the ancient rocks, and in the nature of its fossilised life. For example, if Tyrannosaurus Rex were cold blooded like modern reptiles, they would need lots of sun in the morning to warm up their huge bulk, to obtain enough energy to get moving and catch their breakfast. It would be an advantage for them if the planet were closer to the sun than it is today, such that it would be really hot and sunny all the time. Did dinosaurs like hot weather?

On the other hand, if the Earth had previously been further away from the sun, we might expect to find similar evidence of a cold climate in the rocks and fossilised life. Did tree ferns like cold weather? It seems not, I had one in my garden and a winter frost killed it.

There could be other signs, perhaps more subtle, in the Earth's palaeomagnetic record, which could have been affected by the stronger or weaker solar wind, or in the crystalline structure of certain rocks or minerals.

We might find that the answer is non-committal, both hot and cold.

If we accept that the Earth has indeed been moved, then we must also accept that a great disaster would have been visited upon the planet, and there should be some evidence of that disaster. As the supposedly mythological account in Genesis succinctly puts it, 'the Earth was without form and void.'

We should look for a sudden change in the nature of the flora and fauna that dominated the Earth, similar to the extinction of dinosaurs and the rise of mammalian life, with special regard to the timing and duration of such a change.

This brings me back to the old 'science' of catastrophism. Much of the work done by those antiquated researchers has been lost, or hidden, because it has all been discredited by the authoritarian assertions of Lyell.

I would recommend that this old catastrophism work be resurrected, because there may well be some evidence that answers the case, but has subsequently been re-interpreted.

There must be plenty of potential evidence in fossilised life and in the geology; there must be unexplained gaps in the geological record. It just needs to be examined without the intrusion of Lyell and Darwin and Laplace.

There should have been a geologically short period, not long ago, where there was briefly hardly any life on Earth at all, this might show up as a very small gap in the geological record.

It is true that the Genesis account implies that a substantial amount of terraforming took place, so there might actually be evidence of this. Alternatively a gap in the record might have been 'patched over' by the same terraforming, and the patchwork repair might be detectable.

Also relevant, though likely to be dismissed out of hand as fantasy, is the Biblical claim that the Elohim not only cloned mankind, but also produced all manner of other animals and plants, presumably by genetic engineering, or sowing preserved seeds. If this has any basis in truth, then there should have been a time when all manner of modern mammalian life suddenly appeared, without evolving. This would be a necessary part of terraforming a barren planet, and again, some evidence may be detectable in recent strata.

*

The likelihood is that Earth has been moved, if only by a little, to accommodate the other planets, ensuring that all the orbits are stable, whilst they also conform to the mathematical pattern.

In some ways the moving of the other planets is not a problem, after all we know that it happened, proof is in fig 10; it is the main subject of this book.

It is true that we don't know for sure if our own planet was moved, or when and by how much, but is it really that important?

It is important for one reason, apart from verification of the scriptural claim that the Earth was rendered 'without form and void' for a short space of time. The reason is because nobody is going to accept the notion that we are clones based solely on logic. Science has got so much credibility invested in the human evolution story that they are not likely to voluntarily stop deceiving the public without hard evidence.

It is important not only to show that the Earth has changed orbit, but that it has done so recently enough to exclude the possibility that we evolved. For this we need accurate and verifiable dates that do not depend on the suspect radiogenic methodology.

We are not at war with scientists, but their intransigence may delay first-contact, and we wouldn't want that, would we?

Old bones

The most difficult questions to be answered are those raised by the supposed history of mankind, the human species itself, and here we enter the area where the elite scientists in the dating laboratories wield their greatest power to accidentally mislead.

I may mention that science claims to have identified quite a number of different species of mankind, or sub-species, the distinction is unclear, let me call them all 'quasi-humans'.

There are so many different names for these quasi-humans that it is difficult to grasp how they could all precede us in the evolutionary tree if we are claiming that there is no such tree, we claim to be cloned from the gods.

In addition there is the subsequent bottleneck of the flood and Noah. We are all supposed to be descended from the people who built Stonehenge, so we should all be the same species. Where did Neanderthal man come from? Where did Cro-Magnons come from? How about all the others?

One thing we should note is that science just digs up old bones, in many cases just a fragment of bone, or a tooth. This scarcity of material does not deter science from giving them all very serious-sounding exotic names. These are not real names, they are just names invented to distinguish one box of old bone fragments from another.

The fact is that these names also have a powerful psychological effect. An anonymous collection of old bone fragments is just a box of old bone fragments, but if they are given a name, especially an exotic name, then the content of the box is suddenly transformed into something terribly important.

Homo erectus (for example) is just a collection of old bone fragments, as are all the other supposed sub-species of humanity. These are all allocated dates, or time frames in which they supposedly thrived, based on the nature of the flint tools they used or the sedimentary or volcanic strata they were found in. Dating is achieved by a variety of different methods, including radiogenic isotope methods. Some of these dating methods are quite intricately convoluted and not at all straightforward as one might be led to suppose from the confidence with which they are reported.

The collection of bits of old bone that is named 'Homo erectus' is claimed to be one and a half million years old.

There is no merit in just dismissing these things in the same way that scientists will dismiss the ordered orbits. We must look at them more closely, in order to be able to face up to the inevitable "What about...?" questions.

*

The plethora of different kinds of quasi-humans must really be an embarrassment for evolutionists, but not for me.

The theory of Evolution maintains that every time an egg is fertilized there is an opportunity for a favourable mutation to occur. That is how evolution comes about, and that is how we humans are supposed to have originated.

In order to understand the evolutionist's problem with quasi-humans we must consider the situation regarding our own kind, modern humans.

In total there have been about fourteen billion of our kind alive on Earth, and that includes the dead along with the living (by binary summation). That means there have been fourteen billion fertilizations, fourteen billion individual opportunities for an advantageous mutation to occur and offer the possibility of a new species. In those fourteen billion opportunities for an advantageous mutation, how many have we actually seen? We have seen none. Not one.

There have been plenty of negative and disadvantageous mutations, resulting in disabilities, and there are lots of people in wheelchairs or on crutches as a result, but not a single advantageous mutation have we seen, not one.

Our human evolutionary beneficial mutation rate can then be put at fourteen billion to none – zero.

On the other hand our deleterious disadvantageous mutation rate is rather higher; world-wide there must be tens of millions of people suffering from a disadvantage caused by any one of an uncounted number of damaging genetic changes.

If we now apply the principles of science to determine the quasi-human evolutionary beneficial mutation rate, we would have to estimate the rate for quasi-humans from the observation of a supposed closely related species, namely ourselves. They surely must have experienced the same rate, since they are also human, if only 'quasi'.

That is the only scientific way to do it. Scientists cannot just apply an arbitrary figure for evolutionary rate, surely not?

It follows that in order to evolve, every single quasi-human species must have experienced a similar number of fertilization 'opportunities' as we have, or more.

Of course, all successful fertilizations mean that a new child is born, and this means that the total population of each and every quasi-human species must have been on a par with our own, in the region of fourteen billion, before they can even hope to produce an advantageous mutation and thus evolve. Obviously this didn't happen, or quasi-human skeletons of various types and names would litter the Earth in huge numbers.

And still, they would not have evolved. Fourteen billion to none means what it says – 'none' – zero.

The above argument highlights the ad-hoc nature of evolutionary theory. It is somehow assumed that quasi-humans evolved at a much faster rate than modern humans. In fact, evolutionists frequently vary the rate of evolution to suit their own purposes, rather than follow rigorous scientific rules. I have even heard circular reasoning come from the mouth of an evolutionist. He claimed that the beneficial mutation rate of quasi-humans must have been faster than ours or we could not have evolved. How is that for putting the cart before the horse?

It means they are cheating. They cannot use observed and verified beneficial mutation rates derived from the current human population, which is what they should do. Instead, they make them up ad-hoc as they go along.

However, be that as it may, I have still not tried to explain where I think the so called quasi-humans came from.

*

One advantage enjoyed by science is that of flexi-time. Scientists have often been heard to use the phrase 'given enough time'.

Given enough time, anything can happen. Monkeys can type the complete works of Shakespeare, or evolve into the bard himself and write the original manuscripts.

'Given enough time' is something of a cop-out for science. Anything they wish to happen can happen, given enough time.

Actually this is misdirection, scientific sleight of hand, another deception. Time is not enough on its own.

Opportunities for mutation, fertilization of eggs, are the driving forces behind evolutionary theory, not time. For humans, and quasi-humans alike, fourteen billion opportunities are not enough, and no amount of time can make them enough.

Time alone will never produce a new species.

But evolutionist still invoke 'Given enough time'.

We are not so lucky. We do not know how long ago Stonehenge was built, but we know we are limited to a few millennia; not anywhere near 'long enough' for evolution to take place, because it is self-evident we have not evolved.

In the scenario demanded by the facts and the reasoning in this book, and in the book of Genesis, the entire human population (Noah's tribe) was scattered throughout the Earth at the time 'God' came down to visit the Tower of Babel, and we must accept that this was just a few thousand years ago, shortly after Stonehenge was built, or even during the building of it.

Genesis 11 verse 9

...and from thence did the LORD scatter them abroad upon the face of all the earth.

If we then presume to follow the fortunes of the individuals who were scattered we can see that they would have been in dire straits, with their language confused, and probably scared out of their wits by the sudden appearance of the Chief of the Mighty Ones on the scene.

These would no doubt have congregated in small groups, for company if for nothing else, and the groups would have wandered aimlessly around, finally crossing the channel (in crude boats) and being dispersed throughout Europe. As time passed, they spread themselves further afield, building simple stone circles, wretched imitations of Stonehenge, as they went.

Being in small isolated groups, there would have been a greatly enhanced opportunity for in-breeding, and as we all know, in-breeding can lead to genetic problems.

I have heard it said, and seen it in professional literature, that isolated communities 'evolve' faster than others because there is a greater chance of a favourable mutation. I would say that there is actually a much greater chance of a genetic disaster. The rate of incest and inbreeding in an isolated population will be higher, and greater occurrences of genetic defects would result.

Inbreeding is bad, that is why incest is against the law, and is naturally abhorrent to all right-minded people. It promotes mutations, sure it does, but the vast majority of those mutations will be damaging. I would say ***all*** of those mutations will be damaging, if the human experience is anything to go by.

Isolated, inbred communities do not evolve faster, they degenerate faster.

If inbreeding in isolated communities could enhance the probability of favourable mutations, then surely incest would be encouraged? The truth is, incest enhances the probability of ***disabling*** mutations, and the same would happen in isolated populations.

That particular bit of widely published, peer reviewed, evolutionary science is patent nonsense. This is another example of scientific legerdemain, wherein the public are deceived.

*

Returning to the people who fled from the Elohim at Stonehenge, we can see that it would be natural for them to disperse into small isolated groups, and that such groups would soon become inbred, and start to produce degenerate offspring. This process would have been exacerbated by the recent disaster; the collapse of the ice rings would have destroyed the ozone layer and disrupted the protective geomagnetic field of the planet, thus allowing a massive increase in ionising radiation, which we all know causes mutations.

As time went by these in-bred degenerates would become isolated from the normal population, because it is a natural instinct to shun the different, the strange or deformed. This is not ‘PC’ in our modern age, but it remains true nevertheless.

I do not need to explain to anyone how strong the sexual urges are in men, and these urges and desires would apply to degenerate humans as well as they do to modern man but without the inhibitions of social protocol and morality. In the days before contraception, the isolated groups of inbred humans would themselves have mated, and done so very often, as often as they wished. As a result the populations of inbred genetically degenerated humans would have multiplied rapidly; and would no doubt have given rise to a race of even more degenerate 'quasi-humans' as they are now called.

It might be suggested that such degenerates would be destroyed by predation and by competition; the normal rules of natural selection, but those rules depend entirely on circumstances.

In the given circumstances, soon after a global disaster, there would not be many predators, and, by definition, isolated groups do not suffer from competition because, --- they are isolated.

We see that there is nothing to prevent isolated groups of inbred degenerates from multiplying and passing on their defective genetic code to their offspring, thus producing larger populations of their own progressively more degenerate kind.

As the population of normal humans grew, so alongside them in parallel growth would be found isolated populations of degenerate humans.

There is no way of proving this, but it is in keeping with the simple observation that deleterious genetic changes are very commonly seen amongst modern humanity, whilst advantageous mutations have never been observed in fourteen billion opportunities.

I therefore seriously suggest that these Neanderthals and Cro-Magnon, and Homo erectus, are all the products of genetic deterioration, they are all degenerated from true humans. They did not precede us on the human evolutionary tree, there was no such tree. All of them walked the earth at the same time.

*

In a world dominated by science everything must obey natural laws, so there is no way of accepting the flood, or the survival of such animals as mammoths if there was one.

In a world dominated by powerful intelligent entities like the Elohim, who are capable of terraforming a world and engineering life, anything becomes possible; not by magic or miracle, but by superior science and technology.

What do modern farmers do if they lose all their animals in a natural disaster? They restock and carry on, that is what a modern human would do. I have to consider the possibility that the Elohim would do the same sort of thing after the flood.

Clearly, the Ark of Noah could not support or explain the diversity and number of animals hunted by humans with flint tipped spears, and it certainly cannot explain the huge diversity of life that currently inhabits the Earth. We cannot explain them either, except by calling on the power of the Elohim to engineer and seed life.

This suggestion would be received with ribald laughter by scientists; it is absurd, too ridiculous for words, but then, so is an ordered Solar System.

*

After the dispersion at Babel, the 'normal' strain of mankind survived in the classical way of hunting the food animals provided by 'nature' or by the Elohim.

The degenerate isolated inbred groups may also have survived on nuts and berries, insects, carrion, scavenging, and the odd bit of cannibalism.

If we wish to be scientific, because old habits die hard, there are probably ways of examining the recent geological record with a slightly different premise, to see when the very first mammoths appeared, or the first examples of any modern mammal, for that matter. Again, accurate dates would be necessary, without recourse to the suspect radiogenic methods.

*

If we were to accept the Biblical narrative, then there is a very late possible example of genetic variability in 2Samuel 21 v. 20, where is briefly described a race of giants, wherein genetic changes were passed on to succeeding generations, without anyone claiming it to be an example of evolution.

20…… that had on every hand six fingers, and on every foot six toes, four and twenty in number; and he also was born to the giant.

The giant 'Goliath' is fairly famous in Christian and Jewish lore, but it is less well known that there was a whole family.

22…..These four *(Giants)* ***were born to the giant in Gath.***

*

The degenerate inbred branches of humanity would not have survived; being genetically enfeebled they would eventually have died out.

As the majority 'normal' population grew in numbers, and groups met up with other groups, more diverse marriages became commonplace, the human race secured its genetic integrity and became what we are today.

We have been conditioned to think of ourselves as the peak of creation or the apex of evolution, but in the context of the Bible and of this book, we must also be regarded as 'degenerates', we are degenerated from the antediluvians, if only in respect of our life span, and they in their turn were clones of the Elohim and somewhat less noble than their clone-parents.

The inbred branches of humanity became extinct, and because their old bones are different from normal old bones, whenever they are found they attract the attention of scientists who are predisposed, and very eager, to demonstrate the theory of evolution.

Normal old bones do not attract attention; they are ignored as being 'modern'. The degenerate, deformed old bones are examined in lavish detail, given exotic names and allocated important roles in the supposed 'evolution' of man. Little by little and one by one they are fitted into the pre-existing evolutionary model, and as often as not the dates allocated are derived from supposed evolutionary features, like brow ridges or sagittal crests.

In this way the genetically degenerate old bones gave rise to a lot of peculiar names, and secured their place in the annals of science.

If you strip away the trendy names, all that is left are piles of old bones, and questionable dating techniques.

As an alternative argument, and a much simpler one, we could invoke probability. Given the extreme rarity of an advantageous mutation, zero in fourteen billion, compared with the millions of disadvantageous genetic changes that plague humanity, which alternative has the highest probability? -----

1) That we, by a series of repeated miracles, evolved from small isolated groups of inbred quasi-humans?

2) Or is it more likely that those small, isolated groups of inbred quasi-humans degenerated from us?

You decide.

To help in your decision, it only takes 33 generations, or 'doublings' to get to a population of eight billion, excluding other factors.

This means that, again excluding other factors, and allocating a reproductive generation of 30 years, that population level of eight billion could have been reached by the survivors of the flood in less than one thousand years.

I do not claim that such a population level was actually achieved; I simply wish to point out that there is more than enough time to produce a substantial population of various degenerate sub-humans, as well as producing a high level population of 'modern' humans.

Not only so, but if we assume that groups would disperse in random directions, and if we assume that each group could travel at an average speed of one mile per day, (by land or sea) then the whole world would be within reach of humanity in as little as one century. I do not claim that this actually happened; I am simply trying to ascertain a reasonable time span. It seems to me, all things considered, that one or two thousand years would be more than long enough for the entire globe to be repopulated.

We do not know when the flood occurred or when Stonehenge was built, but it was certainly a long time before two thousand years BC, so there is ample time for jungles to grow and for animals and mankind to spread all around the globe and establish themselves, developing different cultures and ethnic adaptations as they explored the planet and multiplied their populations.

Scientific objections would need to be focussed on absolute dating, not elapsed time, since there is clearly enough elapsed time.

The postulated degenerate sub-humans would carry the same genetic link to modern humans as proposed by evolutionary reasoning. In this proposal of degeneration, the same genetic associations would apply, it is no different from evolution, except that it is a lot quicker; it just works in reverse.

For a genetic change to add a beneficial gene (evolution), it takes a lot of fertilisations, fourteen billion or more.

For a genetic change to subtract the same gene (degeneration) it just takes a few generations of in-breeding, and this could occur at any time anywhere on the planet.

*

The overall assumption of evolution, and it is an assumption, is that the one set of old bones somehow 'evolved' into the other, ignoring the blatantly obvious fact that the only living example of mankind has not evolved in fourteen billion attempts.

*

Scientists would counter this argument with dubious dates, derived from dubious isotope decay methods, or the style of flint tools associated with the bones.

Actually the isotope decay dates might be right or they might be wrong. The problem is that after the debacle of the Stonehenge dates, there is no longer any confidence in them. It is best not to depend on a dubious dating method, and it is risky to base a whole evolutionary structure on such a shaky foundation.

If and when scientists find bones that they suspect are really old, when they get them dated they should perhaps remember what happened with Stonehenge. One old monument might not be considered to be so very important in the grand scheme of things, but the people who devised and implement the dating techniques have control over the entire evolutionary sequence.

I do not suggest or imply that they would deliberately engage in deception, but mistakes happen, and they also have reputations to uphold, they have a lot of credibility invested in the success of the theory of evolution. The main problem with suspect dates is not so much that they are proven wrong, but that they ***could*** be wrong. There is no way of being sure they are right, and as long as there is doubt, then they are useless.

*

Flint tools do not come with dates stamped on them either. There are flint arrow heads that are only a few hundred years old, made by Native Americans, and even more recent ones made a few weeks ago on sale in souvenir shops.

Peoples from Mesoamerica, Australia and Africa were using flint or similar stone tools right up until very recent times. The stone-age is not an age, it is a culture.

You cannot date a people by the style of flint knapping.

A few thousand years ago, an old man, expert at making flint axes, was trying to teach a youngster how to do it. The youngster makes his axes the hard way, with cut fingers and lots of swearing. The old man makes them with a practiced flourish, easy and far more stylish.

A few hundred miles away, and a few thousand years later, in my back garden, someone else is making flint axes, but he hasn't a clue how to do it, he makes the most primitive flint axes known to man.

If all these axes were to become buried in different places, and dug up later by scientists, my axe would be classed as the oldest, Palaeolithic, because it is the most primitive. The young apprentice would be next oldest, his would be Mesolithic, because it is in between, and the old man's would be Neolithic, because his is the most advanced.

What kind of a flint axe would an inbred degenerate make? My guess is that an inbred degenerate might make a crude (and therefore very 'early' Palaeolithic) attempt at an axe.

*

As long as scientists classify 'quasi'-man by his skill in making flint tools, and date them accordingly, then the most degenerate or clumsy fumble-fingered individuals would be designated as the oldest.

I am a Palaeolithic Neanderthal man, judged by that system.

I acknowledge there are other methods of dating some flints. Burnt flint can be dated by Thermoluminescence, but the results are probably as reliable as the 'calibrated' Carbon Fourteen dating used to check them.

*

I am not trying to denigrate science here; I am merely trying to point out that there are fundamental flaws in the established scientific view of the origins of mankind.

Science is often guilty of breaking its own rules, as in the case of evolution. It invents arbitrary 'ad-hoc' evolutionary rates for supposed quasi-humans, ignoring a well-known modern example of zero per fourteen billion.

The principle of uniformitarianism advocated by Lyell and adhered to by modern science is as prime an example of 'a priori' reasoning as anyone could hope to find, and it is applied without question to geology, why is it not also applied to evolution?

The denial of catastrophe is a good example of scientific prejudice, a result of an emotional bias against creationist religion. It is very unscientific to rule out a catastrophic scenario just because scientists don't like the implications.

*

I certainly sympathise with scientists in their desire to date their finds. Without dates it is difficult to establish a sequence of events, it is almost impossible to present a convincing picture of history.

In the case of this present work, I have a fairly simple sequence of events which you should now be familiar with.

It all started long ago with the 'age of chaos'.

There then followed a long period of life and unbridled growth during which dinosaurs and all manner of flora and fauna flourished. We could name that entire period the 'Theory era'.

At some point the Solar System had a visit from some powerful intelligent creatures we have come to know as Elohim. These Elohim gave the Solar System a complete make-over, and renovated the surface of the Earth, finishing it off by creating mankind in their 'own image'. This time of turmoil and renewal can be called the 'Terraforming period'.

The terraforming period was very short, and quickly followed by a time of human development, during which a scientifically advanced civilization arose. We now call this the 'antediluvian period'. This period ended in a catastrophic flood, which may well have triggered an ice age.

The highly intelligent, well educated, civilized survivors built a memorial which is now known as Stonehenge, and were then scattered. Subsequently the population of the Earth split into many small isolated groups, reduced to living a Neolithic life style.

Some of these small isolated groups became inbred and degenerated, leaving poorly preserved remains to be picked over by paleoanthropologists who used the teeth and bits of old bone to promote the theory of human evolution.

The rest of the human race then recovered and slowly developed to its present form.

Once things had settled a little, the Elohim chose one group of people, the twelve tribes of Israel; known as the 'Chosen People' for that reason, and made them custodians of the written records of the Elohim and their interface with mankind.

This record of history has been garbled and corrupted over time, but otherwise the Jews have staunchly kept it safe for thousands of years, through displacement and dispersion, as exiles, through wars and slaughter and genocide. The Jews call it the Torah, and venerate it, and it is this veneration that was instrumental in preserving it.

We non-Jews now call it the Pentateuch, part of the Old Testament, which was once understood, but has subsequently been changed by theologians and ecclesiastical establishments. Over long centuries of time and many translations various religious authorities superimposed an overlay of their own monotheistic doctrines on it. Thus it was transformed into a catalogue of mythology and religion, encrusted with a thick tarnish of such sanctimonious holiness that nobody these days ever reads it for what it is; a history book.

*

If the above account of human history is compared to the established scientific view, it is evident that there is very little difference in what we would see when we look at the physical remains, very little changes.

We could argue endlessly about how lions and tigers and mammoths managed to survive the flood, but the fact is that they obviously did.

The facts in this book speak for themselves, and although there may still be many areas of detail left unmentioned, most of them would fall into place if we had reliable and definitive dates.

The most important thing missing from this sequence is that which scientists also badly need and greatly value; - reliable dating.

Without dates we cannot answer the inevitable questions that start with the words “Yes, but what about….?”

*

We don’t have to answer any questions, unless we want to. There is no need to argue with critics, unless we want to.

Evolutionists can keep their beliefs, except for their explanations of the origin of mankind and modern animals. Creationists can keep their beliefs, except for times that preceded the great make-over.

As for us, well, we do not have beliefs, we do not have faith or theories, instead of these we have three verifiable facts, summarised below.

There are three facts that this book addresses, facts that can be checked and verified by any scientist who cares to investigate. I am confident that they will find very little wrong, if they take the trouble to look.

These three facts are facts that scientists cannot refute because they are true.

This being the case, we do not have to answer any scientific objections. We can counter any criticism by simply pointing to any or all of these three facts, and politely suggesting to the irate scientist that the obligation to explain it rests on his broad shoulders, not ours.

We have the confidence of mathematical facts, why should we bow to mere theory?

The Three Facts

1) **The first fact** is the peg-and-string method of drawing the Stonehenge monument ground plan. This is actually a fairly sophisticated geometry, and I needed a modern calculator to verify that it would work. It is far and away beyond the capabilities of any supposed primitive Neolithic man. Not only does it work, it can be shown to actually have been used by comparing the geometry with the archaeology. It also demonstrates why the C14 dating is unacceptable. If a Neolithic man was responsible for it, then he was not Neolithic.

2) **The second fact** is the relationship between the various features of the monument and the orbits of the Solar System. These are exponential in nature and can be shown to be valid by statistical means. It may be objected that I 'repaired' the monument, and perhaps I did, but only to the extent that science repairs the fragmented skulls they dig up, or the text of crumbling old papyri. It is also validated by the

fact that it led me to discover the equation for the Solar System, which works. Again, it challenges the veracity of the C14 dating. If it be claimed that a Neolithic man was responsible, then he was not a Neolithic man.

3) **The third fact** is the Solar System mathematics. The Solar System itself bears witness to the testimony of this book, and the testimony of the scripture. The scheme of orbits in the Solar System is not only artificial; it is also just a rather large copy of the Stonehenge monument ground-plan. This also casts doubt on the C14 dates of the monument. If scientists would dare to check they will find that this claim is also a fact.

*

I think I will have a drop of Glenfiddich in my tea this time.

Ancient Knowledge

Part Four

Discussion of Religion

If we wish to know more about the Elohim and their interaction with humanity there is only one source of information and that is the Bible.

To that end the next two chapters discuss some elements of the Biblical narrative.

I am mindful of the fact that in the early part of this book I assured you that I was not a Bible thumper, and I meant it. I am certainly not a preacher and I am not trying to teach you religion.

These thoughts, suspicions and fears should not prevent us from considering the statements made in the Bible, which we may read as if it were a history book. The statements made in the Bible may well provide us with a better understanding of what the Elohim are doing.

If you are bored by the Scripture, sensitive about religion or bothered by blasphemy, you should skip to Chapter 15.

I am aware that many people believe in a Spirit God, and many of these may object to this book, but the more perceptive amongst them will realise that nothing said in this book would detract from the faith of true believers.

Chapter Thirteen

The Grand Plan - Smoke and Mirrors

To me, the order in the orbits of the Solar System is like a huge great big neon-lit "Hello!" sign in the heavens. I would love to be able to say 'Hi!' in return, but I do not know how to go about it, other than to write this book.

I have said many times that this book is about ancient knowledge, and is not about religion, and I have not changed my mind. I consider that I have adequately delivered the mathematics, and it is up to you to decide what to do with it, but I fear that neither you nor I will be able to totally avoid religion; it pervades the entire world, in one form or another, and sooner or later it will come knocking on your door.

One might have thought that with the Solar System being artificially ordered, and Babel being shown to be real, and antediluvian civilization being shown to be real, and the flood being shown to be real, and the Mighty Ones creating us, that religious people would be happy to consider these things seriously.

If you think that, then you would be wrong. Modern Christianity believes in a Spirit God, creator of the Universe, and I am maintaining (because those same Christians left me no choice) that the Elohim of Genesis must be real and physical because they used real physical power to move the planets. Even worse, I am suggesting that they are super-powerful visitors from a Galactic Empire; in fact we could not regard them as being anything else if we wish to stay in the real-world and not indulge in superstition.

Such a physical 'God' is anathema to modern advocates of the Supreme Being, so the whole of this book will be unacceptable.

The subject of religion is a very dangerous one; it is like walking on red-hot coals. There are always endless arguments about what words mean, or what ritual we are supposed to follow, absolutely anything anyone says will be instantly criticised, and allegations of heresy and blasphemy will be hurled around like bricks in a riot. It is unwise to venture into religious territory, and ordinarily I would avoid it like the plague, but we need to discuss how it is possible for a group of Mighty Ones to be transformed into the Supreme Being, how the three 'men' who talked to a nomad called Abraham about the destruction of Sodom could become transmuted into the One True Spirit Creator of the entire Universe, and worshipped by the Vatican with all its power and wealth.

Obviously the change is not a real one; the Elohim must remain as they were to start with. The change is one of human perception, and representation.

If we accept that the Elohim are real, and if we can bring ourselves to believe that they have a purpose with mankind, then we might have cause to think that they started religion deliberately.

This chapter and the next examine that possibility, and some of the implications.

*

Once I had recovered from the shock of discovering the mathematics I eventually returned to my armchair, the Bible, and my tea and biscuits, to try to answer the question of how these Elohim could become regarded as the Supreme Being.

The Bible is just a book, full of information on different subjects, and amongst other things it tells about the occasional interactions between the Elohim and mankind. It is the only source of information we have about the Mighty Ones, so if we wished to learn more, we would need to study the Bible in depth. We cannot go into it in too much detail, because it would take a whole book on its own, and most of it appears to be irrelevant, political history, songs, and so on, but there are a few details we can mention here.

The Bible is not religion. It may be regarded as the source for some religions, because religious sects appear to sprout on it like toadstools, the fungal mycelium feeding on the contents, but it is not of itself a religious book.

There must be millions of different religious sects, or belief systems, in the world today, ranging from small isolated cults like the Christadelphians to Ultra-Orthodox Judaism and Orthodox Christianity, countless protestant churches and the TV evangelists of America. There are Coptic Christians in Egypt, and a wide variety of different Christian groups scattered across Africa and all around the planet. These all spring from the writing in the Bible, and they all hold to different beliefs, so it is reasonable to ask which one is right, since they cannot all be right.

From my perspective the observed fact of so many different and diverse beliefs tell me one thing; it tells me that none of them are right. They all believe what they imagine to be right, or what they want to be right, but none of them are actually demonstrably correct.

If the Bible were to be telling us what to believe, then we would surely all believe the same thing? The Bible is not telling us what to believe, it is telling us nothing. It is no more than a record of events, as seen through the eyes and the pen of the scribes who wrote it; religion is something generated in the pious and God-fearing minds of the people who read it, and there we have a clue that might help us understand how things can become changed.

If the pious and superstitious people who read it are the same people in charge of translating and editing the original text, then that would contribute to the 'evolution' of ideas.

*

Perhaps we should have another quick look at some of the pages of the Holy Book, to see what we might see, but I am concerned that I might accidently and carelessly start growing a new toadstool.

Please understand, I am not advocating a new way of worshipping for anyone. My intention is just to discuss religion, not to start a mushroom farm of my own. I do not intend to preach at you, there are just one or two relevant points that I feel I should mention, and you might find them interesting and useful. After all, the world is full of religious people; polite elderly ladies full of zeal with white hair and blue eyes that sparkle with salvation are to be found everywhere, you will not be able to avoid them all.

YAHWEH

There is no such thing as monotheism. This is a misunderstanding.

To start with there were just a group of Elohim, but it wasn't long before the writer of the scripture decided there had to be a leader or boss, the chief of the Elohim. The structure of command was a simple one; the chief Elohim controlled a whole host of other Elohim. The chief Elohim became the Lord of the Elohim, or Adonai ha Elohim, and gradually he became elevated in status in the view of the scribes.

The current structure is the same. The Supreme Being in the modern superstitious version is not alone; he is accompanied by a host of Spirit Angels, and the distinction between a 'Spirit Angel' and a 'god' is rather a blurred one. Even under the supposed monotheistic regime, the Spirit Angels represent minor gods. The lineage of the 'angels' can easily be traced back, through the Old Testament 'Malak' or messengers, to the Elohim.

It is fairly obvious, at least to me, that the most significant change involved the metamorphosis of the Mighty Ones from physical reality to mythology and superstition, in the same manner as the Tower of Babel was transformed from fact to myth.

Over the intervening millennia the organisation of the command structure of the heavenly powers has not changed, only the terminology and the ideas. People no longer refer to the Lord of the Mighty Ones, worshippers now make them 'Spirit' and call them God and His Angels.

The story of Moses and the burning bush (Exodus Chp.3) is of some interest in this connection. Moses came across a burning bush, and it is important to remember that Moses was raised in a Palace in old Egypt and he had never seen a log-effect fire in his life, so he was very puzzled and turned aside for a closer look, to see why the bush was not consumed.

The event is also enlightening because the name of the Chief Elohim (YHWH, Yahweh or Jehovah) is used here three chapters before it was revealed. The first half-dozen verses of Exodus Chapter 3 feature an angel of Yahweh, Yahweh himself, and the Elohim. These are just words, but the English rendition confuses and camouflages the nature of the power behind the burning bush. We are left not knowing if it was Malak (Angel), Elohim (God), or Yahweh (LORD).

The superstitious assume therefore that these are all one and the same; monotheism is generated by default.

After the Elohim Lord had finished telling Moses what was about to happen, Moses asked the Lord what His name was, and the Lord replied "I am that I am." (*Ha**yah** ha**yah** = I am I am*)

The world of religion has made a great deal out of this enigmatic reply, interpreting it to mean that the Elohim Lord is calling himself the 'self-existent one' or something equally mystical, when in point of fact it seems to me to be just a way of saying 'My name doesn't matter, I am who I am', or words to that effect.

Then in Exodus Chapter 6 the Elohim Lord actually does tell Moses his name, only this time it is the Tetragrammaton, YHWH, unpronounced by Jews because it is too holy, but transliterated into English as 'Yahweh' or as here rendered 'Jehovah'. In the KJAV it is usually rendered 'LORD' all in upper case.

3 And I appeared unto Abraham, unto Isaac, and unto Jacob, by the name of God Almighty, but by my name JEHOVAH (YHWH) was I not known to them.

Here the words 'God Almighty' translate as the 'most powerful of Mighty Ones.'

If you are disposed to believe that this is an example of monotheism, then no doubt that is what it will mean for you, but if you start from a scenario of multiple Elohim then this will mean that YHWH is the name of the Chief or most powerful of the Mighty Ones. The Lord of the Elohim, or Adonai Ha Elohim, is here given a name, Yahweh/Jehovah. The word Yahweh is of uncertain meaning and is often reported by the concordances to mean "I am" or "I will be" or even "He who is".

It is worth noting that the full title is 'Yahweh Adonai ha Elohim', which literally means 'He who is Lord of the Mighty Ones', or 'I am Lord of the Mighty Ones'.

In case anyone is in any doubt as to the meaning of this passage in Exodus 6 v. 3 we only need to turn back a few pages to where this Lord actually appeared unto

Abraham and remind ourselves that Abraham greeted three 'men', and gave them food. They washed their feet, and 'they did eat'. (Gen.18 vs. 1-8)

One of these men was described as 'Yahweh/Jehovah' yet God has just told Moses that Abraham did not know Him by that name. This is a good illustration of how the monotheist editors have redacted the scripture to insert 'Yahweh' into places where it should not be.

There is abundant evidence that the scripture has been redacted, or heavily back-edited, *because this name YHWH was in common use in scripture well in advance of the name being revealed and often used as far back as Genesis*. It was used to refer to the 'LORD God' (Literally 'Yahweh Elohim') who made clothing out of skins for the first humans, thousands of years previously.

By using the name of the Chief of the Elohim in this way, transferring it back in time, it makes it look as though the name 'Yahweh' was known from the beginning, again implying monotheism where monotheism did not exist.

*

After the Exodus from Egypt which was aided and abetted by the Mighty Ones, (as reported by the scribe) with plagues and devastation, the Israelites enjoyed a forty year spell of wandering in the wilderness of Sinai, closely attended by Elohim. It is not known if these were the same or different Mighty Ones, but it makes little difference to the story.

It is during this period that I noticed a number of anomalies, further opportunities for editors and translators to introduce confusion.

In Exodus 13, v 21 it is stated that the LORD will lead the Israelites in the form of a pillar of fire by night, and cloud by day. The personal name of YHWH, is used here, and variously rendered as Jehovah or Yahweh in other versions of the Bible, in mine it is rendered LORD.

In Exodus 14 v 19 the scribe refers to the pillar of cloud as being motivated by one of the Elohim, (Malak, angel, Messenger of the Elohim) instead of YHWH, again introducing confusion and suggesting to monotheistic believers that the two are the same.

The anomalous situation described below is even more confused. The editorial interference is illustrated by the fact that some verses feature the LORD, while other verses switch to 'Angel of God', so we really don't know whether it is referring to Yahweh, or the messengers of the Elohim, or the Elohim. The fact that the scribe, (or later editors or translators) confuse the terminology used to describe 'God' suggests to me that they were trying to make a multiple group look like monotheism.

See if you can make sense out of what follows.

Moses and the Israelites are being led through the wilderness by a pillar of cloud by day and fire by night.

In the course of their ramble through that sunny wasteland they were led to Mount Sinai, where there was a significant event; the people were treated to a spectacular exhibition of power.

After they camped at Mount Sinai, they saw:

Exodus Chp.19 v. ***18 And mount Sinai was altogether on a smoke, because the LORD descended upon it in fire: and the smoke thereof ascended as the smoke of a furnace, and the whole mount quaked greatly.***

Apparently it was actually just a theatrical display put on by the Elohim to impress the audience, because, you see, the Israelites had an invitation, and free tickets for a ringside seat, to witness the spectacle.

Some days ***before*** this event, ***before*** Yahweh came down onto the mountain top, Moses went up the same mountain and spoke with Yahweh, who was already there waiting for him.

Chp. 19 v. 11 *(And* ***YHWH*** *said unto Moses)* ***be ready against the third day: for the third day YHWH will come down in the sight of all the people upon mount Sinai.***

Here we have YHWH on the mountain talking to Moses and informing Moses that YHWH will come down onto the mountain in three days.

Moses is also told to prepare the people for the show.

I would like to remind you that when the Elohim came to visit Abraham they did so quietly, as men, there was no display of pyrotechnics, nor any fire or smoke. I take it this means that the display of power at Sinai was just to impress the locals?

The Israelites were duly gathered to watch the spectacle, and thereafter spent a long time in the vicinity of the smoking mountain, believing and accepting that it was the Lord of the Elohim who was on the top of it.

It was shortly after this, according to the scribe, when the Chief of the Elohim allows himself to be seen, not just by Moses, but by at least seventy of the elders of Israel.

Exodus Chp. 24

9 Then went up Moses, and Aaron, Nadab, and Abihu, and seventy of the elders of Israel:

10 And they saw the God of Israel: and there was under his feet as it were a paved work of a sapphire stone, and as it were the body of heaven in his clearness.

11 And upon the nobles of the children of Israel he laid not his hand: also they saw God, and did eat and drink.

The word here translated as 'God' is the familiar 'Elohim or Mighty Ones of Israel'.

*

A little later we come across a very curious contradiction in Exodus 33 and it is worth looking at. Moses is at the foot of the mountain by the holy tent, or tabernacle, which is a kind of portable temple.

9 And it came to pass, as Moses entered into the tabernacle, the cloudy pillar descended, and stood at the door of the tabernacle, and the LORD talked with Moses.

This pillar of cloud is the one described in Exodus 13 that led the Israelites across the desert, where the power motivating it was described as an Angel, but is here described as Yahweh.

11 And the LORD spake unto Moses face to face, as a man speaketh unto his friend

Here we see Moses speaking with the LORD (Yahweh) who we assume came out of the pillar of smoke, **face to face**. Yet just a few verses later in the same chapter, we read this:

20 And he said, Thou canst not see my face: for there shall no man see me, and live.

21 And the LORD said, Behold, there is a place by me, and thou shalt stand upon a rock:

22 And it shall come to pass, while my glory passeth by, that I will put thee in a clift of the rock, and will cover thee with my hand while I pass by:

23 And I will take away mine hand, and thou shalt see my back parts: but my face shall not be seen.

It is small wonder that many people dismiss the whole thing as irrational, but for me it is an example of the multiple and physical nature of the Elohim, for surely here the scribe is talking about four or five different Lords? All but one of these Lords is designated in the Hebrew as YHWH.

1) There is a LORD in the pillar of cloud, which led the Israelites through the wilderness. It was this LORD that spoke to Moses face to face. Exodus 14 v 19 has 'Angel of God' meaning messenger of the Elohim.

2) There is another LORD in the same chapter whose face Moses is not allowed to see, so this LORD is different from '1'.
3) There is a LORD on the mountain, Ex 19 v 3, who Moses climbed the mountain to speak with. It is this LORD who tells Moses to prepare for another LORD to come down on the third day.
4) On the third day, as arranged, the LORD comes down in smoke with the sound of a trumpet.
5) The seventy elders all see the Elohim of Israel, his feet on a sapphire pavement, and presumably all see the Elohim's face; at least we are not told different. Here the word Elohim is used, not YHWH.

In all these events, which are very different in character, the word 'LORD' represents the use of the name YHWH. It seems to me that the name is being used to signify several different individuals.

I count at least four Elohim, three of them variously referred to as YHWH, or Malak/angels, so we may assume they all serve the same aims and purpose, they are a team.

It was natural for me to wonder why Moses was allowed to see the face of the YHWH who came out of the cloudy pillar, but he was not allowed to see the face of the other YHWH.

It is a curious incident, as Moses was fresh from talking to YHWH face to face, (Ex Chp.33 vs. 9-11) and then in verse 20 he was told he wasn't permitted to see the face.

Either the face of the one was terrifyingly ugly, which seems unlikely, since we are made in their image, or, it crossed my mind, if Moses had seen the face he might have recognised it as the face of one of his own people, an Elohim infiltrator posing as an Israelite. This may seem to be rather a fanciful suggestion, but is it as bizarre as believing that the Supreme Being showed Moses his backside?

Whichever way you look at it; it is clear that there are a number of different YHWHs represented here.

I studied these events carefully, and came to the conclusion that the scribe was referring to several different individual Elohim by the same designation of YHWH, perhaps as we might refer to official bodies like the FBI, the CIA, etc. because the individuals all came under the same command, all were a team, working for the same end and the same cause. They were a collection of individual working as one, but they were not one.

We do not have a monotheistic religion in Exodus, and there is nothing that can be interpreted as 'spiritual'. Whatever was going on it was all *very physical, with fire and smoke and cloud and sounds of trumpets.*

My conclusion is that use of the name Yahweh does not indicate monotheism or a Spirit God; it rather indicates the activities of a number of individual Mighty Ones, acting in collaboration one with another, almost deliberately trying to confuse.

This observation set me thinking and things started to get worse, again.

*

The Elohim appeared to me to be fussing around the Israelites like wasps around a beer can. There didn't seem to be much of a pattern to what they were doing. It was all smoke and mirrors, and the 'now-you-see-me-now-you-don't' routine just confuses. It all seemed just a little bit too artificial, stage managed like a modern 'magic' show, but it all served a serious purpose.

It is during the sojourn at Sinai that Moses was instructed to introduce a formal religion; apparently this was not so much to appease the Chief of the Mighty Ones, but more as a focus for the people who were becoming considerably restless and unruly, and wanted to worship a golden calf.

The Ten Commandments, and the other religious and civil laws, were given, along with the tradition of writing books of records. It was in the wilderness that the people of Israel became knit into an emergent Nation.

*

In Genesis 28 v 12 there is an account of a dream, in which Jacob sees a ladder reaching up to heaven, with Elohim/angels going up and down it. Though only a dream, I wondered if it were possible for us, (that means you), to climb a little way up that ladder, like you were one of the angels, and get a higher perspective. Let us try to see things from the Elohim's point of view.

With a higher viewpoint, and with hindsight, what did the Elohim achieve with the display of power at Sinai?

What they did was to take a bunch of escaped slaves, and weld them into a nation which still exists today, Israel. Not only that but they produced the religion of Judaism, and gave the world the Ten Commandments and a code of moral laws.

Israel and the Jews have had a major role to play in the history of humanity on Earth, not least of which was to play host to Jesus and the initialisation of Christianity.

Not a bad result for such a small group of Elohim and a bit of smoke.

We may conclude that with very little effort, just a handful of Elohim somehow managed to create the religion of Judaism and the nation of Israel.

I began to see the outline of a Grand Plan, which is not very obvious at first, because it takes thousands of years to come to fruition.

Just a little bit of thought should tell us that these Elohim would not do things at random. Everything serves a purpose, and these events in Sinai were part of that purpose. Creating Judaism was part of a Grand Plan.

*

As time passed the scribes began to emphasise the hierarchy of the Elohim. There are 'ordinary' Mighty Ones, which begin to be described with the word 'Malak' which means 'messenger', rendered as 'Angels' in the English version, and the Lord of the Mighty Ones, their Chief Mighty One, who is given various names and titles, amongst them the 'YHWH' mentioned above. These names/titles are used indiscriminately, and all refer to the Mighty Ones.

The concept of the supremacy of Yahweh Lord of the Elohim began to develop in the time of Moses, and it seems to have begun with:

Deuteronomy 6 v. 4 ***Hear, O Israel: The LORD our God is one LORD:***

This has often been quoted as indicating the start of monotheism, but it is not quite so grand. 'Hear, O Israel, YHWH our Mighty Ones is one YHWH.'

*

After the adventures of forty years spent in the barren desert eating manna, the Israelites were led to the east bank of the River Jordan, where Moses died.

Joshua took over as leader, and the Israelites crossed the Jordan River and seized the land of the Philistines (Palestine) by military conquest.

The Israelites settled in the land, and the Biblical narrative continues with a great many chapters devoted to the political and religious history of the people of Israel, their leaders and kings. A period of over a thousand years is full of incidents, but throughout all that time the attitude of the Israelites towards the Elohim hardly changes.

The formal worship of the Mighty Ones became comprehensively merged under the name of YHWH Lord of the Elohim, and became the focus of national identity for the Jews, whilst Elohim that were engaged in other activities became described as messengers, 'Malak, or Angels'.

However, the verbal descriptions offering us a graphic representation of the Chief of the Mighty Ones continued to depict him as a man, dwelling in the starry heavens, along with a host of mighty 'Elohim/angels'. Nothing much changed.

*

Many verses demonstrate the conviction of the Jews that the Chief of the Mighty Ones of Israel was a ruler over the stars in a heavenly kingdom, and the prophets often insisted that one day the Kingdom would come to Earth and the Mighty Ones would rule over the world.

For example Zechariah Chp. 14:

9 And the LORD shall be king over all the earth: in that day shall there be one LORD, and his name one.

The theme of the 'Kingdom of the Elohim' coming to Earth is an often repeated one, which extends down the centuries into the teachings of Jesus. It is a prominent theme in modern religion, but these days it is interpreted as a 'spiritual' Kingdom.

This old Biblical representation of the Elohim still held true at the very end of the period covered by the Hebrew scripture. The Chief Elohim of Israel was still accompanied by his Elohim messengers, or Angels, and he still looked like a man and still appreciated noisy trips around the desert on a vintage flying machine. (Ezekiel)

It is also true that about 500 years before Mary meets with the Angel Gabriel, the Elohim messenger was still being described as a man. *(Daniel 9 v. 21 Yea, whiles I was speaking in prayer, even* ***the man*** *Gabriel;)*

It is true that the development of systematic religion had slowly converted the Chief of the Elohim into the mightiest of the Mighty Ones, which is not so much a change of fact but more a change of word and human attitude. From there on the Jews maintained that the LORD - YHWH was the only name that should be worshipped as representing the rest of the Elohim who, of course, still existed as his 'Malak' messengers.

It is worth noting that over the time elapsed from Genesis to Jesus, a period of several thousand years; the basic outline structure of belief did not change greatly. The Elohim remained the same powerful entities that could be seen and heard and interacted with, and they still ruled over a Heavenly Kingdom in the stars. The only change was one of attitude amongst the Jews. The Priestly system initiated by Moses had slowly grown in power, the ritualistic worship had become more complex, and they had begun to put more emphasis on the leader or Chief of the Mighty Ones.

From the viewpoint of the Grand Plan, the Jews had preserved the legacy of the writings and stories about the Elohim for all the centuries that had passed since Moses. They had preserved the Laws and moral guidance, and had maintained awareness of the Elohim, under the banner of their worship of YHWH.

They preserved the records of Genesis, and if they had not done so, I would not have discovered the maths, and I would not be writing this book.

The passing centuries had also seen the expansion of the scriptural record to include such information as the fact that the Elohim rule over a Kingdom in the heavens, and that one day that Kingdom will come to the Earth, and that they will reveal themselves to mankind. (Isaiah 11 v. 9 and Habakkuk 2 v. 14)

These bits and pieces of information are mingled with prophetic utterances about the Messiah, and so together they prepared the way, and introduced these topics to the human consciousness.

It seems to be a long slow process of education, preparing humanity for eventual open contact with the Mighty Ones, at the time when they establish their Kingdom on Earth.

It may be noted that all these things devolved from the theatrical events at Sinai.

If we are perceptive, we can see that the events at Sinai were not as confused or as pointless as they appeared to be, they led inexorably to the Israel that existed in Roman times.

*

So it was that at the time of the Roman occupation of Israel over 2,000 years ago, the Jews had established a form of temple worship that praised YHWH, (Yahweh) the Lord of the Elohim, above all else.

*

Out of interest the singular of 'Elohim' transliterates as 'Elowahh'.

The Hebrew word 'El' literally means 'strength', but over the centuries it has come to be understood as referring to a 'God'.

The two terms 'Yah' and 'El' have been incorporated into many Jewish names, like Micha-el, or Gabri-el, both of which are Elohim 'messengers', or Yahshua which is transliterated as Joshua, meaning 'Yah saves' which was the Hebrew name of Jesus. Many of these old Hebrew names have survived into modern English, but people don't realise. Dani-el, or Daniel, means 'El is my judge' or 'God is my judge'.

The Coming of Changes

One of the most significant changes in human attitude towards the Elohim came about because of the rise of the Greek and Roman powers and the spread of the languages of those two countries.

It was only natural that over time the language and culture of the conquering nations would become prominent. So it was with the Greek and Roman languages in the times of Jesus.

In the Greek language there is no word for 'Elohim', the Greek uses the word 'Theos' which can only be translated as 'God'.

It follows that as we leave the Hebrew scripture and move into the Christian Greek scriptures, the transition from 'Mighty Ones' to 'God' is automatically made by the shift in language, and there is nothing anyone can do about it.

This also happened when the Hebrew Old Testament was translated into Greek, the result being called the 'Septuagint', which also rendered 'Mighty Ones' as 'Theos' or God. The same switch of meaning would also have happened in the fourth century translations of the Bible into the Latin Vulgate, for the Latin word 'Deus' cannot mean 'Mighty Ones' only 'God' or Deity.

The English Bible arrived via the Greek and/or the Latin, so this is why in my King James Version of the Old Testament I see the word 'God' instead of 'Elohim'. It would have been possible for the translators to have adjusted for the shift in language, one assumes that even the Greek and Latin would have plural words, but the translators and editors were already of a monotheistic persuasion so they probably wouldn't see the need.

In this way references to a plurality of Elohim simply vanished from our Bibles, all that remains of the plural form is the context, expressions like 'One of us' and 'In our image'.

We find a similar situation in the Christian Greek scriptures, or New Testament. There is no reference to Elohim or Mighty ones. Everything is rendered in the Greek language and 'Theos' translates as 'God', giving the appearance of monotheism. The 'angels' are retained, so strictly speaking, the old Elohim structure still exists.

These changes are simply vicissitudes of linguistics and human attitude; they do not change the facts of the matter. The Elohim remain unchanged in reality, but for the general understanding of humanity they became a monotheistic Greek/Latin 'God' plus 'angels'.

We should try to remember this change of terminology when we read the New Testament, or overhear people preaching from it. In the Greek language scriptures we have 'Theos' instead of the Chief of the Mighty Ones, and 'aggelos' or messengers, transliterated as 'angels' in place of the rest of the Elohim.

The Grand Plan thus preserved the knowledge of the Elohim and their doings down through the millennia by way of Israel and the religion of Judaism. Just in time, just before Israel was destroyed in AD70, the Grand Plan moved on, to another, grander, stage.

*

Gabriel, Mary, and Jesus

The next stage in the Grand Plan appears to be the founding of Christianity.

In Luke Chp.1 we are presented with Gabriel, whose name means 'Man of Strength' or 'Warrior of God'. Gabriel is an angel or messenger of the Lord, otherwise known as an Elohim, and he came to see a young Jewish woman called Mary.

Gabriel did not arrive at Mary's house by accident; he was sent, and we may deduce that there was good reason for Gabriel to appear at that time and in that place.

According to the narrative Mary talks with the angel as she would talk to any ordinary mortal man.

29 And when she saw him, she was troubled at his saying, and cast in her mind what manner of salutation this should be.

Mary was puzzled by his form of greeting, but she was not disturbed by his appearance. She didn't scream, or faint, she wasn't afraid, so we can assume that Gabriel looked and behaved exactly like a man. In fact, one might suppose, he was very similar to the man Gabriel who spoke with Daniel, (Dan. 9 v.21) and similar to those who spoke with Abraham thousands of years previously, or the Elohim God who made clothing out of skins for Adam and Eve. Nothing much has changed really.

Mary didn't scream, and we may rightly ask how the scribe could possibly have known what went on in such a private meeting, but it seems we are expected to take the scribe's word for it.

This encounter, true or false, reflects the belief of the scribe and his contemporaries, which must mean that the people of Jesus's day still accepted that the Elohim were real and physical and looked exactly like men.

*

Gabriel the Elohim came to see Mary, and here I run into a sticky and delicate situation.

There is a Hebrew euphemism commonly used in the Old Testament scriptures to denote sexual intercourse.

The expression is 'To go ***in unto*** (a woman)' and this can be demonstrated by reference to over twenty eight instances of its use in that way in the Old Testament scripture. (See appendix 1)

One example is found in Genesis 6 v 4 ***when the sons of God came in unto the daughters of men, and they bare children to them...***

And another in Genesis 16 v. 4 ***And he went in unto Hagar, and she conceived:***

There are lots of them, ***Ruth 4 v. 13 So Boaz took Ruth, and she was his wife: and when he went in unto her, the LORD gave her conception, and she bare a son.***

As I say, I count at least 25 other instances in the Old Testament where this expression is used as a sexual euphemism. It is only used as a euphemism in reference to going in unto 'a woman', not in other instances, like going in unto an empty room, or going in unto a palace or a king.

The strange thing is it occurs just once in the New Testament, in Luke 1: 28, where Gabriel has his meeting with Mary. According to the modern Church, it seems that it does NOT mean sexual intercourse took place.

And the angel (Gabriel) came in unto her – and of course she conceived.

Apparently the text was written in Greek, *but the writer was certainly familiar with the Jewish use of the expression*, so one is left wondering why he would use it in such a sensitive verse. I imagine any Jew would read it as being a sexual innuendo, if not an outright suggestion that Gabriel was the father.

Mary herself used another suggestive expression, when she called herself a 'handmaid'.

38 And Mary said, Behold the handmaid of the Lord; be it unto me according to thy word. - Mary gives her consent.

Both Mary and the unknown scribe were presumably Jews, living in Israel amongst Jews, immersed in Jewish culture, and very familiar with the Hebrew writings and their own history. Both would have known that a 'Handmaid' is a female slave, often used as a substitute wife, or a concubine. One good example is given above in Genesis 16 v 4, where Abraham goes ***in unto*** Hagar the ***Handmaid*** to produce a son.

So we see that there are not one but two euphemistic suggestions hidden in the text that strongly suggest that Gabriel was the father. Both of these expressions are everyday terms in the Old Testament, well understood by Jews, but used here in the New Testament just this once.

There is also a hint that these verses may have been edited, because if we give credence to the euphemisms, then Mary gave her consent ***after*** the deed was done, which is not the way it normally works. The whole episode would make more sense if the order of the verses were to be reversed, but we are not allowed to do that, so we won't.

Even if we ignore those euphemistic implications, the scripture claims that Jesus was both the Son of Man and the Son of God, explicitly a hybrid between Elohim and Human, just like the men of renown in Genesis Chapter 6.

… ***when the sons of God came <u>in unto</u> the daughters of men, and they bare children to them, the same became mighty men which were of old, men of renown.***

In this verse we see the same turn of phrase, the same euphemism, where Elohim go 'in unto' human women and they conceive and bare children, who grow up to become men of renown, just like Jesus.

This is blasphemy, but let me put it like this. When I first started my exploration of the book of Genesis I was very cynical and didn't believe a word of it. I subsequently learned, the hard way, that the stories of the early Bible do in fact have a connection with the real world. My research has left me knowing certain things about the origin and history of humanity, which could only have happened if the Bible contained truth.

However that does not mean that every single word is true, as advocated by the blue-eyed ladies who started me on this journey. Throughout my Biblical studies I have always been prepared to take the scribe's words on faith, so to speak, in order to see what resulted, but I have also kept in mind that much of it has been garbled and changed by editors and theological interference. Some of the Biblical narrative has plainly been altered somewhat by the preconceptions of both modern and ancient scribes, but the underlying substratum, the foundation of the Bible, is truth.

Considering all this, and everything else I have learned, leads me to accept that the scribe who wrote the story of Gabriel and Mary was expressing his thought that Jesus quite probably was the offspring of a union between Elohim and human. I have no mathematical calculations to support this conjecture; it is based entirely on the hidden Hebrew euphemisms, which would not have been there at all if they were not intended to be understood in that manner, and the similarity with the old story in Genesis chapter 6, which would have been well known to the scribe and the other parties involved.

It is worthy of note that the Elohim messenger Gabriel was deliberately sent by the Lord of the Elohim. Again, the scribe reveals privileged knowledge that he could not possibly have known.

Gabriel was not just passing by, he did not select Mary by chance, and he spent time alone with her in her room.

Why? Why did he embarrass her by entering her private rooms? If her child was conceived by the mystery of the 'Immaculate conception' as preached by the Church then Gabriel had no need to be there at all.

If the angel was there just to pass on the message, just to give Mary information, as the Church would have us believe, he could have said all that needed to be said while politely standing on her doorstep, he did not need to 'Go in unto her' as he did.

The conclusion has to be that the scribe, and his contemporaries, still held to the old understanding that Elohim could cross-breed with humans. It follows that the scribe considered Gabriel to be a physical personage, a closely related species to humanity.

The above exposition brings to prominence one aspect of the scripture that causes concern. How could it be possible for the scribe to have known what transpired between Mary and Gabriel? Unless there was a third party present, or a spy eavesdropping, the meeting was a very private event. A religious person would say it was by inspiration of God, (so it must be true), or perhaps the Elohim caused the words to be written? Who knows?

The Bible raises these thorny problems, which is one reason why it has been the source of countless arguments.

It is clear that the scribe is telling us that Gabriel is the Father, and it would follow from that, by extension, that when Jesus spoke about his Father in Heaven, he may well have been referring to Gabriel.

The problems of credibility and integrity arise when there is no evidence to support the contentions of the scribe, which means the choice is left to us to believe or not to believe.

There is a middle way, to accept on the basis of a presumption of truth, just to see if it results in anything significant. I did this with Noah and Babel, and it led me to discover the ancient knowledge, so it is sometimes a productive approach.

For example, if we accept that Jesus was indeed the son of one of the 'Elohim', then his teachings become very significant, because now we must understand his words as being a direct message from the Mighty Ones to man. Unfortunately we cannot know for sure, because of the problems with the scribe outlined above. It could be argued that Mary herself let the story be known, in order to account for her out-of-wedlock pregnancy, or we could argue that these things are often the subject of local gossip, and the scribe could have picked up on those rumours.

Whatever the truth of the matter, it all comes down to 'faith' in the end, or taking it for granted that a God-fearing scribe would not tell lies, and it is therefore most likely true.

I mention all of the above just to show that there is still a strong connection back to the old Genesis story; the events and actions are of the same 'character', even to the extent that scribes report things that they could not reasonably be expected to know.

*

About thirty years after the baby was born, when he had grown up, Yahshua (Joshua = Jesus) began to teach the people about the coming Kingdom, which in my understanding is the Kingdom of the Mighty Ones.

The main theme of his teaching is concerned with the 'Kingdom of Heaven'; in fact the word 'Gospel' means 'good news', the good news being that God's heavenly Kingdom is coming to Earth one day.

One thing that drew my attention was his statement that he didn't know when the Kingdom will come; nobody knows; not the Angel-Elohim, only the 'Father' knows. I wondered if this could be because the choice of when it happens is up to us. (Mark 13 v. 32)

He is never very explicit about the 'Kingdom', which leaves the nature of it open to question. If it is the 'First Contact' event that I refer to then it will be physical, as was believed by the Old Testament Jews and the early Christians, but it is always interpreted as 'spiritual' by the modern Church.

If Jesus actually was half Elohim, then he would have been highly intelligent and most likely knew a lot more than he revealed. We must remember that he was talking to people who believed in evil spirits and magic and all manner of other things. If Jesus knew about the ordered orbits, or Babel, he would not have had any good cause to mention them, and they would not have been understood anyway.

His job was to tell the people about the Kingdom of the Elohim, and that is what he did. He told the people lots of other things as well, but I am not going into them.

Throughout his ministry he refers to his 'Father in Heaven' and he teaches those who followed him to also think of God as their father in heaven. This is in accord with the notion that we are cloned of the same flesh and blood as the Elohim 'father in Heaven', and not just animated dust.

In connection with this he gives the first and greatest commandment as being "Thou shalt love the Lord thy God", which is like saying we should love the Elohim, our ancient heavenly parents, as a child loves his mother and father. It is not possible to command love, not even an infinite God can do that, so we must presume it is more along the lines of a desire than a demand.

'Love' is not the same thing as 'worship' in fact the two are mutually incompatible. If we loved the Elohim, we would not worship, no more than we would worship our own Earthly parents.

This is all given a spiritual twist by the religious authorities of the modern era, who insist that we substitute worship in place of love.

If I translate into simple mundane English, Jesus is saying that our progenitor who lives amongst the stars should be regarded as our parent, or father, and we should look forward to the time when the Kingdom of the Stars, or Galactic Empire, comes to Earth, but he doesn't know when that will be.

The general 'pattern' of this teaching by Jesus appears to me to be very similar to the message of Genesis, where we determined that a power that rules the starry heavens and gave us life is presumed to be returning to embrace Earth into his heavenly realm.

In fact Jesus gave us an example of what we might like to pray for.

'Our father that is in the heavens, may your Kingdom come, may your will be done on Earth as it is in the heavens.'

This was in fact his main message, transposed into ordinary modern language; it is the 'gospel' or good news of the kingdom, but this 'Kingdom' is not a metaphysical one, it is not a spiritual one, and it is not in another dimension. It is to be here on Earth, as illustrated by the following quote from Jesus himself:

Luke 21 v. 27 And then shall they see the Son of man coming in a cloud with power and great glory.

If Jesus is a half-Elohim then he is different from us, and he is a suitable mediator to act as a liaison between Elohim and humanity. This was his job, apparently, and this is why he was conceived and born. If he was just an ordinary man then he was quite a remarkable ordinary man.

The words in the Gospels have all been written down by scribes, and have been translated and collated and edited, so just like in the rest of the Biblical record we can expect to find a degree of distortion, but the main message comes across just the same. The teachings of Jesus paint the same picture as we have seen all through the Bible.

The Elohim are our 'parent' in 'heaven' and they are to bring their 'kingdom' to Earth one day.

The above is rather a brief and tawdry account of Jesus's life and teachings, but I promised not to indulge in preaching, so I will say not much more on the subject of Jesus.

The significant observation I would like to draw to your attention is the similarity of the story in its basic essentials, and in its atmosphere, with the preceding Old Testament accounts of the Elohim, all the way back to Genesis. We may perceive that little has changed since Genesis, we have physical Elohim in the person of Gabriel, and a physical Earthly 'Kingdom', so how did we end up with the modern religion where everything is 'Spiritual'?

The Grand Plan required a personage such as Jesus, who deliberately fulfilled all the prophecies of the Messiah, to the point of his own crucifixion, ***to confirm the truth of the coming Kingdom,*** and sow the seed grain for the next phase. The Grand Plan moves to a much bigger stage.

Chapter Fourteen

Culmination - The Kingdom of the Elohim

The observation of order in the orbits leads to the conclusion that there is a power greater than man.

This power is obviously interested in humanity, and we have concluded in previous argument that the Elohim wish to make contact, with a view to including Earth into the expanding 'Kingdom', or Galactic Empire.

The Grand Plan elucidated in the previous chapter culminates in the Kingdom, wherein large numbers of Elohim arrive to join with the skeleton crew who are already here.

It is perhaps no coincidence that the Bible says much the same thing as those proposed events deduced by logic from the observation of an Ordered Solar System. In fact, if we strip away all the magic and superstition and remove the supernatural from the Bible, it says ***exactly*** the same thing, in many places and many times over!

Here is just one example...

Matthew 25

31 When the Son of man shall come in his glory, and <u>all the holy angels with him,</u> then shall he sit upon the throne of his glory:

32 And before him shall be gathered all nations:

I think the people of Earth are in for a shock if they are unprepared for this arrival of 'Holy Angels' who are of course the Elohim colonial power.

We should consider for a moment that the objectives of the Elohim have been made abundantly clear over the ages; they have made no secret of their intentions.

The message in the orbits has been there since before humanity first walked on Earth, yet it has not been read by the world's astronomers. The fact is that the same message was found in Stonehenge and has been overlooked by archaeologists. The same message is in the Bible, repeated over and over again, and has been mangled into mysticism by the clergy.

The message is repeated in every church in the world every Sunday. It is found in preaching and in prayer, in psalms and in songs, and has been available for thousands of years, yet we refuse to accept that it is real.

The Church was established for the sole purpose of spreading that message, that 'Gospel – good news' that the Earth is to be accepted into the Galactic Empire, the Kingdom of God is coming here!

Matthew 6

10 Thy kingdom come. Thy will be done in earth, as it is in heaven.

The Elohim appear to have made every effort to get the message across, and humanity has steadfastly distorted it, received it as myth or superstition or reduced it to nonsense with supernatural ritual and mumbo-jumbo.

The Grand Plan was instituted to bring humanity to the condition wherein they can accept the reality of a greater power. The plan is intended to bring humanity and the Elohim together.

*

It is often stated that the coming of the Kingdom signifies the end of the world, but this is a complete misunderstanding. It is not the world that ends; it is the eon, or age.

Matthew 24

3 *And as he sat upon the mount of Olives, the disciples came unto him privately, saying, Tell us, when shall these things be? and what shall be the sign of thy coming, and of the end of the **world**?*

The word translated as 'world' is **aiōn** in the Greek, which means **'age'.**

Naturally, the Elohim will have governance, they are the superior partners, and this planet belongs to them, as do we, so the coming of the Kingdom is synonymous with the end of the realm of humanity, and the dawning of a new age, it is certainly not the end of the world.

The coming of the Kingdom to Earth is the central and most important theme of the teachings of Jesus, but the message has been lost in the quagmire of superstition that pervades the modern Church.

One of the things Jesus said particularly impressed me.

In Matthew 24 verse 14 Jesus said ***"And this gospel of the kingdom shall be preached in all the world for a witness unto all nations; and then shall the end come."***

I would remind you of something I pointed out earlier, that there were no printers or publishers in the world when Jesus spoke these words. There was no radio, TV, or internet. Jesus did not even write the words down, the scribe did not put pen to parchment until sometime later.

Both Jesus and the scribe would have been aware of roughly how big the known world was, and of approximately how many nations there were in it. He would have been aware of the extent of the Roman Empire, and the Greek Empire before it. He would have known of Syria and Jordan, Persia and India, Egypt, Ethiopia, and beyond.

In those days when every word had to be written with a quill on parchment or papyrus there was no equivalent of the modern publishing industry, so how could the Son of God be so confident that his good news of the Kingdom of the Elohim coming to Earth would be "preached unto all nations"?

No matter how worthy or inspiring the words were, it would have been an impossible dream without the help of the Elohim, and of course, Jesus was more than human, and he must have known his words were part of a plan, and that the Elohim would make his words come true.

If I were to say something similar, if I were to say that this book will be published in all nations, I would be being very presumptuous; I would rightly be accused of arrogance and foolish wishful thinking.

This book that you have in your hands will only be there for you to read if the Elohim help to publish it. As any hopeful author will know, even with a global industry of literary agents and mass communication, it is still virtually impossible to get a book published. So how much more impossible must it have seemed to a man living in the days of Jesus?

Jesus must have known about an Elohim plan, or he would have had no hope of getting his words spread throughout the entire world.

This is where the man known as Saint Paul comes into the Grand Plan.

*

When I look at the dogma and doctrine of the modern Church, I find it hard to see any connection at all with the teachings of Jesus, and this observation also raises a few questions.

It is true that the teachings of Jesus were not acceptable to the Jewish religious authorities because they were regarded as heresy. He was giving the people a different approach to the old Jewish set of divine laws, and even worse he was seen as claiming to be the Son of God, (half human - half Elohim) which the authorities regarded as blasphemy.

After Jesus had departed from the Earth, and was no longer a problem for the Jewish religious authorities, another problem arose. The followers of Jesus had established a small group of believers, they continued to teach his heretical doctrine, and were making nuisances of themselves.

None of this explains how Jesus's teachings could become so altered as to become almost unrecognisable, and here we come to another point in the story where great changes take place.

That small group of the followers of Jesus's original doctrine had an arch enemy called Saul of Tarsus.

Saul of Tarsus

Saul persecuted the disciples of Jesus wherever he could find them, and his one desire was to extirpate the new heretical sect. Saul was vehemently opposed to the teachings of Jesus; there can be no mistake about that.

Acts 9 v. 1 ***And Saul, yet breathing out threatenings and slaughter against the disciples of the Lord, went unto the high priest,***

2 And desired of him letters to Damascus to the synagogues, that if he found any of this way, whether they were men or women, he might bring them bound unto Jerusalem.

It was when he was on his way to Damascus to carry out this mission that something happened, there was an incident. (Acts 9 v 3)

It happened that Saul 'saw the light' and he subsequently claimed that he had received a message from Jesus himself.

There were a few more details, but the outcome was that Saul changed his name to Paul and claimed to be converted. He eventually became a member of the sect that he had formerly tried to destroy.

Paul (aka Saul) joined the early Christians, who still followed the original doctrine of Christ, and after an initial period of mistrust he finally gained their confidence, and it wasn't long before he took on the task of preaching to the Gentiles (Non-Jews) in the Roman world.

He was evidently of a very strong character; his writings show him to be a disciplinarian, and a very clever manipulator of human emotions. It wasn't long before he grew in influence and made a name for himself as chief apostle to the Gentiles, and quickly established small groups of followers (Churches) in many places beyond the borders of Israel.

Of course, outside of Israel most people couldn't speak Hebrew, and had no knowledge or understanding of Jewish history. Paul could preach his own version of the story without much fear of contradiction.

It was Paul/Saul who transformed the doctrine of Jesus into the 'Spiritual' form that the Churches preach today. This is why modern Christianity is called 'Pauline Christianity'. It is because they no longer follow the doctrine of Jesus, they follow the doctrine of Paul.

With his rich style of writing and clever turn of phrase Paul made his teachings very attractive. In this way over a period of years, and with lots of dedicated hard work, the original message that Jesus preached is more or less swamped by the Pauline doctrine that the modern Church espouses.

Where Jesus took a pragmatic and literal approach, Paul changed the meaning of it all by applying a principle of 'spiritualisation', which means he took the literal teachings of Jesus and the Bible and turned it all into an ephemeral non-real mystery cult, a form of numinous worship that religious Christians of all denominations still practice.

For Jesus the 'Kingdom' comes to Earth, it will be here on Earth, with the Mighty Ones in charge of humanity. For Paul it is a 'spiritual' Kingdom, where we all enjoy living in another dimension.

Jesus spoke of the resurrection as being a literal flesh-and-blood resurrection of the body, and immortal life as being physical, and a selective process. He even went to the trouble of getting himself crucified so he could be resurrected, setting an example.

Jesus describes the resurrection in Luke Chp.20 thus:

35 But they which shall be accounted worthy to obtain that world, *(aiōn)* ***and the resurrection from the dead, neither marry, nor are given in marriage:***
36 Neither can they die any more: for they are equal unto the angels; and are the children of God, being the children of the resurrection.

He says that the resurrected are equal unto the 'angels' which we know are Elohim, and we have a depiction of one such in the episode of Gabriel and Mary, which I have just described in the previous chapter.

Did Gabriel appear to be a 'spirit' or some kind of ghost?

Like all the other Biblical characters who described Elohim, Mary's description made Gabriel appear as a normal, flesh and blood, physical, person.

Are we to suppose that Jesus' own mother did not tell him what Gabriel was like? Are we to suppose that Jesus did not know?

Paul changed Jesus's plain teaching into a spiritual resurrection of the 'soul' and, where Jesus said it was for those 'accounted worthy', Paul made it open to anyone who had 'faith'.

In fact, close comparison of the teachings of Jesus and the teachings of Paul reveal that Paul contradicted Jesus and the followers of Jesus, on just about everything, but cleverly disguised the changes by the dexterous use of 'spiritualisation', supported by an impenetrable thicket of theological argument which very few people claim to understand, even today.

Above everything else Paul departed from the style of all the preceding scribes. The Biblical scribes all reported events, or facts. Paul took a different approach, he did not tell of events, Paul told us quite forcibly what he thought we should all believe.

We must also recognise that Paul's writings are very powerful, they are very convincing for anyone who is predisposed to the supernatural, but they all too often contradict Jesus, which is a polite and pretty way of saying that if Paul is right then Jesus is mistaken, or, as Paul would put it, we are mistaken in our understanding of Jesus, we should all listen to Paul's enlightened spiritual interpretation of Jesus's message.

The original followers of Jesus were Jews, they came from a Jewish culture, were steeped in Jewish history, and they understood the teachings of Jesus in a Jewish, Old Testament, sort of way. They would have understood what Jesus meant about the Father, and the heavenly Kingdom, and they would have understood that his teachings connected all the way back to Noah and the creation story in Genesis.

Paul separated from the Jerusalem Christians, and started to spread his metaphysical understanding throughout the Gentile world. Jews would not accept his preaching, but the non-Jews did. He travelled around all over the place, preaching his own brand of 'Christianity' as he went.

The common languages of the day were Greek or Latin, so the teachings of Jesus and the background of the Old Testament could no longer be properly expressed outside of Israel. Paul preached to the Gentiles, but he could not deliver the same perspectives, he could not have used the concept of Elohim or Mighty Ones, because the Greek word Theos did not convey the same meaning, so Paul taught spiritual monotheism.

Paul would not be troubled by this, because he had developed his own transcendent doctrine, which he spread far and wide, eventually preaching in Rome itself. That was the beginning of a credo that eventually gave rise to the Roman Catholic Church, and the concept of a Universal Monotheistic Spirit God.

Modern Christianity is called 'Pauline' Christianity because it follows the metaphysical spiritualised mystery cult of Paul, and pays only lip-service to the teachings of Jesus.

So now we have a world dominated by the Pauline ethereal mystery religion, which no longer recognises the hard-headed teachings of Jesus himself. As for the group of original followers of Jesus in Jerusalem, they disappeared from the story, and were seldom heard of again.

We could say, as many religious people do, that Paul was right, that he was speaking by inspiration of the 'Holy Spirit', and he fulfilled the prophecy by bringing the word of God to the Gentiles, or we could argue that he achieved his original ambition and destroyed the heretical teachings of Jesus and the early followers of Jesus.

One thing is certain, although Paul retained the hierarchy of the ancient Elohim, with the Chief and his subservient Mighty Ones, (Angels) he had elevated their status beyond anything that ever came before. For Paul, the Chief of the Elohim is now the Supreme Being, promoted and spiritualised, and now the Kingdom is a spiritual Kingdom of the spiritual Heavens, and everything becomes 'spiritual', but not in the original meaning of the term.

Paul's writings are very poetic, full of power and confidence, and they are quite mesmerising, but they differ markedly from the language of Jesus and the rest of the Bible writers. His letters are very clever and persuasive, but they do not tell the same tale as the rest of the Bible. The concepts proposed by Paul do not appear to be in the same context as the teachings of Jesus the Son of the Mighty Ones.

Let me explain it in another way.

The very Son of God, the Son of the Supreme Being (as reported) tells us things; his teachings are recorded in the Gospels, and we would expect that the words and teachings of the Son of God himself would be held to be of absolute authority by his followers.

Paul would have known that Jesus was acknowledged to be the Son of God, and therefore of supreme authority on Godly matters, yet he avows to have had a message from that same Son of God while on the road to Damascus. Apparently, judging by Paul's subsequent doctrine, this Son of God and supreme authority on Godly matters wanted Paul to preach a contrary view, thus undermining and destroying the very Gospel that the Son of God himself spent three years teaching.

It seems like a strange thing for Jesus to do, be he resurrected or not.

Something is not right somewhere.

The teachings of Paul were so strange and mysteriously spiritualised that they appear to me to represent a complete break with the traditions and beliefs of many thousands of years, though naturally they are treasured by the Church that he established. Paul is revered as Saint Paul, the bringer of enlightenment and the person who explained and revealed the 'true' meaning of the word of God, but what he actually brought was metaphysics and magic in place of matter-of-fact reality.

Over the years following Paul's death his extraordinary spiritualised distortion of the Biblical narrative became very popular amongst non-Jews, and spread throughout the Roman Empire.

When the Roman emperor Constantine the Great (306 to 337 A.D) converted to Christianity, it was Paul's spiritualised mystic belief system that he adopted.

Paul's elaborate supernatural variant of Christianity was so richly embellished with flamboyant and baroque 'spiritual' adornments that it soon became firmly established and flourished into the Papacy and the Roman Catholic Church.

The original teachings of Jesus, and his followers in Jerusalem, were overshadowed and eclipsed by the rise of Pauline Catholicism.

Where the traditional story of the Bible was matter-of-fact and physical, and resulted in my discovery of the order in the orbits, the Pauline form of Christianity shifted everything into the realm of metaphysics and superstition, and offers no opportunity for a return to pragmatism.

So we can see how the physical Elohim became transformed into the monotheistic Supreme Spirit Being of modern theology. For the most part it was the work of one man, Saul of Tarsus, also known as Saint Paul.

If we remember our principle, that I am to give the scripture the benefit of the doubt, then we must accept that it was the Elohim, or in fact Jesus himself, that gave this mission to Saul/Paul on the road to Damascus.

It would seem strange, if taken at face value, that the Elohim, who we take to be physical, should instruct Paul to preach the 'Spirit'.

Why would they do that?

The Elohim want us to find out about them, and they are not going to get very far if the story is confined to the dusty alleyways and back-streets of Jerusalem.

Severely hampered by the absence of modern mass communication media, they needed someone like Paul with his fanatical drive and ambition to create an attractive and dynamic means of broadcasting and advertising the scripture, a means such as Pauline Spiritualised Christianity, which would serve as a gaudy vehicle to spread the rest of the Biblical information all around the world.

*

Paul was basing his teachings on a variation of the teachings of Jesus, and Jesus in his turn was building on a variation of the teachings of Moses and the Jews, and Moses traces his ancestry back to Abraham, and before him, Noah, who built Babel in an attempt to preserve ancient knowledge about the Elohim.

Perhaps you can see a long sequence of connected events, which stretch back through time to the antediluvians and the original Elohim?

We should accept that the Elohim are in charge of this world, and always have been. We humans develop 'naturally', or at least we think we do, and we would be resentful if we believed that we were being controlled and guided by a superior being, but we are being guided none the less.

It is clear that at Mount Sinai the Elohim started the Israelite's religion deliberately, a religion which eventually became Judaism, and they also started Christianity deliberately, by bringing Jesus into the world. It is not hard to think that they started Pauline Christianity deliberately as well. His vision on the road to Damascus changed the world.

It is credible that without Saul/Paul and his fervent zeal, Christianity would probably have remained as a minor Jewish heretical sect. This is very likely to be the truth of the matter, and for that reason we can say that Saul/Paul undoubtedly was actually subjected to a direct contact with the Elohim while on his way to Damascus that fateful day.

That is what the scribe claims to have happened, and as a result the story of the Elohim and the Good News of the Kingdom of God coming to Earth has been spread all over the globe.

The words of Jesus in Matthew 24 have come true because Paul made them come true with his zeal, his indefatigable energy and religious drive, and the attractive flamboyance of his spiritualised vision of God. There may still be a remote corner of the planet where the Bible is not known about, but for the most part it has at least been heard of just about everywhere. Even if it is not understood, or people do not read it, or do not believe it, they know it exists.

There can be no doubt, the spread of the Bible around the world was the result of Paul's efforts to 'spiritualise' the message of Jesus.

*

We can look a little deeper, and go back to that single brief visit of the Angel Gabriel to Mary's house, and ponder on the fact that Mary was not chosen at random. Because of the Elohim, Gabriel and that brief encounter, the entire world has changed.

It is also because of that other single incident on the road to Damascus, because of that single moment in history two thousand years ago, that people in Nebraska go to church on Sunday, and it is because of that same incident that we now have TV evangelists, and a world populated by people who have at least heard of a superior being, and who have become psychologically receptive to the idea that superior beings might exist.

It is thanks to the efforts of Paul and his very attractive religion that a great many Christians are preparing for the end of the world, getting ready for the 'rapture', whatever that is. There are literally millions of believers who have seen the signs of the times and are fully convinced that God's Kingdom is nearly upon us.

If we look at the world in this way, to see behind the events, and examine the results, it is possible to detect faint traces of the work of the Mighty Ones as they strive to implement the Grand Plan and prepare humanity to accept and welcome the arrival of the Elohim and the Kingdom age.

*

In this view of events, we may see Paul and his spiritualised religion as being a product of the Elohim after all, but that doesn't mean we have to embrace it for ourselves. Pauline Christianity is just a device, a vehicle to carry information about the Elohim around the world, and that objective appears to have been almost completely accomplished.

The stages of the plan can be followed, but only by trying to think like the Elohim.

If the Mighty Ones arrived tomorrow in power and glory, then thanks to Moses, Jesus, and Paul, there are billions of Christians who will be willing to believe, and will probably be so enthralled that it will not even cross their minds to ask if the 'God' is physical, and there are many billions more, even agnostics, who have heard of 'God' and would not be totally unprepared if it turned out to be true.

Any human who accepts the reality of a 'God' will be partially receptive to the arrival/revealing of the Mighty Ones.

There are many others who have been conditioned by the special effects of popular science fiction films to accept the arrival of powerful 'aliens', and followers of the cult of UFO's would not be expected to reject the Mighty Ones.

There are still many people in the world who would **not** be inclined to welcome the Elohim, including for example, atheists, communists, politicians and military commanders, and so I cannot estimate how long it will take, but the world is now heading in the right general direction, slowly moving towards global unity, and even more slowly, being habituated to the news that the Kingdom of Heaven is coming to Earth.

Armageddon

Logic and reason suggest that the Elohim would be better off communicating with a united world, a society that would fully welcome their arrival, but humanity has never been united and certainly not united in their religious beliefs.

The Biblical prophets are full of tales of war and destruction, of judgement of nations, and the rendering of recompense. People are proud and independent, and may not like to be governed by a super-powerful Elohim regime. There will be many humans who will resist them, and suffer accordingly.

There is some talk in the Bible of Armageddon, which by tradition is the last Great War; it is waged against the Elohim by those who oppose them.

Armageddon is only mentioned by name once, and is actually the name of a place, but it has come to signify the war itself and the destruction of the unworthy.

Revelation 16 v 16: And he gathered them together into a place called in the Hebrew tongue Armageddon. (v.14, ***the battle of that great day of God Almighty).***

It would seem that although we might hope and strive for unity of purpose amongst the nations, humanity will be intransigent to the last.

Spirit versus Pragmatism

My assertion that the power that put the order into the Solar System consisted of super-powerful visitors from across the void of the starry heavens is not at variance with the statements of the scribes in the Old Testament scriptures, nor is it in disagreement with the story of Jesus.

In fact, the discovery of the artificial order in the Solar System brings the written words of the Bible story into the real world, and confirms it as valid truth.

The differences between the actual writings in the Old Testament and the beliefs of modern religions are very great, but the biggest and most significant is the modern assertion that everything is 'spiritual' or supernatural.

To be perfectly honest I am not completely sure of what is meant by the term 'Spirit'. It seems to me that believers are claiming that it is all imagined and that none of it is real, but they are going to believe it anyway.

My opinion is my own, and I do not mean to intrude on the beliefs of others, so if you are inclined to believe in the 'Spirit' then you must understand these things in your own way, as I am sure you will.

If a devout Christian were to be approached with the allegation that his beliefs are imagined, invented fantasy, the believer would probably smile knowingly and offer to pray for the enlightenment of the poor deluded critic, but there is no reason for making such an approach in the first place. People are entitled to believe what they want.

One point of invariance across the millennia is the belief in, and expectation of, the coming of the Kingdom of God. Differences arise in the understanding of the nature of that Kingdom, but the awareness of it is not in dispute.

*

We may rightly ask how this dependence on 'spirit' as a foundation for Christian belief could possibly be derived from the teachings of Jesus, who admittedly used the term, but very sparingly, and usually in the appropriate context of a 'life-force', or 'living', and sometimes in the context of 'character'.

Modern Christianity, as generated by Paul and taught in the Catholic and Anglican Churches, owes very little to the teachings of Jesus or the writings of the ancient scribes. It owes everything to the mystery cult of Paul, with a liberal addition of Saints, Mary-worship, relics, miracles, holy water, icons, and all manner of mystical trappings.

It is now possible to understand how the simple message of interstellar colonisation revealed by the ancient scribes came to be transformed into a global mystery cult.

There are about 2.2 billion professing Christians in the world, of which about half are Catholics, so it seems I am in a minority of one.

All of these follow the Pauline doctrine in one form or another, and worship the One True God, the Infinite Spirit, who is the Supreme Being. This being the case, I feel that I should confront the subject head on, and see what transpires.

Someone has an idea that there is this huge life-force, a nebulosity, a vast intelligence that created the Universe; a Supreme Being. Fine, Ok, I can go along with that. But why worship it?

One may accept that a Supreme Being is worthy of our gratitude and respect, but to claim that in some way it would be impressed by our infrequent worship or the meaningless incense and ritual of the Church is beyond my comprehension.

Worshippers will continue to worship no matter what I might think. A true worshipper would not be reading these words anyway, they would not have got past the blasphemy in chapter one, which is mainly why it was there.

The notion of a 'Spirit' God has a distinct advantage over a physical Elohim, in that the Spirit God is totally subject to the will of the believers.

'God is Spirit' says religion, 'God also has a Spirit,' says religion, so it seems that the Supreme Being, now called a 'Spirit God' who is made of Spirit, also ***has*** a Spirit, called the Holy Spirit. We must also include the Son, who is also a Spirit, despite being last seen as a resurrected flesh-and-blood body. These three Spirits are really only One Spirit, known as the Trinity, or Godhead, who is/are accompanied by a heavenly host of Angels, all of whom are also Spirit, and they all dwell in a Spirit dimension called 'Heaven', which is no longer the realm of the stars. If we wish to worship Him and be spiritually saved and enter into His spiritual kingdom we must worship Him in spirit, and obey all His spiritual laws.

If we question this gobbledegook we are told that it is a mystery only revealed unto true believers. How does one become a true believer in the first place, if what one is supposed to believe is not revealed until after you believe it? Nonsense piles upon b=nonsense.

A Spirit God is whatever the believers want Him to be. He can be infinitely good, and infinitely forgiving. If we murder or rape or steal, we have but to confess our sin and we will be forgiven.

Nobody really knows what is meant by 'sin' except that it is rather naughty. A lot of 'Sin' depends on the particular sect one 'belongs' to.

If we have enemies, or people we don't agree with, our Supreme Being will be vengeful, and support us in our efforts to exterminate the un-believers. A Supreme Being will do anything, and be anything, but He will always be on the side of the faithful, He will always support the particular sect that devised and determined His personal characteristics.

In wars, the Supreme Being is always on our side, but the enemy think He is on theirs, so whoever wins praises the Supreme Being, and thanks the Lord for the victory. The losers bury their dead and offer up prayers to the same Spirit God, begging Him to accept the soul of the recently slaughtered.

*

In the Bible, 'God' did not start out as the Supreme Being, as you should know by now. He started as the Mighty Ones, the Elohim, who ordered the orbits of the Solar System and cloned mankind in their own image.

Since the whole religion thing got started an awful lot of confusion has crept into the Bible to befuddle the faithful. Pious editors have edited the original, superimposed their own beliefs on it like a sticky varnish of doctrine and dogma from a much later age, and this in its turn has led to a whole load of apparent contradictions, all of which were further confused by the attempts of theologians to explain it all.

Despite all these changes, the Bible still retains a sense of dignity and great significance; it still conveys information, which is disregarded by many.

Nowadays the Elohim have been forcibly evicted from their former home amongst the stars, promoted to Supreme Being, or Spirit God, and sent to live in an alternate dimension, where they can't cause any trouble. Fortunately the Elohim don't seem to mind being so misrepresented, in fact they appointed Paul to preach that very doctrine.

Notwithstanding all that, even though the Supreme Being is now regarded as being outside of the Universe in another dimension, and infinite in power and majesty, He is still held to be at the beck and call of believers, who constantly demand that He answer their myriad prayers and grant all their various wishes, and intercede on their behalf in any trivial disputes with other believers.

The significance of all this is that the modern 'Spirit' God is totally under the control of the worshippers, and those who have established themselves as being the leaders of the faithful. These self-appointed 'most-reverend' representatives of the Almighty always claim to be teaching 'by the grace of God', and in 'His service'. They claim that they are empowered to lead the congregation by appointment of the self-same Spirit God that they manipulate.

Here is a profound dissimilarity between the Elohim of the Bible and the modern Spirit God. The Elohim were not slow to criticise and condemn the people of Israel for wrongdoing. The Elohim of Israel rounded on the Jewish people many times, and hotly condemned the whole nation for its back-sliding and lack of righteousness, something that the modern Spirit God can never even contemplate doing.

Therein rests the weighty difference between an invented God who serves the purposes of the inventor, and a real powerful Lord that makes his displeasure known, in no uncertain terms.

The Infinite Almighty God has no mind of His own, not any more. God is compelled to forgive sinners; He is no longer permitted to pile burning coals of fire on their heads. The Supreme Spirit is no longer empowered to judge reprobates and wrongdoers, the Human Rights Act has seen to that.

The problem I have with a Spiritual God is not whether or not He exists; my problems are centred on the observation that the modern Spirit God is entirely subservient to mankind. This cannot be the case if the Spirit God is real.

If the infinite Spirit God is real, then humans should be doing what He says, not the other way around. A real God, a real power, must assert real influence; just like the real Elohim who put the real Solar System into real order.

The Blasphemy Paradox

This will only work for you if you understand that the mathematics really does demonstrate that the Solar System order is artificial.

The paradox goes like this, I hope you can follow it:-

Note 'A' - It is often claimed by theologians and believers that the existence of a Spirit God cannot be proved, or disproved.

I have mathematical evidence that demonstrates that someone put the Solar System into artificial order, and since this evidence is derived from the Bible, I would like to suggest to the Church and believers everywhere that this mathematics proves the existence of the God of the Bible.

However, all of those 2.2 billion Christians who believe in a Supreme Being must object to this, because they all agree that God cannot be proven to exist.

If a Spirit God cannot be proven to exist then it must follow that whoever it was that put the Solar System in order, it was not the Spirit God, or He would be proving Himself to exist, and He cannot do that, so it must be someone else who put the orbits into artificial order.

This ‘someone else’ cannot be another Spirit God, because there is only one Spirit God, it follows that someone powerful that is not a Spirit God must exist, and we may call this someone ‘Elohim’.

If the Elohim cannot be a Spirit God, then they must be physical beings.

This is the position taken by this book, the Elohim of the Bible are physical beings. This assertion will be a problem for religious people.

These Mighty Ones who put the Solar System in order are identified as the Elohim or God of the Bible, and that must mean that the God of the Bible is physical.

If physical beings are presenting themselves as the God of the Bible, then the Church and the 2.2 billion Christians must consider that the physical Mighty Ones that put the Solar System in order are imposters.

Pretending to be God is blasphemy. So if the God of the Bible is a physical imposter then Christians must hold Him to be guilty of blasphemy.

But the authority of those 2.2 billion Christians is based on the God of the Bible, and so if the God of the Bible isn’t really the Spirit God of the Bible, if He is physical and an imposter, then their authority is annulled, so they are no longer qualified to comment on religious or Biblical matters, and therefore are not authorised to accuse the God of the Bible of being an imposter and a blasphemer.

The only way the Church and 2.2 billion Christians can restore their authority is for them to accept that the power that ordered the Solar System was the Spirit God after all.

The Spirit God would then be again proving Himself to exist and He cannot prove Himself to exist, because part of the Pauline dogma is that salvation is by faith, and faith depends on not knowing for sure. It follows that if God proves Himself to exist; the resulting sure and certain knowledge that God exists destroys faith and removes salvation.

The Church's God will never allow faith and salvation to be destroyed, so a genuine Spirit God would never prove Himself to exist, so then the God of the Bible must be a blasphemous imposter after all. But if God is a blasphemous imposter then there is no point to faith and no meaning to salvation, and that poses a dilemma.

So the Pope, the Church, and 2.2 billion Christians all have to say that the mathematics of an ordered Solar System is not the work of a Spirit God, because if it were, then the Spirit God would be revealing Himself, He would be proving Himself to exist, and destroying the salvation that comes through faith.

If then it is not the work of a Spirit God, then it must be the work of a physical Mighty One, or group thereof.

If Christians accept physical Elohim, and ignore the blasphemy, then they can salvage faith, and restore salvation by faith, but at the same time they destroy the Spirit God that they have faith in, and so destroy the salvation they hoped to obtain through their faith.... [And so on and so on ad-nausea.]

In fact the above argument actually proves that the Spirit God does not exist, because if He did exist He would not allow someone to put the Solar System in order, because that proves that He does exist, and according to the theologians, if He existed, he would not allow anyone to prove He existed, so He would not allow the Solar System to be ordered.

Since it is a matter of observation that the Solar System is actually ordered, we can safely conclude that the Spirit God of theology does not exist.

But, according to theologians, we cannot prove He does not exist, so we would have to accept that He does exist, and did put the Solar System in order.

That means we must go back to 'Note A' at the beginning of this section and start over, or.....

Exit from Blasphemy Paradox

*

So, the Catholic Church leaders are not the only ones who can indulge in absurd gobbledegook. I can be quite good at it as well.

It is much simpler, and avoids paradoxes, if we just accept that the power that put the Solar System in order is physical.

Putting paradoxical argument aside for one moment, it is clear that as and when the Elohim agree to show themselves, there are going to be a lot of red faces in the Vatican.

*

We are then faced with the problem of why the Elohim do not trouble to correct mankind, why did they engage Paul/Saul to preach the 'Spirit'? Why cause humanity to worship a Spirit?

It is probably for the reason explained above; it was the best way of indoctrinating the maximum number of people into accepting the possibility that the world will one day be ruled by a superior power.

If we look at the effect it has had on the world, we can see that it certainly worked as a ploy to spread the 'Good News' to all the nations of the Earth, as predicted by Jesus.

While mankind is so engrossed with worshipping a paradoxical Spirit nobody stops to consider that there might be some really powerful and very physical superior beings lurking in the cobwebs of ancient knowledge, but at one and the same time the way is still prepared for the arrival of the Elohim, in power and great glory.

We could not easily continue with our way of life if we fully understood that the Elohim were real. Believe me; I know how hard it can be.

*

Now we really should look at the bigger picture, and if we do that then we find that our perspective on these matters might well change.

If you were to turn back to the first chapter of this book, you will find written there a few paragraphs describing how the Bible has shaped the civilisation of the Western World. Most, if not all of that shaping has been done by Saul of Tarsus, otherwise known as Paul, and his Spiritualised version of Christianity.

We should try to climb a few more rungs up the heavenly ladder and see the bigger picture; try to get an even higher perspective and take a wider look at the results of the Pauline Christian religion.

The Grand Plan culminates in the Kingdom, and the purpose of the Grand Plan is to bring the Earth and its inhabitants into the Galactic Empire.

Isaiah 11

9………. for the earth shall be full of the knowledge of the LORD, as the waters cover the sea.

Habakkuk 2

14 ………For the earth shall be filled with the knowledge of the glory of the LORD, as the waters cover the sea.

Ezekiel 38

23 Thus will I magnify myself, and sanctify myself; and I will be known in the eyes of many nations, and they shall know that I am the LORD

*

There must come a time when a majority of people in the world ask the Mighty Ones to show themselves, and then the human race will know for sure that the Elohim exist. I make this claim because it seems to me to be the sensible way for the Elohim to behave, but I could be wrong. If they simply turn up uninvited their arrival would probably provoke a lot of trauma and hostile reaction.

I am assuming they will wait for us to recognise them and accept them, because the whole point of Jesus and Paul is to educate people to that end, to create a world religion that teaches the coming of the Kingdom.

All the different religious sects have developed different ideas about what is meant by the Kingdom of God, and I am not going to discuss any of them. I will however point out that there appears to be three versions of the Kingdom in the Bible.

1) One espoused by the Old Testament prophets held that the 'Kingdom of God' is when the Elohim come and rule over the Earth. There is also the 'Kingdom of Heaven' which is the Elohim domain/empire in the stars.
2) The second is the one proposed by Jesus. This is similar to the first, because God comes to rule over the Earth. The main difference is that people can be elevated in status, changed in some way whilst alive, and by the dead, who are resurrected to be like the angels. I can understand being changed while alive, by some kind of genetic alteration, but resurrection is a bit of a problem for me. I suppose it is remotely possible without invoking magic but it would depend on how long the subject had been dead, and the medical and technological expertise of the Elohim.

3) The third is as Saul/Paul and modern Christianity would have it, that the Kingdom is a spiritual heavenly place, a different dimension where our immortal souls go after death.

*

If I was asked for my own view I would go with the first or possibly the second. If asked what it will be like I would have to say I don't have the faintest idea, to be honest. I can conjecture, and did so earlier in this book, but that is guessing. We could become elevated to the status of Elohim, or we could be servants, or we might just carry on with our normal lives, I do not know.

Let me suggest that a small advance party of Elohim spent a lot of time and energy travelling across interstellar space to get here, and then they had to put the planets in order, which took more time and effort. They terraformed the Earth, and covered it with animals and plants, and then they cloned humans and told them to be fruitful and multiply and fill the Earth. ***A small group remained here and spent thousands of years raising us and educating us, and trying to make us receptive to the idea of joining a Galactic Empire, and having a greater power coming to rule over us.***

Altogether the amount of time and effort the Elohim have put into this project has been beyond imagining, yet it was apparently all for one purpose. The grand culmination is the coming of the Kingdom.

From this I can only conclude that the Kingdom must be something worth all that time and effort. Certainly the Elohim must think it is worth it, or they wouldn't have bothered, and I am confident that it will be good for humanity as well, or at least, I hope so.

*

There is also the 'doomsday' scenario that deserves some minor comment.

Acts 2

20 The sun shall be turned into darkness, and the moon into blood, before that great and notable day of the Lord come:

Matthew 24

29 Immediately after the tribulation of those days shall the sun be darkened, and the moon shall not give her light, and the stars shall fall from heaven, and the powers of the heavens shall be shaken:

Religious pundits will provide many interpretations of these weird celestial events, but from my profane viewpoint I would say that one would expect a severe distortion of the local space-time continuum if a large interstellar FTL starship were to suddenly slam on the brakes as it arrived in our Solar System.

*

To summarise, the original story of the Bible was not a religious one, it was a story of super-powerful space travellers, interstellar colonisation, terraforming, and cloning.

The Elohim have spent thousands of years trying to educate mankind to the coming of the Kingdom of Heaven to Earth, and we call the process of education 'Religion'.

*

The physical power of the Mighty Ones is written in the planets, and revealed in my chapter 10 and figure 10. It is also in the Psalms:

Psalms 19:

1 The heavens declare the glory of God; and the firmament sheweth his handywork.

2 Day unto day uttereth speech, and night unto night sheweth knowledge.

Apart from Paul, who makes the whole thing mysterious, magical, and spiritual, throughout the entire Bible the story is consistent with the Mighty Ones being physical in nature. The same applies to the sporadic claims by the scribes and the prophets that one day these Mighty Ones will establish their kingdom on Earth, or in other words, the Earth will join the Elohim Kingdom/Empire in the heaven of stars. The story of the prophets and the scribes is consistent; the Kingdom of Heaven will come to Earth – literally. We are all the children of the living Elohim, we are the offspring of the Mighty Ones, and nothing can change that.

*

Let's have one final tea break.

The story so far is that the group of Elohim engineers who ordered the Solar System and terraformed the planet have moved on to the next job, leaving behind a skeleton crew to manage humanity until the main party of Elohim settlers arrive to establish themselves as Earth's new government.

The arrival of these ambassadors of the Elohim will constitute the start of the Kingdom age.

One odd thing that I noticed as I read through the Bible was that the skeleton crew of Elohim or 'angels' appear to be very small in number. When the scribes report the appearances of them, they are usually described as being in very small groups of two or three, and mostly as individuals. They appear at widely separated time intervals, and act to produce major changes with apparently minimal effort.

There were the three that Abraham encountered, and a small number in the Sinai with Moses and the Israelites. There was one that met with Ezekiel, and it only took one to meet with Mary, and just two in the tomb of Jesus, (John 20 v. 12) and two at the ascension, and one that accosted Saul on his way to Damascus.

I would like to remind you that I am still following the principles I started with, I am taking the word of the scribe as if were true, on the basis that these scribes were honest God-fearing people.

If what the scribes write is true, then the world is currently in the hands of no more than just a few dozen Elohim, and it was these few that started Judaism, created Christianity, and used Saul to spread the Gospel of the Kingdom all over the world.

One single Mighty One appears to have said just a few words to Saul on his way to Damascus, and with consummate ease thereby created the entire Christian religion as it exists today, including the Roman Catholic Church, and 2.2 billion believers, and all the social and moral laws that stem from it.

This surely demonstrates how accomplished the Elohim are, and how easy it is for them to manipulate the human race. These examples I give are in the religious domain, but what else have they done? In how many other ways have humans been guided?

Do they direct our politics? Do they start and finish our wars? Do they secretly give us technology? .... I don't know.

There could actually be rather more of them than I at first thought, they would need to have enough personnel to monitor human activity and progress, or they would not be in a position to direct the course of our development. Judging by the number of UFO sightings in the world, I suspect there are rather a lot mingled amongst us in all walks of life.

*

Isaiah 65: 1: ***I am sought of them that asked not for me; I am found of them that sought me not:***

Sometimes when I am bored I like to entertain myself by trying to think of ways to identify the individual Elohim who must still be at work, posing as mere mortals.

I have not yet found a way. There appears to be no distinguishing features, no wings, no halo, and no racial characteristics, nothing that could be used to identify them.

There are scriptural stories about angels appearing in dreams, but that doesn't count, no more than the 'visions' which have all the characteristics of technological projections of some kind. The Elohim I would like to identify are those that are real and walk this Earth, like Gabriel, and those mentioned in Hebrews:

Hebrews 13 v 2 Be not forgetful to entertain strangers: for thereby some have entertained angels unawares.

How can it be possible to entertain an angel/Elohim unawares unless they look and behave exactly like humans? Is it not clear that the scribe who wrote these words considered Angels to be indistinguishable from ordinary humans?

Daniel 2 v 43 ...they shall mingle themselves with the seed of men...

I imagine there must be some differences in DNA, and they would need to be careful not to leave any samples for analysis, but apart from DNA, distinguishing between an Elohim and the normal 'seed of men' seems to be nearly impossible. They would be incredibly intelligent, of course, but they would probably hide their intellect from mere mortals. They would be very knowledgeable about almost everything, but again, they would hide their knowledge when in contact with ordinary people.

They do not grow old, but if they move house frequently, nobody would notice their rate of aging was very slow or non-existent. They could evade official documentation easily, and change their appearance from time to time.

Even if I suspected that a certain person was one of the Elohim, there would be no point in confronting him with my thoughts, no point in asking him, he would simply deny it, and of course anyone who makes unsolicited claims to be an Elohim must be regarded with grave suspicion. They will never reveal themselves until the time is right.

I find myself in a situation where I know that there are 'people' like Gabriel, who look and behave exactly like human beings, but who are not quite the same. We can only identify them by the outcome of their work, which extends over centuries, but it is fun to play 'Spot the Elohim'.

End of final tea break.

Some odds and ends.

When I first started reading the scripture my understanding of it was about the same as that of any other disinterested individual, but things have changed since then. I have now studied the entire book, and because of this I have been able to make one or two observations that you might find interesting.

I noticed certain features that occur throughout the Bible, from Genesis to Jesus, concerning the way the scribes write. (I do not include the 'letters' in the New Testament in this analysis, they are of a different character.)

Firstly, the scribes always seem quite happy to write about proceedings which they could not conceivably have had knowledge of. They write as though they were first-hand eye-witnesses, even when they could not possibly have been present at the events they describe. From early in Genesis where God said "let there be light," through to where Gabriel is talking to Mary, and even later, where Jesus is talking to Pilate. At first I just thought the scribe was writing down what he and his contemporaries believed, and there may be some truth in that, but it is not the whole truth, because the scribes pull the same trick right the way through the Bible.

Secondly, I noticed the scribes were all extremely confident. They never appear to express doubt. They will write about the doubts of others, like 'doubting Thomas', but never show any reservation about their own statements. Most people who write, including myself, will often use words like 'possibly' or 'could be' or 'it appears to be', and throughout this book I am conscious of the fact that I have probably used these expressions fairly often. The Bible scribes do not appear to ever doubt themselves. It seems that words expressing self-doubt are never used by the scribes, not ever, anywhere in the Bible. But I could be wrong.

Thirdly, I got the distinct impression of a coupling between the various scribes. By which I mean that we assume there were many different scribes that were writing the original stories over a period of thousands of years. These accounts may have been collected and copied by later scribes, but the collation should not have obscured the natural differences in style one would expect from different authors. The scribes of the Bible all appear to adopt the same, or closely similar, style all the way through, and the various scribes all support each other and even quote each other. For example compare Psalm 22 v 1 with Matthew 27 v. 46.

Experts would contest this statement, referring to 'Yahwist' and 'Elohist' writers, and that is something I have observed myself, but the 'style' to which I refer appears to be independent of these differences.

Fourthly, the scribes never seem to speculate, or explore options. Whenever they 'explain' something, the explanation is confident and brief, "As it is written" or "In order that the scripture might be fulfilled." This may appear to you to be in keeping with the scripture, but if it was written by a number of different scribes, we would expect at least one of them to demonstrate a little eccentricity.

Fifth, the pattern of scripture is followed. As smoke fills the Most Holy part of Moses' portable temple, or tabernacle, in the Sinai wilderness, so also it does in the temple of Solomon, centuries later, in the Israelite capital, Jerusalem. Even the proportions of the design remain the same.

Lastly there is continuity, the same story-line all the way through, in broad terms it recounts the development of humanity from our origins as clones through to our return to the Elohim who made us, when they establish the Kingdom of Heaven on Earth.

No doubt these are the things that give religious people their notions of 'Inspired by the Spirit' and 'every word is literally true'. We may accept that the above observations could combine to give the faithful the impression that the Bible is divine.

The prophecy is something else that inspires religion, especially when it always seems to be fulfilled. If someone like Joel the prophet, in his Chp. 3, says that Israel will be returned to the land after the diaspora, and in 1948 the State of Israel is reborn, religious people tend to take note.

Whatever else one might say about the Bible, and I have to admit some of it is rather boring; considering that for the most part it was supposedly written by uneducated primitives, stone-age or bronze-age rustic peoples, it is quite a remarkable book.

*

If we just pop back to Genesis for a minute, to where the Elohim say, “Let us make man in our own image,” we may notice that they don’t actually tell us ***why***.

We are left to guess, or try to deduce, the ‘why’ of it all.

We may recall that we are ‘as one of them’ but we do not live for ever, so if we are in fact to be fully in the image of the Mighty Ones, it follows that at some stage we must become as them, totally.

From this it may appear that the world is a kind of breeding colony for the Elohim, and to be honest I cannot think of any other reason for all the effort they have put into creating us, but I cannot perceive the next stage with any degree of clarity.

Later in the Bible when the Jews have started a formal religion, as I have just mentioned above they had a temple in which the presence of the Elohim was said to reside. The Lord was always hidden behind a veil, and concealed in a cloud of smoke, so his voice could be heard but he could not be seen.

The veil and the smoke still conceal the Elohim from the world, in a larger sense; they are hidden from us, and the future is concealed, but we may still make some deductions about their intentions.

*

If we keep in mind the main content of this present book, that the Solar System is artificially ordered, we might come to the conclusion that the Elohim do not do things by chance. They utilise chance, randomness, in much the same way that they hide in the cloud behind the veil. Random events disguise the order, and make things look natural.

If we assume that my deductions are correct, that the Elohim have a purpose with humanity, they are not likely to be operating on a basis of chance. I am suggesting that they know what they are doing, and act deliberately to achieve their ends.

It is also not logical to assume that we are the only planet to be colonised. It is reasonable to suppose that Earth is just one of a large number of planets to be colonised, the Elohim did not engage in a project involving just one single planet.

I pondered all these things, and after a lot of thought, and tea and biscuits, I came to the conclusion that the book on my lap was not just a record of events. It was not just divine instruction, it was not just a history book, it was not just a revelation, nor was it only teaching salvation, it was far too complex and coordinated than it needed to be for any of those objectives.

It finally came to me that it might be the record of progress of a development plan, if not the development plan itself.

Consider this possibility for a moment, and you might see it as I do.

The Solar System is artificially ordered, but the order is hidden beneath the exponents and a scattering of random asteroids, so it all looks natural.

I see in the structure of the Bible a similar set of circumstances, there is a skeletal framework, an ordered progression from the beginning to the end, showing the various stages in the development of the story of Israel and through them the rest of humanity. This ordered skeletal framework is liberally decorated with seemingly chance events, giving the false impression that the plan of action is no more than a record of natural occurrences; disguised by the interference of editors and translators it all looks ordinary.

The prophecies are followed by fulfilment. A prophetic utterance or even the suggestion of one is fulfilled by the devout people who came after.

Prophecy followed by fulfilment is just another way of describing the steps in a planned sequence. It is as if someone has written a sequence of instructions, or a program of events that must happen in the development of humanity. At times the prophetic 'instructions' in the planning are completed by Elohim, at other times by other characters, like Moses or Jesus, but the outcome is the same. The scripture is fulfilled; the grand plan takes another step forward.

It is possible to demonstrate from comments made in the Gospels that everything Jesus did was planned in advance. This would include his betrayal by Judas Iscariot, his crucifixion, his death and resurrection, and as before mentioned in my chapter 6, his ascension.

Theologians and believers would use words like 'foreordained' or 'foreknown of God', but to me these words all mean the same thing, they mean that everything was pre-planned.

To arrange a crucifixion, a death, and a resurrection, would take some detailed and careful planning, and some critics would say there are clues in the text to suggest that it was all faked.

Nobody is going to invent a story that can be shown to be faked, so if the story of the crucifixion does contain such clues, we can be very certain that it was not invented. So, faked or not, we may be assured that it really did happen. In fact the possibility of a faked death gives the story a lot more credibility, not that it makes much difference to the theme of this present book.

Jesus did nothing by chance, just about everything he did was done deliberately to fulfil what was written, which is another way of saying he was obeying instructions. There are many examples of this happening, a good one is in Matthew 21 where Jesus sends his disciples on a trivial errand to fetch him a donkey, and even this minor task was allocated in order to fulfil a prophecy.

4 All this was done, that it might be fulfilled which was spoken by the prophet,

Statements like this occur scores of times throughout the gospels and can be seen as describing a deliberate obedience to instructions.

Another good example is the one mentioned earlier, where Jesus foretells with confidence that the Gospel shall be preached in all nations. His words are equivalent to an instruction, as if read from a book of instructions.

The instructions are first found in the Old Testament in Isaiah, which, according to historians, was written about 500 years before the time of Jesus:

Isaiah 42

1 Behold my servant, whom I uphold; mine elect, in whom my soul delighteth; I have put my spirit upon him: he shall bring forth judgment to the Gentiles.

6 I the LORD have called thee in righteousness, and will hold thine hand, and will keep thee, and give thee for a covenant of the people, for a light of the Gentiles;

Isaiah 49

6 And he said, It is a light thing that thou shouldest be my servant to raise up the tribes of Jacob, and to restore the preserved of Israel: I will also give thee for a light to the Gentiles, that thou mayest be my salvation unto the end of the earth.

(A Gentile is everyone non-Jewish.)

Jesus was familiar with this instruction, and knew it was time for it to be initiated.

The next step is to ensure that the instruction is carried out. Paul was selected to carry out that step in the plan because of his excessive fervour. All that was required was to turn his burning passion and zeal away from hostility, and use it to advantage, use it for preaching.

Paul was carrying out instructions.

I have already suggested that the development of the scripture and the people of Israel are mirrored in the development of humanity as a whole. We are what we are because of the Bible.

*

The Bible appears to be a plan of action, and if it is then it was probably devised and first written long ages ago and far away across the heavens.

If it is an action plan for the colonisation of planets, then it has been implemented on thousands of different worlds already. The same drama has been played out time and time again. On strange planets in other stellar systems people like us, human-clones would experience a similar Garden of Eden. The names would be different, the geology would be different, even some of the events might be different, but the underlying stratagem is the same. We are not the first, and we will certainly not be the last.

The plan is implemented as a routine.

It is a flexible plan; it comes as a skeletal framework decorated with a wide variety of optional random extras. The plan progresses in stages, and as each stage is completed the next one starts, until it reaches the end objective, which is the fulfilment of everything, the culmination in the coming of the Kingdom, which is the bit I cannot clearly see, not even with my head in the clouds, but it involves open and direct contact with the Elohim.

To the casual observer the Bible plan looks perfectly natural, and the pundits explain it all away as primitive religious nonsense; but when we strip away the random elements we can see the articulated bones of the skeleton.

We can perhaps see that the development of Humanity is also following a plan. It is not entirely random.

If we wonder how a plan can be implemented over a period of thousands of years we only need to remember that the Elohim are immortal.

As pointed out by the scribe in 2 Peter 3, immortals are not bothered much by the passage of time.

8 But, beloved, be not ignorant of this one thing, that one day is with the Lord as a thousand years, and a thousand years as one day.

*

Conclusions

Once we understand the maths, and can perceive that the Solar System order is artificial, then everything else follows from simple logic.

The Elohim are not going to leave the project to pure chance. There has to be a plan, a plan that has been implemented on every planet the Elohim colonise, the same plan that has been applied here on Earth.

*

The ‘ancient knowledge’ comes to a focus in chapter ten of this present work, it is valid and I will stand by it. Everything else about the Elohim is deduction based on those calculations. I do not ask or expect you to accept my comments without questioning my reasoning. I am sure you are intelligent enough to carry out your own analysis and come up with your own extrapolation.

If you prefer to think in terms of Spirit, then you are free to do so. I am no expert on Spirit; I don’t even claim to understand it. In any case, the narrative parts of this book contain logical extrapolation, deduction, and conjecture, not doctrine or dogma.

It is logical to suppose that the Elohim will achieve their objectives, contact will be made, and their Kingdom will come to Earth, but I cannot really see the future, no more than anyone else.

Throughout this narrative I have been referring to ‘Elohim’ and ‘Mighty Ones’ for want of a better name. This gives the impression that they are somehow different from us. They are not. I would like to repeat something I said earlier, to remind you, these are not aliens, these are not spirits; these powerful people are the same as us.

Their Grand Plan is to colonise the entire Galaxy, by terraforming planets and by spreading intelligent life, in the form of humanity.

Once a planet is fully developed, and the population suitably receptive, the main body of colonists arrive, and set up home. The Elohim become benign rulers, and impose peace and righteousness on the colonised planet.

The Kingdom that is preached in the Bible and in the Churches is well named, for these Elohim are so superior to their cloned offspring that when they establish themselves on a planet they quite naturally take control.

This is the story of the Bible, but it is also the story of the mathematics in chapter ten of this book, and the story of the monument called Stonehenge/Babel, it all blends together into one consistent and homogenous whole.

We are indeed the children of the living god in all significant respects, and when the Kingdom finally arrives, it would seem to me to be a little like when we were very young, at kindergarten, with our caring parents waiting at the gate, ready to bring us home.

*

Chapter Fifteen

A Horror of Great Darkness

After we left the building of Babel, as the people were scattering across the Earth, the story continues with a long genealogy, which ends with a man called Abram.

Abram later had his name changed to Abraham, who we know as that great patriarch of Judaism.

It is with Abram that the story of Israel and the Jews gets started, and the Bible has a lot to say about Abram, but there is just one passage that I wish to discuss, briefly, because it introduces something that I think could be important for you. The matter is one of concern to me, but I am not sure how to approach it.

It is in Genesis 15, and we find Abram in his tent, engaged in a conversation with God about the future. Abram was worried that he had no heir, but that is not what I wish to talk about.

The story is a bit confused, and we must expect that, it is after all a very old story.

It is late at night, and God takes Abram out of his tent

5 And he brought him forth abroad, and said, Look now toward heaven, and tell the stars, if thou be able to number them: and he said unto him, So shall thy seed be.

There then follows a ritual, which is incomprehensible to me.

It must have been a day or two later, because it is evening, and the sun is setting, so Abram is outside under the starry sky when he fell asleep.

Genesis 15 v 12 …and, lo, an horror of great darkness fell upon him.

It is somewhat enigmatic, but it drew my attention because I confess I have also suffered an experience that I could describe as a 'horror of great darkness', and I could empathise with Abram. I hasten to point out that I am not identifying with that great patriarch, I am not trying to draw any connection between myself and Abram, and I certainly do not mean it that way. I am not a nomad.

I am simply saying that I suffered a similar 'horror of great darkness'; and it is not very nice, and I worry that it might happen to you as well.

It might not, I cannot say, but I still worry.

It may well be that when you have finished this book; you might just dispose of it as a waste of money. If that is the case, then there is no need for me to worry.

On the other hand, if you take the book seriously and get deeply involved in the calculations, you might suffer what I suffered. If that should be the case, it would be well for you to be warned in advance. Forewarned is forearmed, as it were. This is why there is a warning on an early page.

I was concerned then, and I am still concerned now, that what happened to me might also happen to you.

It happened when my subconscious mind caught up with what my conscious mind was thinking, and understood it was all real, understood it all with vivid clarity.

The whole thing came together into one whole, and the meaning of it became very tangible and crystal clear.

The mathematics gave me vision, and I saw with the eye of the mind the appalling power of the Elohim.

I felt abruptly sick, a severe cramp seized my stomach and I had to make emergency use of the waste bin, and right then and there the horror of great darkness came over me.

It was not a religious experience, it was not at all like I would imagine 'seeing the light' would be like; it was more akin to being suddenly overwhelmed and swept giddily into a limitless black void of frightening proportions.

I hung in the black emptiness, a feeling of intense dread turned my bones to ash, my flesh dissolved into dust, and I dangled in oblivion like an empty skin bag while something powerful beyond imagining scrutinised every miserable mote of my wretched soul.

And then I was tossed aside like discarded litter, I was dropped into the abyss; I fell through infinity, and jolted awake.

I found myself lying on the carpet with my face still in the waste bin.

I did not return to normal straight away, my head was spinning and my whole being was suffused with fluttering shadows of terror. The shudders of cold fear persisted long after the world returned to solid reality, whatever that might be.

My heart raced, I shook and trembled, my strength had left me, I was so wobbly and feeble I could hardly stand up.

I felt as though I had experienced a glimpse of something beyond space, beyond the Elohim, something that defies turgid words, where logic and reason and equations all became emptied of meaning.

I was still incoherent some days later, when a friend came to visit.

I did not go mad, though she might have thought so. I could not speak; I could not tell her what was wrong.

The reaction was physiological, but I was able to retain control of my mental processes, so I think I remained sane. It is hard to tell.

The worst bit was that I could not explain to her. I could not even tell her not to worry, I couldn't tell her anything. She would not have understood anyway.

I am confessing all this because I am concerned that it may happen to you.

My friend drove me to the doctors, and he diagnosed a severe attack of food poisoning, and I was happy to accept his diagnosis, I was prepared to leave it at that.

For a while it seemed that there may be much more to the universe than the things described in these pages. The experience left an indelible mark on my mind and on my memory; it did not fade with time.

It seemed to me that there was a power greater even than the Elohim, and if so, then it is something nobody would wish to argue with.

It occurred to me that there is no reason to suppose that there is a limit to the powers that could exist in this universe. After all, scientists will tell us that the universe is billions of years old, and our entire human existence is no more than a fleck on the surface of such a huge expanse of time. Our best brains would be on a par with bacteria compared with the mental abilities of a race that is eons older than our own. There could be an ascending hierarchy of super-powerful intelligences out there, and we have no reason to suppose otherwise. There could even be a Supreme Being.

I suffered a few moments of doubt, wondering if there could really be a Creator Spirit, Lord of All, or was it just mental overload?

Only a fool would say in his heart that there can be no Supreme Being, but there is no reason to suppose that such a being would have any interest in mankind.

If there is an ultimate power, a Supreme Being, then such a power is well beyond the reach of exponents and equations, and beyond the scope of this book.

My brief but disturbing brush with eternity gave rise to such thoughts, and filled me with a strange feeling of insignificance; it left me vacant and drained of energy.

It also put an end to my mathematical researches.

*

Later on I took the view that it was all down to overwork, mental fatigue, and a stale pork pie. The experience shows how the mind can play tricks and how superstition can get started and take hold.

I managed to convince myself that it was internal, it was a mental aberration brought on by stress and exhaustion, call it what you will, it was not real.

*

A couple of years have passed since then, and now I am fully recovered and able to analyse it and to better understand what actually happened.

We all have our own individual ‘world view’ that we acquire from birth. Our understanding of the world, our place in the world, is what shapes us and gives us a feeling of identity.

We all feel that we ‘know’ certain things, without consciously bringing them to mind. We understand what the world is like, what it is all about.

Our world view makes us who we are. It builds our personality. It is part of what makes us. If we share a similar world view with others, we feel an affinity with them. They are those we hold dear.

The horror of great darkness is what happened to me when that world view was shattered.

When all that we thought we knew is shown to be false; when the world view that is an integral part of our personality suddenly collapses like a house of cards; that is when the horror strikes and takes hold.

Of course, if your interest in these matters is purely superficial, then nothing much will happen. If that is the case with you, then there is no problem.

It is also the case that there is a profound difference between reading something second hand, and being the person at the pointed end, so to speak. I was immersed in it, and being so immersed I was carried away with the intricacies of the calculations, I did not really have time to keep up with my own progress. It was only when I sat back to review all that I had done that the horrors caught up with me and struck me down.

*

In a perverse sort of way, I rather hope you can understand as I understand, but if you do, then there is always the possibility that you might experience something along those lines. Let us hope that it is a milder form.

If you do happen to get struck by the horrors, then I am here to tell you not to worry too much. It won't last for long; you won't go mad, and you will recover in a very short time.

After a while the new world view will settle into place, and then you will remember the old, learn to adjust, and get on with your life.

*

After a year or two resting, I resumed my studies, I restarted the work, and eventually I decided to write this book, so that others may judge the value of these matters for themselves.

I did not actually finish the mathematical investigation of Stonehenge or the planetary orbits, although I think I found enough to show that there really is something greater than mankind in this Solar System and on this Earth. The mathematics and the astronomy provide evidence of the Elohim, they are real, and they would seem to me to be physical, but that understanding cannot rule out the possible existence of an even greater, more remote power that perhaps is as far above the Elohim as the Elohim are greater than us.

I know there is more information waiting to be discovered by other people who might be interested in pursuing these matters. The Stonehenge inner monument ground plan has a strong connection to the Heel Stone, but I did not find the time to investigating that aspect.

There will almost certainly be more in the way of quirky mathematics in the Solar System to be found.

There are many aspects of science, in particular geology, and history, that I have only touched on and of course there are huge areas of scripture and religion that I simply haven't dealt with.

There is plenty of scope for more work to be done, should anyone be interested, I have only scratched the surface.

Now I would like to return to the narrative, if I may.

*

Before Abram had his horror of great darkness, he was shown the stars of heaven. The image generated by the words suggests that God took him by the arm, dragged him from his tent, and pointed at the starry sky.

And he brought him forth abroad, and said, Look now toward heaven, and tell the stars, if thou be able to number them.

We cannot say if this is what gave Abram his attack of the horrors, but it could have been.

Psalm 115 v 16 The heaven, even the heavens, are the LORD'S: but the earth hath he given to the children of men.

Surely this is a clear enough statement that the realm of the stars belongs to the Mighty Ones? The very God who was pointing them out to Abram was the owner, or represented the owner, so it is a fair assumption that Abram knew that.

It also indicates that the Elohim have given the Earth to us, to live on.

Isaiah 66 v 1 Thus saith the LORD, The heaven is my throne, and the earth is my footstool:

Again, we have a clear statement referring to the heavens as being in the ownership of the Chief of the Mighty Ones, and the Earth is also subject to his dominion.

The use of the word 'throne' is interesting, because it is often used as a synonym for the power of a ruler, or the domain over which he rules.

Here in these two verses, and there are many more, we have a fairly clear statement that the Elohim Lord is ruler over the starry heavens.

The verses I quote were written down long after the time of Abram, but they reflect the beliefs that Abram would have held.

*

The above references are an example of what humanity believed for thousands of years. Up until quite recently it has always been believed that 'God' lived in 'Heaven'; which was said to be 'up there' above the sky in the realm of the stars, in outer space.

Since the advent of modern science, and in particular since the time we started sending robotic probes into space, scientists have found no evidence of 'God' so we have decided to evict God from the heavens and relocate Him to another dimension.

Science has even demoted Him from a superpower to a superstition.

*

Let us ignore that for now. The Elohim are reported to be the rulers over the realm of the stars, which by any definition is a vast volume of space.

Since there is really no merit in ruling over barren planets and unpopulated desert worlds, we must conclude that the Lord of the Elohim is referring to his possession of the heavens as being more along the lines of having authority over a great many **populated** stellar systems.

In plain language, the Elohim are from a Galactic Empire, and the Empire is crawling with life.

This conclusion is in accord with a logical extrapolation from the single fact that our System is ordered, and it is also in accord with the record of the ancient scribes.

Someone very powerful came here, a representative of a vast stellar empire, or kingdom, and set our planets in order.

Isaiah 45

18 For thus saith the LORD that created the heavens; God himself that formed the earth and made it; he hath established it, he created it not in vain, ***he formed it to be inhabited:*** (Made it habitable? GC)

*

We may reasonably conclude that the starry skies beyond our Solar System belong to the Elohim. They are Elohim starry skies.

So when God took Abram from his tent and pointed to the stars of heaven, he was actually pointing to Elohim stars, Elohim skies, and His own kingdom, where His throne is.

That is what the scripture claims, anyway.

Logic and reason dictate that they are ***populated*** starry skies, so perhaps that is what gave Abram the attack of the horrors.

"So shall thy seed be".
His seed would be as the stars of heaven; as the populated Elohim stars of the Empire of the very God who was standing beside him.

Or, God just meant he would have lots of descendants.

*

There must be hundreds of thousands of Solar Systems like ours in the Galactic Empire. The starry skies are seething with Elohim and their offspring, humans like us.

Unfortunately we mortals are effectively prisoners in the Solar System. Despite any advances in technology, unless we find the secret of immortality we can never travel to the stars. The only way we will ever be able to make that journey is to become Elohim ourselves, and that is beyond us at the moment.

For the Elohim, a trip of a hundred light years would be the equivalent of a trip to the local pub, but for us, it would be an impossible excursion.

If you stand outside on a clear night, and look up at the starry skies, look in the direction of the Milky Way, you will see what Abram saw, you will be looking up at the Elohim Empire, you will be looking up at Elohim skies and you will be looking at our ancestral home, for we are the children of those who live amongst those stars.

-------------------------*-----------------------

Well, that is it! You have stayed with me all the way through and I really do appreciate your company. I doubt very much if you and I will ever meet, but if we do, perhaps in a pub, I'll buy you a drink. Or even better, *you* can buy *me* a drink. Just one very small glass of Glenfiddich, as it comes, would be very nice. I like Glenfiddich.

I expect we could have an interesting chat, but that will never happen, sorry to say.

For now it is time to wrap things up.

*

I started the introduction to this little book with the statement that the book was about a treasure hunt. I stated that the book actually finds the treasure, in the form of ancient knowledge.

You should now have gained knowledge that is ancient, so I have fulfilled my promise. Now you want to know if it is genuine treasure or fake.

The treasure is confined to part two of this book, in chapters 8, 9 & 10, and is genuine, pure gold, all the way through, but the only way for you to be sure of that is for you to either test it yourself, or to have someone you trust test it for you.

I want you to test it, or have it tested; I want you to subject it to close scrutiny, because I want you to know that it is the real thing.

If you are near a place of education a mathematics teacher would be the best person to ask. Ask them to check some aspect of the math in Part Two, or all of it, and see what they say. They are likely to rubbish my methodology and my presentation, but these things do not matter. What matters is for you to know that it is true, and not some clever deception.

If you ask any other kind of teacher you are likely to get a short and rude answer, but in general, a mathematics teacher should give an honest appraisal.

I would trust a mathematician, but none of the others.

If you have satisfied yourself that it is genuine, then that is all I can reasonable ask of you.

The ancient knowledge in Part Two is the main feature of this book, it has been verified, and I hope you can understand it.

The rest is all comment and deduction based on my peculiar brand of logic, and should probably be ignored, since it cannot be verified.

I would prefer to have confined myself to the mathematics, but unfortunately it seems that some people expect books to have words in them, and I hope you can understand that as well.

*

So what do we do with it?

We have an elaborate peg-and-string exponential mathematical model of the orbits of the planets that has stood and crumbled on Salisbury Plain for thousands of years. From it we obtain the information that we live in an artificially ordered Solar System.

It tells us more than just astronomy though, doesn't it?

It throws a light on our past, surely? It says that some long time ago there lived a person who knew all about the orbits of the planets, and he had sufficient brain power to design this clever peg-and-string model.

He was not a Neanderthal; he was not Australopithecus afarensis; he was an intelligent and well educated man from an advanced civilization.

That much is certain.

The monument sheds light on our past history; it tells us that the story concocted by scientists and historians is false.

It also sheds light on our possible future, as I have discussed at length in preceding chapters.

Can this all be true?

I have given you the treasure, but I have not been able to polish it for you, only you can make it sparkle.

*

Do you ever ask yourself existential questions? I mean questions like 'Why am I here?' and 'What is the purpose of life?' If so you are not alone. Many people ask these questions, including myself.

The answers provided by established science tend to be nihilistic. They would say that there is no reason for life, we evolved by random accident. They would argue that there is no purpose to life, other than to survive and reproduce.

The story related by the monument is rather different.

The monument confirms the story in Genesis. It tells us that there is a power greater than modern man. We call that power 'God' or 'Angels' or 'Elohim' or 'Mighty Ones' for want of a better name. We do not know what they call themselves, other than perhaps 'YHWH', which is the name that was first revealed in the time of Moses.

The astronomy derived from the Monument provides us with a string of logic that suggests to us that these Mighty Ones wish us to know they exist. From this we deduce that they wish us to join with them in some way.

This is not religion; this is straight forward reasoning on the facts as presented by the Monument.

So there are alternative answers to the existential questions, we do not have to accept the dismal answers provided by science.

We were created to become members of the Galactic Empire. Our purpose in life is to become Elohim.

We cannot know for certain if we will succeed, because that is in the remit of the Mighty Ones, but we can make an effort to move in that direction.

We can try, if we wish.

*

I said at one stage that if you are reading this book then it must have been published, and then I said, that first-contact had been initiated.

I do not consider myself to be a naïve kind of person. I do not expect the world to receive this work with any kind of enthusiasm. In fact, it is pretty obvious that most people won't be at all interested.

People are concerned about their immediate circumstances, like paying the mortgage, paying tax, getting divorced and so on. Most people do not have the time or the inclination to consider material of this nature.

I do not have the ear or the eye of the authorities, I cannot speak to governments. Nothing will change as a result of this little book.

Scientists will ignore it, as will the religious authorities. If any discussion takes place at all it will not take place in the corridors of academic learning, or in the palaces of religious power.

But then, I wonder if it is really necessary for those in authority to accept this situation? All that the Elohim would need and require is that enough individuals, ordinary common people, accept them. The authorities must then respond to popular demand.

Why would the Elohim be respecters of persons in power? They selected Noah to survive because he was 'righteous' (Gen 7 v 1) and Enoch 'walked with God'.

It would seem that character is more important to the Mighty Ones than power or political influence, so my earlier thoughts that our leaders need to be convinced might not be totally true.

*

You and I know what this is all about, but nobody else will be interested. This little book has revealed one or two secrets. The secrets are open secrets, the easiest secrets to keep. Even though it is all in the open, all available for public examination, a secret that nobody believes is the perfect secret.

Which is a pity really, because we all know that the world is going to end fairly soon. Not because of the 'repent the end is nigh' doomsayers, but because the global human population is seven billion and growing rapidly. We are severely over-populated.

To exacerbate the situation, the world still operates a growth economy, which means that business and industry must keep growing profits, which in turn requires a growing market. A growing economy and a growing population requires a growing energy consumption, which in turn means an increase in the rate of consumption of resources, and the consequent growth of pollution and shortages.

If nothing else fails, one day we are certain to run out of oil, which means that we will have no fuel for the growth, processing, and distribution of food.

People appear to be blissfully unconcerned about these observations, perhaps because the world seems to carry on as it has always done.

In recent years 'climate change' has hit the headlines and governments have tried to bring that looming problem to the attention of the public, with limited success.

The population must continue to grow at an exponential rate, so there is no question that sooner or later the earth will no longer be able to support us.

It appears to me that the end of civilization as we know it is inevitable. It is just a question of when.

I have read many and varied proposed solutions to this dire future, but none of them address the problem of population growth, or the fact that business and industry is founded on growth. A business of any kind must grow its profits or it will go under.

Finding new sources of power is a red herring, because more power will simply provide more food and fuel to promote more population growth.

The question is not 'what to do about it?' but 'how does this relate to the content of this book?'

*

I worry. I worry about all sorts of things.

I believe the Mighty Ones know what they are doing, but I worry that I might have said the wrong thing, or made a mistake somewhere in my reasoning. I hope the Plan that I have described is real, and that things will work out, but I cannot be certain.

I worry that the Plan might fail, like it seems to have failed in antediluvian times. We are not looking at miracles. The Elohim are powerful but not omnipotent.

Suppose mankind will not recognise or accept the Elohim, what then?

If I might remind you of a few things I said in earlier chapters, the order was put into the orbits as a message for intelligent mankind to read. Dolphins and dogs cannot read it. I worry because as I write, mankind hasn't noticed it either. What happens if they don't ever read it?

The Elohim are telling us they exist, from which we may reasonably conclude that they actually want us to know they exist. The Solar System would have been left genuinely random if they wanted to hide forever.

If they want us to know they exist, then that must mean that at some stage they intend that contact should be made.

The question then arises as to when such a contact will occur.

I have previously intimated that such a contact must be at our instigation. They are not going to force themselves on us, they made that mistake once before and it ended in disaster.

Perhaps we can now see the problem.

Earth is headed for another disaster, where civilization, and perhaps even the entire human species, is destined to become drowned in its own effluent, yet the Elohim cannot interfere.

We might try to put ourselves into the Elohim's shoes and ask ourselves what they can possibly do to save the colony that they have worked so hard to create. The Grand Plan has worked, and brought us this far, but what about the next step? I cannot see the future.

It must be very frustrating for the Elohim, to be forced to obey rules of their own making, and sit back and watch while the world destroys itself. There are a few things they can still do, nudging in the right direction, as they have always done, but they cannot interfere openly. If they were to suddenly appear and take charge, the detrimental effects on the majority of the population would be immense. The intrusion would seem like an invasion.

They left the message in the planets, in the heavens, so that one day humanity would read it and understand. They must be hoping that their colonists will read it soon, and start to change their ways, and save themselves before the last chapter in the human story reaches its inevitable conclusion.

It is a race between the forces of overpopulation on the one hand, and the acceptance by mankind of the message in the planets on the other.

The recognition and acceptance of the Elohim will allow them to openly respond.

The Plan, as mentioned earlier, may not yet be fully completed, I am not in a position to say, but it is certain we are getting very close to the fulfilment of all these things.

Planet Earth will become part of the Galactic Empire, indeed in many ways it is already, it always has been, the people of Earth don't know it yet, that's all.

*

I regret to say, I do not believe any of this.

None of it will happen. I hate to appear to be the pessimist, but it all sounds like invention, the dream of a mad man. Even if you, my last remaining reader, support my findings and my reasoning, the rest of the world will say I am mad, and continue along the path of self-destruction, regardless of any attempt to change things.

Men will say it is a crazy fabrication; it is a fantasy; it is science fiction.

No, it is none of these. Stonehenge is a fact, the order in the Solar System is a mathematical fact, and the rest is logic and reason based on those facts.

Only time will tell, but there are definitely such entities as Elohim, they certainly have the power to travel across the Galaxy, and they have demonstrated the ability to move planets like Jupiter and Uranus and put them into order with Venus and Mars.

*

I do not have a crystal ball; I cannot say what the future holds, either for you as an individual or for humanity as a whole. What I can say, with some degree of confidence, is that mankind must change its attitude towards its own history and its own place in the universe, or we will go the way of the antediluvians.

Did the antediluvians suffer an accident that the Elohim failed to stop, or did the Elohim actually bring the flood deliberately to wipe the slate clean?

Either way, these Mighty Ones showed no concern for the death of a whole world of people. What are we to make of that?

It is perhaps not so much that they were callous or vindictive, but more perhaps that the world was a lost cause.

Again, it is not for me to judge the Mighty Ones, but others might do so.

You must make up your own mind.

It seems to me to be a simple choice that is placed before humanity.

The story of mankind is in its last chapter and our species will not survive the problems that assail the modern age, so if we carry on ignoring the Mighty Ones, we will perish, just as the antediluvians perished, perhaps not with a flood, but in some other way.

I do not wish for humanity to perish. I confess I do not have a great love of humanity, but I do not wish for it to vanish from the Earth.

I would wish that humanity would recognise and respect the reality of the Mighty Ones, that contact would be established, and that we could become one with them.

*

The two silver-haired elderly ladies that called at my door never came back, I never saw them again. As I write these few final words, I am an old man, so I doubt if I will ever get the chance to thank those gentle visitors, but they might call on you one day. If they do, please be kind to them, because without them this book would never have been written.

If you wish to dump this book in a charity shop, and forget you ever read it, then that is your choice, but if you value the content then you should understand that it is up to you to carry it forward towards first contact. Do not rely on me, for I will most likely be dead and gone by the time you read these words.

So how can you carry this work forward, should you wish to?

I have said, and I repeat, it is not my purpose to start a new religion, and I meant it. No worship, no hymns, no priests, no churches and definitely no dogma or doctrine.

We have mathematics and hard facts both on the ground and in space. What need have we of faith and the odour of sanctity? No cult religion, don’t even think it. The Elohim are physical, to be respected, not worshipped.

If you wish to continue this work, what you could do, is not to preach the word, but simply to find mathematicians and ask them to explain parts of the math. When one has explained it, find another. Make a nuisance of yourself; eventually someone will take notice. Do not forget that there will be others who have read this book and are like-minded; all you need do is identify them.

Not only that, but you can entertain some personal hope that your own future will be different than it might otherwise have been.

Knowledge has an effect, all on its own. The transition from 'not knowing' to 'knowing' is an easy one to make, it happens in an instant and is one-way. Once you know, if you survive the horror of great darkness that may well come with the knowing, you cannot go back to your previous state of ignorance.

Knowing something is not like 'faith' or 'belief', which are often just temporary changes, and can be lost, undone and forgotten.

Knowing something is permanent, and brings with it permanent changes to you as a person. Once you understand the reality of all this, you will feel isolated, because you know something that other people, friends and family, do not know, and you cannot talk to them about it for fear they will think you to be mad.

When you hear talk of evolution, or religion, or archaeology, you will feel strange inside, because you will know that falsehoods are being spread.

All these things will change your life, and we hope it will be for the better, but something else will happen as well.

You will know that the Elohim exist, and ***they*** will know that you know.

So, in a manner of speaking, you will have initiated first contact.

I am going to close soon, but I have one last word.

Your life has meaning, and if you will, your life serves a purpose.

You are not an animal, you did ***not*** evolve from an ape; you are a god.

You are of the stuff of the Elohim, you were made by the Elohim, and the Elohim know you already.

Thank you for helping me to carry my burden.

I must say goodbye now.

Have a good life.

THE END

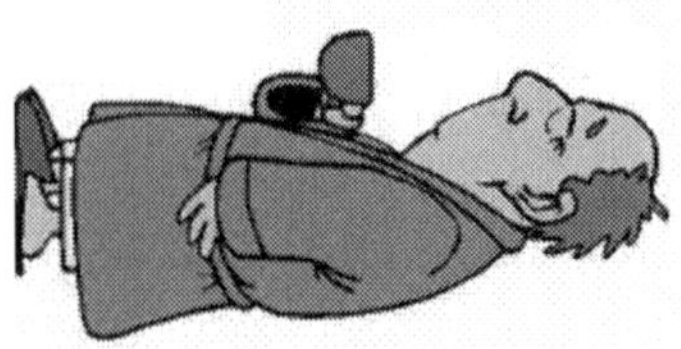

Appendix 1

Sexual euphemisms used in the Bible

Old Testament and New Testament

Genesis 6

4 There were giants in the earth in those days; and also after that, when the sons of God came ***in unto*** the daughters of men..

Genesis 16

2 And Sarai said unto Abram, Behold now, the LORD hath restrained me from bearing: I pray thee, go ***in unto*** my ***maid***; it may be that I may obtain children by her. And Abram hearkened to the voice of Sarai.

4 And he went ***in unto*** Hagar, and she conceived: and when she saw that she had conceived, her mistress was despised in her eyes.

Genesis 19

31 And the firstborn said unto the younger, Our father is old, and there is not a man in the earth to come ***in unto*** us after the manner of all the earth:

32 Come, let us make our father drink wine, and we will lie with him, that we may preserve seed of our father.

Genesis 29

21 And Jacob said unto Laban, Give me my wife, for my days are fulfilled, that I may go ***in unto*** her.

23 And it came to pass in the evening, that he took Leah his daughter, and brought her to him; and he went ***in unto*** her.

Genesis 30

3 And she said, Behold my ***maid*** Bilhah, go in unto her; and she shall bear upon my knees that I may also have children by her.

4 And she gave him Bilhah her ***handmaid*** to wife: and Jacob went ***in unto*** her.

16 And Jacob came out of the field in the evening, and Leah went out to meet him, and said, Thou must come ***in unto*** me; for surely I have hired thee with my son's mandrakes. And he lay with her that night.

Genesis 38

2 And Judah saw there a daughter of a certain Canaanite, whose name was Shuah; and he took her, and went ***in unto*** her.

8 And Judah said unto Onan, Go ***in unto*** thy brother's wife, and marry her, and raise up seed to thy brother.

9 And Onan knew that the seed should not be his; and it came to pass, when he went ***in unto*** his brother's wife, that he spilled it on the ground, lest that he should give seed to his brother.

16 And he turned unto her by the way, and said, Go to, I pray thee, let me come ***in unto*** thee; (for he knew not

that she was his daughter in law.) And she said, What wilt thou give me, that thou mayest come ***in unto*** me?

18 And he said, What pledge shall I give thee? And she said, Thy signet, and thy bracelets, and thy staff that is in thine hand. And he gave it her, and came ***in unto*** her, and she conceived by him.

Genesis 39

14 That she called unto the men of her house, and spake unto them, saying, See, he hath brought in an Hebrew unto us to mock us; he came ***in unto*** me to lie with me, and I cried with a loud voice:

17 And she spake unto him according to these words, saying, The Hebrew servant, which thou hast brought unto us, came ***in unto*** me to mock me:

Deuteronomy 21

13 And she shall put the raiment of her captivity from off her, and shall remain in thine house, and bewail her father and her mother a full month: and after that thou shalt go ***in unto*** her, and be her husband, and she shall be thy wife.

Deuteronomy 22

13 If any man take a wife, and go ***in unto*** her, and hate her,

Deuteronomy 25

5 If brethren dwell together, and one of them die, and have no child, the wife of the dead shall not marry

without unto a stranger: her husband's brother shall go ***in unto*** her, and take her to him to wife, and perform the duty of an husband's brother unto her.

Joshua 23

12 Else if ye do in any wise go back, and cleave unto the remnant of these nations, even these that remain among you, and shall make marriages with them, and go ***in unto*** them, and they to you:

Ruth 4

13 So Boaz took Ruth, and she was his wife: and when he went ***in unto*** her, the LORD gave her conception, and she bare a son.

2 Samuel 3

7 And Saul had a concubine, whose name was Rizpah, the daughter of Aiah: and Ish-bosheth said to Abner, Wherefore hast thou gone ***in unto*** my father's concubine?

2 Samuel 12

24 And David comforted Bath-sheba his wife, and went ***in unto*** her, and lay with her: and she bare a son, and he called his name Solomon: and the LORD loved him.

2 Samuel 16

21 And Ahithophel said unto Absalom, Go ***in unto*** thy father's concubines, which he hath left to keep the house; and all Israel shall hear that thou art abhorred

of thy father: then shall the hands of all that are with thee be strong.

22 So they spread Absalom a tent upon the top of the house; and Absalom went ***in unto*** his father's concubines in the sight of all Israel.

Ezekiel 23

44 Yet they went ***in unto*** her, as they go ***in unto*** a woman that playeth the harlot: so went they ***in unto*** Aholah and ***unto*** Aholibah, the lewd women.

Amos 2

7 That pant after the dust of the earth on the head of the poor, and turn aside the way of the meek: and a man and his father will go ***in unto*** the same ***maid***, to profane my holy name:

New Testament

Luke 1

28 And the angel came ***in unto*** her, and said, Hail, thou that art highly favoured, the Lord is with thee: blessed art thou among women.

38 And Mary said, Behold the ***handmaid*** of the Lord; be it unto me according to thy word.

Appendix 2

SOME RELATIONSHIPS CONNECTING THE MEAN ORBITS OF THE PLANETS

These notes give details of certain mathematical relationships connecting the lengths of semi-major axes of planetary orbits (assumed to be elliptical). Such relationships do not follow from known natural laws, being obtained by observation rather than derivation.

Throughout, equations are presented in exact form but, in most cases they relate to approximate quantities calculated from other approximate quantities or data.

Data Throughout, Astronomical Units (AU) are employed.

The lengths of the semi-major axes of the known planet's orbits are taken from Norton's Star Atlas. One is obliged to assume that the accuracy of the data is indicated by the number of decimal places given.

In the table below, semi-major planetary axes lengths, (the arithmetic mean of aphelion and perihelion distances) are denoted by Z;

Z-values have been converted into x and y values, where

Table 1 .... $x = Z^{(3/2\pi)}$ **and** $y = Z^{(9/4\pi)}$

Planet	Z value	X value	Y value
Mercury (Me)	0.3870987		**0.5067562**
Venus (V)	0.7233322		**0.7929725**
Earth (E)	1.0000000		**1.0000000**
Mars (Ma)	1.5236915	1.2227197	**1.3520425**
Jupiter (J)	5.2028039	2.1977496	
Saturn (S)	9.5388437	2.9354505	
Uranus (U)	19.1818710	4.0976543	
Neptune (N)	30.0579240	5.0777748	
Pluto (P)	39.4390000	5.7809400	

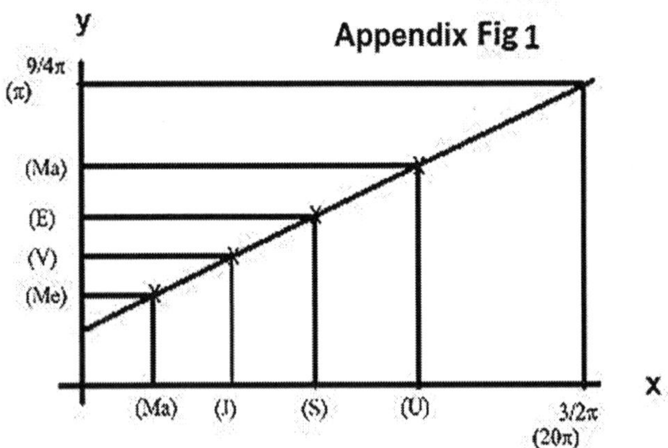

In appendix fig 1, corresponding y-values for Mercury, Venus, Earth, and Mars are marked on the graph y axis, and corresponding x-values for Mars, Jupiter, Saturn,

Uranus, Neptune, and Pluto are marked on the X axis. Additional points P1, P2, P3 and Px are also marked. (The graph is not drawn to scale)

The apparent near colinearity of the four points **(x_{Ma},y_{Me}), (x_J,y_V), (x_S,y_E)** and **(x_U,y_{Ma})** suggests that a good fitting linear equation in x and y may be determined.

Thus, consideration is given to a straight line of gradient **1/ln30** which passes through the point

$((20\pi)^{3/2\pi},(\pi)^{9/4\pi})$........................ (1)

The equation of this line is

$(y-(\pi)^{9/4\pi}) = (\ln 30)^{-1}(x-(20\pi)^{3/2\pi})$, which simplifies to :-

<u>y=0.2940141 x +0.1472341</u> .... (2)

Equation (2) is the first important finding of this investigation; the differences between known and equation calculated y-values for the four points are found to be very small, and consequently the corresponding pairs of Z-values also differ by small amounts.

The linear regression equation for the four points was found to be

<u>y = 0.2933088 x +0.1464114</u>...................... (3)

With correlation coefficient r = 0.999900, and from this, corresponding Z-values for Mercury, Venus, Earth and Mars were also calculated. The results obtained from both equations are shown in Table 2 with percentage differences (with respect to the data Z-values) being included.

Planet	Z (data)	Z (equ 2)	% difference	Z (equ 3)	% difference
Mercury	**0.3870987**	**0.3870718**	**0.007**	**0.3852757**	**0.471**
Venus	**0.7233322**	**0.7238812**	**-0.076**	**0.7208603**	**0.342**
Earth	**1.000000**	**1.0144079**	**-1.441**	**1.0103543**	**-1.035**
Mars	**1.5236915**	**1.5236281**	**0.004**	**1.5177892**	**0.387**

Table 2

It can be observed that in three of the four cases, the Z values obtained from equation (2) are more accurate than those obtained by use of equation (3). This suggests that equation (2) may be employed with some confidence to predict other Z values.

P1, P2, P3, and Planet X

Referring to Figure 1 and using the x-values for Neptune and Pluto in equation (2), we can now determine the y-values (and hence the corresponding Z-values) for P1 and P2. Thus for P1, y = 1.6401715 and Z = 1.9954545 and for P2, y = 1.8469120 and Z = 2.3552069.

The first of these Z-values is very close to the nominal inner boundary of the asteroid belt, but P2 does not appear to be of any significance. However, if we suppose that a point P3 on the y-axis corresponds to the nominal outer boundary of the asteroid belt at Z = 3, then the corresponding y-value is $3^{(9/4\pi)}$ = 2.1964075 and, substituting this into equation (2) then gives us an x-value of 6.9696435 (marked as X_{px} on Figure 1). If this relates to an 'unknown', Planet Px, then the Z-value for this planet is given by

$$\mathbf{X_{px}}^{(2\pi/3)} = \textbf{semi-major axis} = \textbf{58.3466693 AU} \quad \ldots\ldots\ldots\ldots (4)$$

Does such a planet exist ?

Interval Differences of x and y

With reference to Figure 1, let

$y_V - y_{Me} = a = 0.7929725 - 0.5067562 = 0.2862163$

$y_E - y_V = b = 1.0 - 0.7929725 = 0.2070275$

$y_{Ma} - y_E = c = 1.3520425 - 1.0 = 0.3520425$

$y_{P1} - y_{Ma} = 1.6401715 - 1.3520425 = 0.2881290 = a$ (to within 0.67%)

$y_{P2} - y_{P1} = 1.8469120 - 1.6401715 = 0.2067405 = b$ (to within 0.14%)

$y_{P3} - y_{P2} = 2.1964075 - 1.8469120 = 0.3494956 = c$ (to within 0.73%)

This repetition of a, b, c, along the y-axis is another observation that has no ready explanation. Also the repeatability of the similar x-axis set of differences A,B,C, now follows, where

A/a = B/b = C/c = ln30 .... (5)

Through equation (1) several relationships exist between the x, y, and hence Z-values for pairs or groups of planets, for example, from equation (1)

$y_{Me} = 0.2940141\, x_{Ma} - 0.1472341$ and

$y_{Ma} = 0.2940141\, x_{U} - 0.1472341$

In terms of Z, these equations become $\mathbf{Z_{Me}^{(9/4\pi)} = 0.2940141\, Z_{Ma}^{(3/2\pi)} - 0.1472341}$ and

$$\mathbf{Z_{Ma}^{(9/4\pi)} = 0.2940141\, Z_{U}^{(3/2\pi)} - 0.1472341}$$

Eliminating the Z_{Ma} between them now gives an equation connecting Z_{Me} and Z_U; it follows that, by solving this equation for Z_U, we can determine Z_U from a known value of Z_{Me}.

Although this does not provide us with new information, since it is derived from the original fundamental equation (2), a similar observation can be applied to relationships which involve the repetitive characteristics of a,b,c or A,B,C. Orbits are interrelated by simple addition and/or subtraction of these values, in a variety of combinations.

However, in what follows, two additional relationships are determined which, apparently, do not derive from previous results.

An Equation for Venus

From the previous section, **b/a = 0.2070275 / 0.2862163 = 0.7233253,** which is almost equal to Z_V (taken as 0.7233322) . This difference is less than 0.001%

However, b = $[Z_E^{(9/4\pi)} - Z_V^{(9/4\pi)}]$

And a = $[Z_V^{(9/4\pi)} - Z_{Me}^{(9/4\pi)}]$

Thus we may take

$$\mathbf{Z_V = [Z_E^{(9/4\pi)} - Z_V^{(9/4\pi)}] / [Z_V^{(9/4\pi)} - Z_{Me}^{(9/4\pi)}]} \text{.............. (6)}$$

This equation can be solved for Z_V using an iterative method, (Assuming Z_V is an unknown) and the result (0.723331002) is within 0.00017% of the figure for Venus mean orbit given by Norton's Star Atlas.

However, formation of the equation requires prior knowledge of Z_V, and it's relationship with Z_E and Z_{Me}.

Nevertheless, the equation is not predicted by theory, and is apparently unrelated to previous findings.

Pythagoras

Consider $a^2 + b^2 = (0.2862163)^2 + (0.2070275)^2 = 0.1247802$

And $c^2 = (0.35204525)^2 = 0.1239339$

Thus

$\mathbf{a^2+b^2=c^2}$...................(7)
to an accuracy of better than 99.3%

It follows that

$\mathbf{A^2 + B^2 = C^2}$............... (8)

These Pythagorean relationships (for a,b,c and A,B,C) could be illustrated by reference to corresponding similar right-angled triangles.

Kepler's Third Law

Since the semi-major axes (measured in astronomical units) of the planetary orbits convert to period by the application of Kepler's third law, it follows that in most of the equations the semi-major axis Z-values could be replaced by orbital period, in years, provided the exponent is changed accordingly.

$Z^{(9/4\pi)}$ is interchangeable with $P^{(3/2\pi)}$

And $Z^{(3/2\pi)}$ is interchangeable with $P^{(1/\pi)}$

(Where P is orbital period of respective planets in years)

Summary and conclusions.

It would seem that the orbits of the Solar System are interrelated in a number of different ways. This is an observed and verified fact that requires explanation.

We may reasonably conclude that the origin, laws, and dynamics of the Solar System are not yet fully understood.

INDEX

Abduction *202, 203, 204, 211*

Abraham *80, 191, 228, 434, 439, 440, 442, 456, 458, 480, 501, 517*

Abram *80, 517, 518, 524-527, 543*

Adam *37-39, 48, 171, 190, 456*

Aliens *39, 189, 202, 357, 358, 483, 515*

Altar stone *99, 102, 104, 267, 269, 270, 284, 292, 293*

Angel *189, 191, 212, 226, 227, 355, 437, 438, 441, 444, 445, 447, 448, 450, 451, 454-457, 460, 462, 467, 468, 474, 477, 488, 498, 501-503, 530, 547*

Animals *39, 41, 50, 59, 65, 66, 67, 98, 171, 173, 218, 234, 363, 369, 383, 384, 392, 406, 416, 420, 426, 499, 540*

Ape *150-152, 180, 234, 370, 371*

Aphelion *104-106, 108, 113, 284, 285, 291, 292, 324, 549*

Ararat *64, 66, 71, 74, 76, 84*

Ark *52, 64, 67, 68, 416*

Armageddon *484*

Asteroid *106, 186, 285, 328, 352, 509, 552*

Atheist *38, 151, 194, 224, 484*

ATKINSON Prof R.J.C. *7, 95, 101, 102, 215, 245, 252, 256, 267, 269, 277, 281, 284, 285, 289, 293, 294, 383, 387, 388*

Aubrey *89, 96, 98, 106, 245, 247, 249, 250, 252-255, 261, 266, 268, 269, 283, 290-292, 294, 384*

Australopithecus afarensis *530*

Babylon *47, 63, 64, 73, 74*

Back-sight holes *99, 102, 104, 108, 267, 269, 284*

Blasphemy *197, 431, 434, 459, 471, 487, 491,* **493, 494**

Bluestone horseshoe *99, 102, 104, 267, 268, 284*

Bluestone circle *99, 105, 267, 277, 285*

Bones *186, 407, 408, 418, 420, 421, 513, 519*

Breeding *176-179, 185, 413, 420, 507*

Carbon Dating *10, 382, 384, 385, 388, 390, 392, 393, 423*

Catastrophe/Catastrophism *45, 46, 178,* **395-397**, *399, 402, 405, 423, 424*

Chalk ***89, 98,*** *119, 242, 244, 246, 272*

Cherub (as machine) *174, 226, 228*

Clone *38, 39, 169-174, 176, 177, 180, 182, 183, 186, 196, 209, 362, 363, 371-374, 376, 382, 406-408, 418, 463, 489, 499, 506, 513, 515*

Clothing *39, 41, 173, 212, 218, 363, 440, 456*

Colony *170, 178, 180, 182, 184, 190, 196, 359-361, 507, 535*

Colonial *362, 363, 373, 468*

Colonist *173, 360, 373, 380, 515, 535*

Cosmos *16, 137, 232, 339*

Creationist *26, 53, 67, 166, 167, 186, 222, 391, 399, 423, 426*

Daniel *200, 451, 453, 456*

Dark Star *135*

Darwin *150-153, 182, 183, 206, 207, 225, 340, 387, 395, 400, 406*

Death *172, 198, 200, 205, 209, 210, 379, 392, 479, 498, 510, 537*

Degenerate *83, 413-420, 422, 424*

Devil's toe nail *398*

Diamond *392-394*

Dinosaurs *60, 182-185, 360, 361, 368, 397, 399, 404, 405, 424*

Dolphin *368-370, 534*

Dog *129, 130, 161, 286*

DNA *44, 186, 362, 374, 503*

Earth - *throughout*

Eclipse *89, 96, 98, 245*

Eden *27, 43, 171, 182, 199, 513*

Elijah *202*

Elohim - *throughout*

Engineer *125, 186, 196, 406, 416, 500*

Enoch *48, 197, 202, 205, 532*

EQUATION for Venus *162,* **319-321**, *353, 354, 555*

EQUATION main 143, 155, 308-310, 316

EQUATION main simplified 316

EQUATIONS Stonehenge 121

Europe *74, 83-85, 413*

Eve *171*

Evolution *53, 151, 152, 182, 186, 206, 210, 340, 361,* **366-370**, *380, 382, 388-390, 396, 400, 401, 407,* **409-426**, *539*

Ezekiel *226, 228, 451, 497, 501, 547*

Flint axe *286, 287*

Flint tool *408, 416, 421-423*

Fossil *60, 184, 185, 360, 397-399, 403-406*

Gabriel *451,* ***455-461****, 465, 474, 475, 482, 503-505*

Galaxy/Galactic *195, 197, 200, 358, 359, 367, 370-372, 374, 433, 464, 467-469, 499, 515, 526, 527, 531, 536*

Galapagos Islands *210*

Genetic *44, 177, 178, 180, 186, 200, 205, 210, 362, 406, 410, 413-415, 417, 418, 420, 498*

Gentile *85, 473, 476, 477, 511, 512*

Geology *152, 216, 397, 401, 406, 423, 513, 524*

Geometry *117, 120, 215, 217, 245, 252, 262, 263, 281, 286, 287, 365, 382, 384, 386, 387, 394, 427*

Hawkins G.S. *245*

Helicopter *564*

Heel Stone *96, 135, 285, 523*

Heresy *434, 471*

Homo Erectus *371, 408, 409, 415*

Hutton, James 339

Ice *54-59, 66, 398, 414, 424*
Ice age *57, 58, 66, 398, 424*
Ice rings/cloud *54, 55, 414*

Inner Monument *266-273*
Inner Solar System *105, 106, 121, 132, 286, 288, 303*
Intelligence *187,* **363-370**, *373, 381, 383, 487, 521*
Isaiah *452, 496, 502, 511, 512, 525, 526*
Israelites 440-450

Jacob *439, 447, 512, 543, 544*
Jehovah *438-441*
Joel *507*
Judaism *20, 48, 435, 448, 455, 481, 501, 517*
Jupiter *105, 106, 187, 281, 285, 303, 313, 402, 537, 550*

Kant *339*
Key *103, 241, 395*
Key, Dumb *116, 118, 241, 242, 263*
Key, Golden *139*

Ladder *447, 496, 512*
Laplace *150, 151, 153, 183, 339, 395, 400, 406*
Lyell *150, 151, 153, 183, 339, 387, 395, 396, 400, 405, 406, 423*

Mammoth *393, 416, 426*

Mars *54, 102-106, 185, 190, 284, 285, 291, 302, 303, 345, 353, 354, 537, 550-552*

Mary *451, 455-462, 474, 475, 482, 486, 501, 505, 547*

Mercury *102-105, 284, 291, 292, 314, 315, 319, 321, 322, 324, 353, 354, 402, 550-552*

Mesolithic *422*

MESSAGE First Contact 187-189, *234, 381, 463, 538, 540*

MESSAGE in Monument ***125, 130,*** *141, 165, 166*

MESSAGE in Gospels *464, 465, 468, 469, 473*

Migdal *63, 76-83, 85, 88, 91, 95, 115, 235*

Monkey *411*

Moon *54, 55, 65, 190*

Moses *191, 217, 438-449, 451, 480, 483, 501, 506, 510, 530*

Mud *60, 64, 397, 398*

Mud Brick (buildings) *75, 81, 88*

Neanderthal *408, 415, 423, 530*

Nebular Hypothesis *149, 339, 340, 360, 400, 403*

Neolithic *83-85, 104, 107, 108, 113, 114, 116, 120, 121, 151, 244-246, 252, 278, 297, 364, 382, 387, 401, 422, 424, 428*

Neptune *105, 106, 118, 285, 550, 552*

Nibiru *135*

Nimrod *70, 71, 80*

Numerology *145, 304, 341*

Old Earth *151, 399*

Olive branch *65*

Olives, mount of, *469*

Oort cloud *135, 285*

Palaeoanthropology *152, 216*

Palaeomagnetic *405*

Palaeolithic *422, 423*

Paradox *491, 494, 495*

Paul (see Saul)

Peg and String *117, 120, 125, 126, 146, 235, 261*

Perihelion *103-106, 108, 113, 284, 290, 291, 324, 549*

Plain *73, 89, 529*

Pluto *105, 106, 118, 120, 121, 125, 216, 217, 285, 328, 550, 552*

Priest *193, 205, 216, 231, 451, 472, 538*

Psyche *198*

Psychiatrist *193, 208*

Psychology *5, 203, 205, 408, 482*

Psycho-slave *208*

Pyramid *311*

Pyramid-ology (see also Numerology) *341*

Pythagoras *153, 155, 159, 236, 319, 321, 325, 330, 354, 365, 555*

PYTHAGOREAN GRID 153-155, 314, 322, 323, 325, 328, 341

Px *324, 328, 345, 550, 553*

'Q' holes *267, 277*

Quasi-human *407, 409-412, 415, 419, 423*

Radiocarbon *382, 384, 385, 388, 390*

Radiogenic 382, 389, 390-394, 407, 408, 417

Resurrection *474, 475, 498, 510*

R-holes *99, 105, 267, 285*

Sarsen stone 98

Sarsen Circle *98, 99, 105, 106, 244, 252, 265, 266, 272, 277, 285, 286, 385*

Saturn *54, 105, 187, 285, 302, 311, 315, 323, 324, 352, 355=357, 550*

Saul *472, 473, 479-481, 495, 496, 498, 501, 546*

Seasons *404*

Sinai *440-442, 447, 448, 452, 481, 501, 506*

Skin clothing *39, 41, 173, 218, 440, 456*

Slaughter stone *99*

Sodom *188, 191, 228, 434*

Spacecraft (see also UFO) *206, 358*

Strata 184, 185, 406, 408

Summer *57, 102, 404*

Sun *65, 66, 103, 104, 185, 402-404, 518*

Swedenborg *339*

Tabernacle *443, 506*

Temple *71, 76, 78, 88, 387, 443, 452, 506, 508*

Tides *65, 398*

Triangle *322, 324, 331, 556*

Trilithons *98, 99, 104, 106, 135, 267-269, 284, 285, 291-293, 302, 304*

Turkey *64, 83, 84*

UFO *190, 208, 315, 483, 502*

Uniformitarianism *150, 151, 340, 395, 396, 423*

Uranus *105, 108, 113, 114, 285, 290, 302, 315, 353, 354, 537, 550*

Venus *102-105, 108, 162, 284, 319-321, 324, 331, 353, 354, 402, 537, 550, 551, 552, 555*

Venus Equation, **319**, see under ‘Equation’

Vernier circle *216, 253-256, 261, 277, 285*

Water *42, 51, 52, 54-59, 63-66, 141, 153, 184, 218, 226, 397, 398, 486, 496, 497*

Weapons *208, 225*

Winter *404, 405*

X-Files *202*

‘x’ Axis (Graph) *101, 127, 322, 324, 347*

'**y**' Axis (Graph) *101, 127, 319, 320, 322, 324, 347, 353*

'Y' Circle/holes *99, 101, 105, 112, 261, 261, 263, 285, 290*

Yahshua *453, 462*

Yahweh *437-442, 444, 446, 449, 452*

YHWH *78, 438-442, 444-446, 449-452, 530*

'Z' Circle/holes *99, 105, 112, 252, 263, 264, 268, 272, 285, 384*

Ziggurat 74